GRAMSCI'S DEMOCRATIC
Contributions to a Post-Libera

The prison notebooks of Antonio Gramsci serve as the foundation for Sue Golding's in-depth study of Gramsci's contribution to radical democratic theory. Her analysis encompasses English, Italian, and French debates on the subject, as well as political and philosophical discussions on the limitations of liberal and socialist democratic theory.

Golding explains how Gramsci arrives at the conclusion that a fundamentally pluralistic 'post-liberal' democracy – that is to say, one that is 'open,' fluid, and based on an immanent and heterogeneous will of the people – is not only possible and preferable, but actually obtainable.

The consequences of his analysis are dramatic: on the one hand, Gramsci is able to provide a conception of the structure which is no longer static or reducible to a formal economic moment; it is, instead, profoundly political, since it becomes both the repository and expression of change as well as the terrain upon which a better society can emerge. On the other hand, he is able to incorporate as fundamental to a post-liberal democratic theory a number of concepts often overlooked in the theoretical discussions of socialist democracy.

Gramsci demonstrates that if one is to take seriously historical materialism and the kind of democratic society to which it points, one will necessarily be faced with a clear choice. One can either accept a flawed but strategically powerful methodology based on the dialectics of a philosophy of praxis or, more to the point, take as a given the profundity of the political and the radical diversity this implies, and search for a new logic. In the concluding chapter, Golding takes a look at the possible resolutions offered by way of a discursive (or what has come to be known as postmodern) philosophy outlined in part by the surrealists and further developed in the work of Laclau, Mouffe, Foucault, and Derrida.

SUE GOLDING is a Research Fellow at the Centre for Theoretical Studies, Essex University, and Visiting Scholar, Department of Political Science, University of Toronto.

GRAMSCI'S
Democratic Theory
Contributions to a
Post-Liberal Democracy

SUE GOLDING

UNIVERSITY OF TORONTO PRESS
Toronto Buffalo London

© University of Toronto Press 1992
Toronto Buffalo London
Printed in Canada

ISBN 0-8020-2799-7 (cloth)
ISBN 0-8020-7674-2 (paper)

Printed on acid-free paper

Canadian Cataloguing in Publication Data

Golding, Susan R.
Gramsci's democratic theory

Includes bibliographical references and index.
ISBN 0-8020-2799-7 (bound)   ISBN 0-8020-7674-2 (pbk.)

1. Gramsci, Antonio; 1891–1937. Quaderni del carcere.
2. Democracy.   I. Title.

HX289.7.G73G6 1992   321.8   C91-095554-9

This book has been published with the help of a grant from the Social
Science Federation of Canada, using funds provided by the Social Sciences
and Humanities Research Council of Canada.

Contents

Foreword

For well over the last half century, the obscure and passionate prison writings of Antonio Gramsci have continued to inspire political scholars and activists deeply committed to social change. But, during the first decade after his death, Gramsci's writings were taken more as a symbol of having endured the brutality of fascist imprisonment than as original and rigorous contributions to a complete rethinking of marxist theory. So compelling were the circumstances in which he wrote, that, at the outset, Gramsci was considered primarily as a heroic figure of the anti-fascist resistance whose intellectual influence was limited to, and scarcely distinguishable from, the leninist tradition with which he was identified. It was in the aftermath of the Second World War, with the first publication of the *Prison Notebooks*, that the subtle nuances of his political philosophy began to be debated in earnest; though even then, and for the next twenty years, he was cast mainly as an Italian intellectual, whose work provided the ideological ground of the Togliattian innovations in the PCI (Italian Communist Party). Emphasis was placed on the necessity, for example, to reconceptualize the role of the 'partito nuovo,' the 'national tasks of the working class,' the crushing defeat of the factory council movement, and so forth.

Only by the late 1960s, and particularly by the 1970s, at the height of Eurocommunism, did his influence cut through and transcend national boundaries. His analytic and strategic contributions around the question of organic and conjunctural crisis, or the uneasy relation of civil society to the state, or the fact that classes were forged always at the point of struggle, made Gramsci one of the major marxist theoreticians of the twentieth century. These and many other of his concepts provided the intellectual tools necessary to rethink socialist strategy in a way that could account for the uniquely fluid power imbalances of contemporary advanced industrial societies. Finally, by the 1980s with 'the crisis of Marxism,' the advent of post-structuralism, and the general debates concerning post-modernity, a significant and new turn takes place: Gramsci's contribution is understood as an important shift away from a weak marxism dominated by totalizing categories. Here we find, then, the formulation of a political vision no longer eclipsed by an essentialist outlook.

The present book by Sue Golding is an outstanding contribution to this last perspective. There are three aspects in which she makes an original contribution to Gramsci's scholarship. First, she locates Gramsci's work within the literature concerning democratic theory, in relation to both the limits of liberalism and what might be considered the best areas to be retrieved and strengthened. This is important not the least because most of the existing literature has studied Gramsci's work only in relation to a marxism devoid of any democratic content. Second, she clearly points out the relevance of Gramsci's work for contemporary debates – such as deconstruction or radical pluralism and the question of contingency – debates that for so long have been considered very distant from her subject-matter. The logic of undecidability and supplementarity in Derrida, the genealogical approach of Foucault, as well as the specificity of the hegemonic articulations that I have tried to point out in my work with Chantal Mouffe, are brought to the fore in a very successful attempt to show their implicit operation in Gramsci's work. In particular we find a dramatic rereading of his concept of the will and the role of a fluid dialectical structure in relation to economics and ideology, and an insistence on the political moment as the core expression for both the possible and the real. Finally, the wide historical canvas within which Golding inscribes her subject makes her acutely aware of the unresolved tensions in Gramsci's thought and the incompatible elements that he tried – unsuccessfully – to combine. In this respect this book is more than a mere exercise in intellectual history: the contours of a post-liberal conception of democracy, which are presented in the last chapter, are a very promising contribution to political theory. The author announces a new book, *The Cunning of Democracy,* in which her theoretical approach will be represented in full.

Sue Golding has made an extremely valuable contribution to Gramsci's scholarship. Her work deserves careful consideration and discussion.

Ernesto Laclau

Acknowledgments

This book could not have been completed without intellectual guidance and support from Frank Cunningham, Gad Horowitz, Dusan Pokorny, and the late C.B. Macpherson. I would also like to express my deepest gratitude and admiration to Chantal Mouffe and Ernesto Laclau, who, in breaking new and uncharted territory for a radical democratic theory, not only provided a variety of theoretical avenues to pursue, but also gave generously of their time and friendship.

In addition, I would like to express my gratitude to the various institutions that provided research facilities, funding, or both: first, to the University of Toronto, Department of Political Science, which saw to it that this project would receive generous funding; second, to the graduate library facility at the university, the Robarts Library, and, in particular, to Elaine Genius and the late Richard Swanton, who kindly assisted me in acquiring the less readily accessible documents I needed. I would also like to offer my appreciation to the staff at the British Library Reading Room in London, England, where much of the research was completed; and, as well, to Cambridge University, which kindly gave me permission to study with Professor Raymond Williams while doing research in London. In this context, too, I would like to thank the University of Toronto Press, and, in particular, Virgil Duff, for his continuing encouragement and support. In addition, I would like to extend a deep note of thanks both to Noreen Harburt and to Beverley Beetham Endersby, whose sustained and careful editing improved the quality of this book.

My appreciation must also be expressed for all the unreserved time and intellectual, political, and moral support that my friends and colleagues gave by way of conversations, letters, telephone calls, and dinners, or simply because of their continuing political commitment despite all odds. These people include: Shannon Bell, Julia Blazdell, Philip Derbyshire, Sky Gilbert, David Gitlin, Rachel Holmes, Samuel Hollander, Asher Horowitz, Ryan Hotchkiss, Chris Lee, Ruth Martin, Gayle Rubin, Simon Watney, Jeffrey Weeks, the *Body Politic* collective, and all the outrageous souls at Buddies in Bad Times Theatre in Toronto. I would like also to extend a profound appreciation to my family: to my sister, Judi, and my brothers, Frank and Ken; to my mother, Joyce E. Golding, for all her love and support; and, most of all, to the memory of my father, the late Dr E.I. Golding, particularly for his courage, humour, intellectual curiosity, and down-to-earth wisdom.

Finally, I would like to express my deepest appreciation to Bob Gallagher, who stood by my work at every turn, who was always prepared to argue a point with me, to dissect the logic, to ignore the hardships and applaud the victories – in short, who played editor, academic, and, most of all, friend. It is to him that this work is dedicated.

Sue Golding
Toronto 1991

Preface

When one first approaches Gramsci's *Quaderni del carcere* a curious double spectacle confronts the uninitiated. Embedded in the many thousands of pages, each written in the highly censored atmosphere of a prison cell, is the passionate urgency of a political strategist striking out against the fascistic turn of events in Italy (and elsewhere) and beckoning to those 'not in the know' to organize and resist. Here one meets the militant tactician, the marxist-leninist par excellence. But, at the same time, one also encounters the finely tuned scholarship of a radical intellectual who questioned and alternatively incorporated a whole series of theoretical concepts that often seem markedly distanced from the marxist-leninism grounding his philosophic astuteness and political common sense. In relying on such concepts as 'ethicality' or 'immanence,' or even 'the distincts,' one seems to find traces of a slightly refurbished idealist, one who might appear to be casting his intellectual net closer to the analytic proposals of Hegel and Benedetto Croce rather than to those of Marx or Lenin.

These apparent contradictions have led novices and scholars alike to attempt to discover the 'real' Gramsci, 'discoveries' that, as we shall see, have little to do with the immense contribution and impact the prison notebooks have made on political theory in general and on democratic theory in particular. Then again, there are those who carefully resist the temptation to label Gramsci's political and philosophical work one way or the other, but try instead to find the one key that will unlock the otherwise daunting obscurity encumbering almost every fragment. In so doing they often miss the more subtle nuances and turns of phras-

xii   Preface

es Gramsci used in order to develop the layered complexities – and fundamental radicalism – of a philosophy of praxis.

Rather than try to trace a coherent and singular thread through his work, this book investigates one of the most pressing practico-theoretical problems Gramsci himself was to identify over and again in the *Quaderni*: the fact, as he so eloquently would lament, that the 'old was dying but that the new could not yet be born'; the fact that a crushing fascism seemed to be triumphing in lieu of a democracy based on and expressing the intellectual and creative potential of the people. This 'fact' gave him more than pause for thought; and, indeed, his reflections, steeped as they were in the analytic and historical complications of a rising fascism, offer more than just a commentary on the reasons behind either the emergence of fascism or the total defeat of the working-class factory council movement. They offer a profound contribution to theorizing what a better society based on and expressing the will of the people might entail; and they do so without, at the same time, repeating the limitations found in either a liberal or an idealist – or, for that matter, a marxist-leninist – framework.

Indeed, it would not be overstating the case to say that, in Gramsci's prison notebooks, we are given a series of vital and challenging concepts, which, taken together, begin to articulate the basis for what has come to be known as a 'post'-liberal democracy. His is a theory about democracy that incorporates the central premiss that society, and indeed, 'the people,' must be understood not simply as entailing a specific historicity – without a natural order or essence – but as necessarily born out of and sustained by an open, creative, and immanent intellectual as well as practico-political 'will.' His theory takes this 'will,' itself diversified and fractured, as both the ground *and* the horizon – as both the 'is' and the 'ought' – of a democratic possibility.

And yet this focus on a subjective will is neither innocent nor without its consequences: for not only does it challenge certain liberal and idealist assumptions, it rethinks the entirety of marxism itself. Questions around objectivity and science and truth are reinscribed to include, indeed to privilege in a certain sense, the subjective moment. In turn this provides not only a fundamental rewrite of dialectics as historicized immanence, but grounds political agency in a radical pluralism and fluid diversity of the social structure itself.

This book delineates what is entailed in Gramsci's provocative proposition. It tries to show why a 'radical' openness, diversity, and contingently formed consent must become the integral basis for a post-liberal democracy, and why, in becoming that basis, a kind of social ethics, which Gramsci quite simply calls 'progressive,' can be established.

Moreover, it tries to do so by following the methodological and theoretical route Gramsci took, the dilemmas he encountered, and the resolutions he finally offered. But it also discusses how, in the end, he is
caught in a trap from which he cannot escape. We will return to the
intricacies of this dilemma shortly.

To establish the parameters of the task at hand and set Gramsci's
explorations in the proper context, the general limitations of both liberalism (with its liberal-democratic variant) and idealism are briefly
outlined in chapter 1, while the heart of the argument is developed later, in chapters 2 through 5. Relying in part on the work of Hobbes and
Locke and the way in which C.B. Macpherson, among others, positions
liberalism, the analytic difficulties are divided into three interrelated
areas: i / the problem of taking as a given an abstract concept of the
individual based on the notion of an 'equality of reason,' an abstraction
that – not inadvertently – gives credence to establishing a society inextricably based on the inequality of ownership; ii / the subsequent need
to provide a notion of obligation to an external agent, usually in terms
of a sovereign or a state (or both) so as to account for, or at least give a
theoretical pretext for, the ideological cohesiveness of a society fractured by that inequality; and iii / the attempt by Macpherson and others to relocate a concept of democracy based on the self-development
and intellectual capabilities of the individual without having to accept
the concomitant position of class inequality or obligation to an external
authority.

To begin to tease out these themes, we look first at Hegel's general
attack on utilitarianism and his specific attack on Kant's and Rousseau's incorporation of obligation and communal ethicality. Here we
explore why Hegel proposes that an obligation based on an external
authority or, conversely, rooted in a general will or transcendental subject cannot properly 'ground' or give content to ethicality. In Hegel we
find, instead, that the content of an ethical reality, of the 'what ought to
be,' can only be realized by sidestepping the usual requirement of external agency to obligation, alternatively replacing it with the concept
of a collective will as something that cannot be severed or made distinct
from *Sittlichkeit*. That is, Hegel presents a notion of the will that can
neither be understood outside of ethical substance itself nor find its
realization apart from the ethical state. As we shall see, this proposition,
albeit in an idealized form, becomes extremely attractive for Gramsci.

But the obvious question for Gramsci becomes whether it is possible
to avoid the idealism of Hegel and still find substance or grounding in
a communal ethicality, a grounding that is located on, or in some way
linked to, the complex terrain of an immanently historicized present. In

short, the question becomes how the 'better' society, i.e., the 'what ought to be,' can become located on the terrain of the 'is,' without either proposing an external authority or essence or, for that matter, without casting the argument in terms of a teleological unfolding of the ethical state bound to a static or homogeneous conception of history.

In the *Quaderni*, Gramsci carefully lays out the argument that the ethico-political society must instead emerge as a contingent relation to historical circumstance, nuanced by the fractured will of the people. Moreover, he argues that this relation is itself a subjective process that entails no essence or abstract generality; indeed, it is immanently created out of the practico-political struggles that take place always on, within, and between what must be understood as a 'discontinuous' terrain of a historicized and contingent reality. Given this position, Gramsci argues that not only would a radical democracy have the possibility of coming to fruition, it would integrally entail the possibility of being maintained and reproduced as such.

For Gramsci, then, the philosophy of praxis also outlines, systematically, how an 'open link' between the ethico-political society and the collective will of the people can be institutionalized or made permanent in a way that does not deny the contingent identity of 'the people.' We have here a conception of the 'better society' and the people who constitute its identity – indeed, identity itself – as one that can be brought into existence only through a complete recognition of the social over the natural as a bearer of truth. To put it slightly differently, we find Gramsci placing politics (and political struggle) as the core relation to any truth, or, more to the point, as the core relation to all aspects of the real.

The implications of this specifically Gramscian move are developed in detail, beginning in chapter 2. Here we find that this reinstatement of the political emerges in part from his assessment of the age-old debates around the severing of nature and history, a double disruption that Gramsci formulates with and against a particular reading of Vico's development of science and Croce's later adaptation of it in terms of historical 'error.' What becomes important here is not simply the point that all truths are historically (and thus politically) contingent, but that there is a specific logic to that contingency, one that must necessarily entail negation or error in any formulation of truth. Indeed we have here a rendering of a 'not-truth' as being something quite different from a vacuous Other in relation to any truth game. It is also, at its core, political. These discussions form the basis of chapter 2, and, as we examine in chapter 3, have profound implications for Gramsci's reconceptualizing not only of science and error, but of reality itself, now posed as more closely resembling probability and law of tendency than rigid or homogeneously inscribed factuality.

Rethinking the real in these terms not only highlights the specificities of negation, but also recasts the problem in terms of a (historically particular) fluidity or movement. Indeed, we are confronted now with a more nuanced concept of immanence or becoming, one that recasts the marxist dialectic itself as directly political without, at the same time, seeming to reinstitute a teleological 'ought.' Moreover, in so recasting the dialectic on the terrain of a political 'becoming,' that is, on the terrain of a historicized immanence constituted by and expressing the unity of truth as both truth and error, Gramsci not only refocuses the philosophy of praxis towards strategic questions of practical political activity, but he is able to draw attention to the crucial concept of the collective will. For Gramsci, the will becomes both the expression and the function of that practical political activity.

The methodological ramifications of this decision are set out in chapter 3; the two different readings of the collective will are discussed in detail in chapter 4. On the one hand, we find that Gramsci poses the will as neither arbitrary nor general, nor, for that matter, as privileging an ontologically a priori social agent. For Gramsci, the collective will is necessarily heterogeneous, one whose 'unity,' i.e., collectivity, is precisely born out of and constituted by the political. On the other hand, and inasmuch as this will is a product of a historicized immanence and thus a synthesized or cohesive expression of a specific 'the people,' Gramsci argues that the will becomes the necessary vehicle representing (and maintaining) an open and radically pluralistic society. Following this line of reasoning, the 'real' democracy for Gramsci becomes precisely the expression of a particularized collective will embodied in the social whole rather than an ethical will embodied in the state, as others have argued.

Two subsequent positions emerge from this rendering. On the one hand, given that this collective will cannot be an arbitrary or general will, inasmuch as it is rooted in – and is an expression of – the historical subjectivity of a particular 'the people,' Gramsci is able to incorporate the 'is' with the 'ought'; that is, he is able to give *content* to ethicality. On the other hand, he argues that only in the attempt to make more coherent and directive this collective will can the people continue to create in reality what exists at the moment as mere possibility, i.e., to bring to fruition – and be able to maintain – a radically pluralistic society. For Gramsci, then, the practico-political task becomes one of making more unified the collective will of a people, should that coherence become 'unhinged' or, for whatever reasons, not yet exist in reality.

But Gramsci is not ignorant of the fact that this position, however much he might wish that it be grounded in an immanent politics/history, might still seem closer to Hegel's realization of the ethical-state. Nor is he prepared to resolve that dilemma either by having to accept an a priori communal ethicality or, secondarily, by having to accept a crocean notion of progress. The former would force him into posing the 'ought' as an abstract ethical ideal; the latter, as the teleological unfolding of a history/anti-history dialectic with no room to determine the content of ethicality except to say that whatever might be taken as 'good' would simply be that which might emerge as such.

Gramsci is determined to show that only in profoundly radicalizing the notion of social totality – and not the notion of 'social' per se – can one avoid the relative nihilism or abstract ethicality inherent in an idealized teleology. Turning to Marx's preface to the *Critique of Hegel's Philosophy of Right*, 'Theses on Feuerbach,' and other works, Gramsci reassesses the notion of totality in terms of the base/superstructure dichotomy. But rather than construe this dichotomy to mean a privileging of the base (itself wrongly interpreted, argues Gramsci, as an opaque and somewhat static notion of 'mode of production' from which various ideological and political practices could be deduced), Gramsci recasts the entire formulation. Starting with the concept of 'base' as an economic system, he argues that it, too, must now be understood to be more heterogeneous and fluid, more closely resembling a 'structure' whose coherence emerges out of a politically contingent suturing.

Given this position, then, Gramsci suggests instead that the economic, as a structure, is itself part of a unity whose meaning can only remain an abstraction if severed from or posed 'outside' dialectical synthesis. To put it slightly differently, he argues that the structure cannot be singled out or divided off from the superstructure, nor can it somehow (logically or otherwise) be considered more important than the latter. Rather, he shows how these are two distinct moments of a dialectical movement, where each component part of the unity is itself a synthesized entity, emerging from the practico-political struggle of hegemony. These components can no more be severed one from the other than can their individualized moments be understood 'outside' of the coherent synthesis they express. Indeed, it is only in their unity – a unity fraught with error and contingency – where social 'truth' becomes meaningful. It is only in their unity where a social totality becomes actualized, i.e., becomes both possible and concrete.

As it stands, this clarification and subsequent development might not seem particularly unusual, and certainly not worrisome. It does provide a way to reject the rigid determinism or homogeneous epiphenomenalism that led to a reducing of all political and ideological factors to an immediate economic moment or, conversely, to reflections of that base. Moreover, by re-emphasizing the constitutive nature of a 'base' in terms of a dialecticized structure, Gramsci is able to defeat a reductionist notion of economics itself, replacing a flat or empirical notion of quantity with Marx's more fluid 'qualitative' economics, one that necessarily entails the specificity of history.

In fact in re-evaluating Marx's base/superstructure as pluralistically contingent and historically immanent, a series of concepts that differ quite dramatically from their predecessors emerges: concepts around the role of the intellectuals or the party or the state, concepts around ideology and hegemony. Indeed, all concepts concerning power, political struggle, and change now contain the integral trace of a subjective heterogeneity and contingency. Gone is the notion of 'false consciousness' and, with it, various ahistoricized universalisms around objective truths. Gone is the notion of classes as entities that are 'always already' pregiven and locked into fixed power games. Gone is the notion of power itself as an entity to be uncovered or avoided or seized or abolished. In their place we find concepts nuanced by the relation of specific forces and crises, that is, nuanced by distinct and concrete processes wholly linked to the political, itself understood as an integral moment of a (dialectically synthesized) structure. 'Real' or 'organic' change in the gramscian sense becomes precisely that which emerges 'within' a social totality, as opposed to something that might be brought forth from 'outside,' as if by a vanguard or external authority, or as a result of a unique or accidental set of circumstances.

But now we come to the troubling difficulty: in relying on a notion of the social order as a totality, dialectical or otherwise, Gramsci becomes caught in a kind of gordian knot from which he is unable to escape. For, while he wants to argue that any democracy configured as a 'real democracy' must emerge from the organic and heterogeneous *Sittlichkeit* of a specific 'the people,' he wants also to argue that that specificity must be linked to and expressed by the working class. That is, he wants to pose the working class as, ipso facto, the bearer of this radical totality, and he wants to press that argument forward not simply on the basis of strategic or practical political grounds, but in terms of a precise analytic necessity.

Insisting that the working class must be *the* inheritors and standardbearers of historical truth means, in part at least and despite his at-

tempts to avow the contrary, to accept as necessary an already given
communal ethicality teleologically unfolding prior to the political moment. For, in order to 'ground' the ethical content of this radical vision,
Gramsci is forced to accept, among other problems, a privileging of an
originating and transcendental political subjectivity, now cast somewhere 'outside' the structure. It is a kind of 'chicken and egg' problem
regarding ethicality itself, where truth and the practical political activity
of expressing, changing, or maintaining the radical meaning of what
ought to be and why (not to mention how and for whom) must now be
accepted in purely abstract and a priori terms. Instead of an immanent
and contingent social order sutured by hegemonic struggle and all that
this has implied, we find the notion of a totalized and statically 'objective' system taking precedence over and against the notion of an 'open
link' as the fundamental requirement for a democracy empowered by
the will of the people.

Does this mean that Gramsci's work for a post-liberal democratic
theory is for naught? The short answer is no. And, in the concluding
remarks of chapter 6, Gramsci's contributions and the possible choic-
es we can take in light of the more recent debates by Foucault and Derrida are set out and assessed.

Gramsci's Democratic Theory

Contributions to a Post-Liberal Democracy

ONE

Setting the Problem

Perhaps we can come at the whole thing best by asking, with tongue not entirely in cheek, whether it is now proper to promote a concept of post-liberal-democracy ... [That is] ... is the theory as it now stands adequate in justifying the liberal-democratic state and society as they now are or as they might be improved, or do we *need* a still further changed theory, so changed as to merit a new name? In other words, do we *need* a post-liberal-democratic theory? I shall suggest that the answer is yes.[1]

In his characteristically succinct fashion, Macpherson was able to single out one of the most pressing problems in contemporary political theory: the need to conceptualize in all its complexity a democratic theory that could go beyond its liberal-democratic roots. It was not that liberalism had outgrown its own parameters. It was rather that liberal-democratic theory could not successfully come to terms with what had been identified as one of the most fundamental prerequisites of a liberal-democratic state, namely, the creating and maintaining of a progressive society-state), that would be constituted by, and represent in all its diversity, the will of 'the people' and their fundamental equal right to creative self-development. Liberal-democratic theory could not achieve such a coming-to-terms without either institutionalizing a 'tyranny of majority,' as de Tocqueville and others had ominously envisioned,[2] or making the market mechanisms of exchange and profit fundamental prerequisites for a society based on individual creativity and growth.[3] Others have argued that liberalism and its liberal-democratic variant could not successfully come to terms with a conception of a pluralistic democracy without accepting both.[4]

Let us, for the moment, take as a given the point Macpherson suggests in the passage quoted above: that the limit to liberalism does indeed exist and that we are now in a position where the need to articulate a post-liberal-democratic theory, one that can 'retrieve' the best parts of the liberal-democratic tradition and focus them in the context of a socialist discourse, is paramount. Given this position, the question then becomes: Can that retrieval take place without, in the end, lapsing into liberalism or simply resurrecting it in a different form? Moreover, in attacking liberalism in this manner, is this retrieval something that stands outside of marxist theory or something inherent in its philosophical and political underpinnings?

These are not new questions, and one could reasonably argue that they have been at the forefront of the political and intellectual agenda for at least the last thirty years,[5] or, as some would argue, even longer.[6] Indeed, it can be said that the resolutions, or attempted resolutions, to these questions are central concerns throughout Gramsci's prison notebooks. But in order to get a fuller understanding of how Gramsci grapples with them and why they are so central to his work, it is worthwhile to clarify not only what the limits to liberalism might include, but also the general attacks launched by Hegel against some of those limits. For as we shall see, Gramsci was committed to his own clarification of a socialist democracy and of the philosophy of praxis that would articulate such a democracy. Indeed, he was committed to it very much along the lines of an absolute historicism that incorporated an idealism of sorts and, in so doing, was pitted heavily against a reductionist or orthodox marxism without, at the same time, rejecting historical materialism or its dialectical methodology.

Clarifying the 'limits' to liberalism

In presenting the position that liberalism and its liberal-democratic variant had reached full potentiality and could not provide for a more comprehensive democratic theory, Macpherson pointed out both the positive and the negative aspects of liberal theory. On the one hand, as a coherent, but still heterogeneous, body of political philosophy, it expressed a new concept of both the individual and society as distinct entities whose raison d'être was more closely linked to reason than to the pre-Enlightenment cosmological and hierarchical ordering of life. On the other hand, it had done so, argued Macpherson, at the cost of having to accept the concomitant position that, as the embodiment of 'possessive individualism,' the liberal society could reproduce itself only along propertied, and hence class-divided, lines.[7]

To put it quite simply, liberal theory forwarded, in part, the notion of a human nature whose essence could be derived in terms of man's ability to reason, as opposed to one founded on a God/authority axis. In this context, it would thus support the view that all individuals were created equal. But it also put forward the argument that this human nature entailed an aggressiveness and drive for mobility or, to use Hobbes's more expressive description, 'a need for appetites and constant motion.'[8] From this position it could be deduced that equality, on the one level, might bring with it, on another, a society rooted in the scarcity of goods, since inevitably some of the people might take, given their insatiable 'appetites,' more than their due and possibly, in so taking, prevent others from getting anything at all.

On the one hand, then, reason was thus understood to be the necessary instrument used to guide – and not tame – those appetites. And, in that respect, it became precisely a *calculation of means to an end*, and not, as it had been considered in the past, an end in itself.[9] But coupled with the kind of human nature described above, it also became, on the other hand, a way to accept as 'natural' the variety of practical activities required to reproduce successfully the market mechanisms of that society; namely, the exacerbated disparities between those who had access to the means of production and those who did not, all couched in an environment of squalor and meanness, exploitation, alienation, and even pettiness. The cruelty of sociality emanating from that position would now be considered as something not inherent in (or emerging as a result of) specific relations of production. Rather, it could be interpreted as merely a reflection of the general nature of the human condition, itself thought to be transhistorical.

Holding to the concept that the individual must be understood in terms of a universally abstract human nature or 'man-in-general,' distinguished through one's reason and massive appetites, led also to the positing of an abstract notion of society, whose essence was itself constituted precisely by that general, however disparate, essence of man. Hence society was seen to be an expression or representation of simply what was natural and, indeed, therefore, 'what ought to be.' Society, now integrally pitted against an abstract and universalized state of nature – so neatly described by Hobbes as 'nasty, brutish, solitary and short' – could thus be regarded as the protector of the individual against the travesties of 'nature.' Moreover, and despite an inherent logic in the system leading to, and indeed requiring, ipso facto, a reproduction of inequality emerging from the varied appetites of its inhabitants, its demise would necessarily throw one back into the tumultuous void of greed and war, that is, back into the (mythical and timeless) state of nature.

Among the many consequences to which these assumptions led was the specific theoretical and practical problem of seeking legitimation for a society both historically rooted in the unequal distribution of property ownership and exchange and constantly undermined by the competitive quest to amass individual material wealth.[10] Clearly for Hobbes and for Locke, as well as for other early seventeenth- and eighteenth-century liberals, this contradiction would in part be settled by invoking the consensual aspect of the social contract, insisting that each citizen, by having so 'agreed,' albeit by dint of civil law and *convenance*, to a withdrawal from the state of nature, would necessarily have created by that agreement an obligation to the sovereign state and a concomitant acceptance of inequality as the price for that security and freedom.[11]

In light of the obvious requirement for some kind of political obligation, an array of resolutions was established that in reality merely seemed to beg the question of a divided society based on the so-called equality of reason. For, though one would find differing conceptions of the state of nature, the social contract, and the kind of societies that would, as a consequence, emerge – indeed, albeit vast differences that might be implied or expressly stated with the concept of 'the people' itself and who, therefore, might be given a stake in societal power, property, and law – an appeal to an external agent or authority still had to be invoked in order to promote the cohesion and stability of the social whole.[12]

One finds with Hobbes, for example, an insistence on accepting and forwarding as fundamental, an absolute obligation required of the individual to the state or state-as-government. Without this specific duty towards the sovereignty of the Leviathan state, its structure would necessarily collapse, and one would thus be thrust back into the tortuous existence found in the state of nature/war.[13] By contrast, Locke's position brought to bear a different degree of obligation, in part because he distinguished between the government and the state. This distinction allowed him to develop a concept of obligation that did not necessarily imply a total commitment to the governing body, but only to the welfare of the state as a whole.[14] Indeed it provided him with a conception of obligation that included as fundamental to a functioning democracy the citizens' right to depose a government, since delegitimating a government, or, indeed, changing it, did not now, necessarily, jeopardize the state or engender a civil war.[15] However, attempting to overthrow the state apparatus itself, or to disfigure any part of the system that ensured its maintenance and growth, would constitute, of course, an entirely different matter.

Despite this significant alteration by Locke, it still remained that the notion of obligation on the part of the citizenry fulfilled the essential function of providing cohesion to a splintered and heterogeneous society. In fact, both positions managed, though Locke's state sovereignty remained markedly different from the hobbesian leviathan, to incorporate a divided society as a given – indeed, to incorporate it as an 'ought.' But the logic of this position needed not, and indeed did not, equate total obligation towards the state with a concomitant right to a total access to political power within the state. To have extended that kind of mandate might possibly have endangered the reproduction of the status quo in society, that is, might possibly have endangered the unequal divisions of power and property, and thus disrupted the inherent divisions around class, race, and sexual privilege. 'Far am I from denying in theory,' wrote the eloquent Edmund Burke,

> ... the real rights of men. In denying their false [democratic] claims of right, I do not mean to injure those which are real, and are such as their pretended rights would totally destroy ... [For] in this partnership, all men have equal rights, but not to equal things. He that has but five shillings in the partnership has as good a right to it as he that has five hundred pounds has to his larger proportion. But [the former] has not a right to an equal dividend in the product of the joint stock; and as to the share of power, authority, and direction which each individual ought to have in the management of the state, that I must deny to be amongst the direct original rights of man in civil society, for I have in my contemplation the civil social man and no other.[16]

This problem of having conceptualized an abstract but essentialized nature for both the individual and the society, coupled with its requirement of an absolute obligation to an external authority so as to cohere and provide legitimation to a perpetually dividing civil order linking equality of reason with greedy appetite and fear, clearly posited a serious limitation to any attempt, practical or otherwise, at increasing the participation of those originally disenfranchised from state or civil power. Indeed, it clearly established that this form of liberalism had the tendency to diminish or disregard entirely the whole sordid question of democracy itself, if, that is, democracy were to mean the intellectual growth and collective participation of all 'the people' in a free and equal way.

And yet, one of the great virtues of Macpherson's work on possessive individualism and the contradictions the concept engendered was to clarify just how far removed democratic theory could be from liberalism, without dismissing the historic roots of a democratic vision linked to that liberalism. Conversely, one of the most important aspects of his investigation was in pointing out the way in which democracy did indeed become intrinsic to the liberal state of the later eighteenth- and nineteenth-century Europe and how (and why) it was able to produce a coherent, though, again, not homogeneously inscribed, political philosophy that could now be labelled 'liberal-democratic'.[17]

By showing that contemporary democracies were hybrid products with a specific political history, he was also able to articulate the way in which concepts around civil liberties – for example, freedom of press, speech, and religion – or those involving a human right to creative potentiality and intellectual growth had been linked to, but were not necessarily a fundamental expression of, liberalism itself. Indeed, he was able to show not only that the linking of what might be considered 'democratic' to this entity called 'liberalism' was precisely the outcome of political struggle on a variety of fronts, but that what constituted the very meaning of democracy was also, and precisely, born of political struggle.[18] The result was the now increasingly obvious conclusion that, if certain forms of liberalism tended to perpetuate the disenfranchisement and inequality of the people, and if, in contrast, democracy itself was not necessarily a synonym or even a direct result of liberalism per se, it seemed unquestionable that there might be certain elements within liberal-democratic theory worth incorporating into a system that could perpetuate equality on a number of levels, not the least of which involved property, economic justice, and the right to govern.

It would seem reasonable, in other words, given the historic specificity of liberal democracy, to acknowledge the best parts of that tradition, particularly around civil rights and the notion of self-development – around, that is to say, the diversity of humankind – without having to accept the market assumptions that seemed inherent in this notion of modernity or without also having to accept as a priori a transhistorical notion of human subjectivity and the ethical social order of which it was a part. Could we now, in other words, come to develop a democratic theory historically rooted in a specific conception of the individual and society based on what is 'right' or 'good,' without having to presuppose the rule of one class over another or ground that theory in a generalized (and abstract) 'truth' about humankind? Could we now begin to develop the type of post-liberal democracy Macpherson had envisioned, one that could move beyond liberalism, that is, the kind of democratic theory that ought to – indeed, must – 'treat democracy as a kind of society and must treat the individual members as at least potentially doers rather than mere consumers, must assert an equal effective right of the members to use and develop their human capacities [inasmuch as] each must be enabled to do so, whether or not each actually does'?[19]

For Gramsci, the answer was an unqualified yes, and, in his prison notebooks, he began to tease out such a theory, detached from market assumptions and abstract assumptions of human nature and authority. To articulate such a theory, he set the framework in terms of a philosophy of praxis that polemicized the notion of history, science, and the dialectic found in both the early and later writings of Marx and Engels. But even though the answers to these kinds of questions were posed in the affirmative, still there were (and continue to be) a multitude of difficulties in trying to make that leap.

The second impasse

It could be said that, at least on the ethico-political level, there remained, in particular, one very glaring obstacle. This obstacle was precisely the difficulty of grounding the 'what ought to be': it was the problem of connecting the ethical assumptions inherent in the search for, and attempts to establish, a better or progressive or, indeed, democratic society as such and for whom in a way that neither presupposed an a priori or metaphysical given nor ignored the specificity of history in the creating of that (or any other) meaning. It was precisely the practical problem of taking seriously Marx's claim that history – and not thought – delineated the foundation and terrain upon which people would be able to understand their circumstances and change them for the better.

Yet, if we look at the problem closely, embracing history as the foundational component is exactly where the ethico-political predicament seems most exacerbated. For, in connecting the 'is' with the 'ought' in a way that can acknowledge the very fluidity and legitimacy of history itself, one can encounter the dual trap of either having to accept a relativity of history-as-truth and thus (seemingly) be accepting a vulgar nihilism or, conversely, having to pose an external truth somehow existing as an already established category and hence (seemingly) be accepting a pregiven moral agent as the standard-bearer of the communal good.

The former, it would seem, requires having to accept as ethical the dubious argument that anything created in history is good. The latter would seem to lead us squarely into the first limit discussed above, that is, the posing of an external agent/authority as an archimedean point above the horizon of the social, necessary to legitimate any existence or truth. In either case, establishing ethicality would require some kind of founding essentialism or dogma, or both, having thus only exchanged the old ethical standard-bearers (be they God or the state, or even reason) for that of a sutured and homogeneously inscribed 'the people.' The one would seem to lead back to an overactive idealism privileging concept over history – despite intentions to do exactly the reverse; the other, to an insistence on a reductionism so crude as to rob the historical materialist dialectic of any meaningful content.

In short, the impasse would come down to this: if one were to accept the two points discussed thus far – i / that there is no pre-established or natural order to the social, and, more directly, ii / that the criterion from which the whole of reality could be understood is precisely a historical expression of political process (rather than a product of an abstract will or normative ordering) – it would then seem that, in order to give concrete content or substance to the 'what ought to be,' one would have to ground the notion of progress on some form of the particular, that is, on some form of specificity emerging 'within' the social itself.

For, as we have noted, to ignore the centrality of history and its specificity would be, in part, to ignore the divisive cleavages of modern society and present them, instead, as if a product of a universalized essence of man, and hence as an 'ought' *sui generis*. This would require, as was earlier noted, accepting a notion of obligation to an external agent or an appeal to an 'other' in the form of extrinsic authority. But on the other hand, it would seem that if one were to take seriously the claim that reality is itself a constitutive historical product, a synthesis of the past forming the terrain of the present, a terrain where the social whole would itself continually be forged from a people whose subjectivity was also historically bound, one might have to accept, inadvertently or otherwise, some form of relative nihilism. That is, one might be forced to accept a conception of ethics as that which is created as such or as one based on hindsight. Or, perhaps worse, one might have to accept a preconstituted category of the 'good' that in the end could only hypostatize history or the people, or both.

As we will see in the more detailed discussions in subsequent chapters, Gramsci grappled with this impasse at length and, moreover, tried to resolve it in part by shadow-boxing, as it were, with the agenda already established in Hegel's rendering of the communal good. That agenda concerned, in part, the ontological suppositions implied if one takes as a given the constituent nature of 'truth' and, by extension, whatever the ethical content a collective or communal good would of necessity entail based on that particular given.[20] For Hegel, this impasse was brought to bear when, as he argued in the *Phenomenology* and elsewhere, the logic of utilitarianism could not but collide with the absolute freedom and the radical autonomy suggested in the work of Kant and Rousseau.[21] It was a 'collision' that produced an impasse precisely because neither could develop, as Hegel saw it, a content to their respective communal goals.

In brief terms, the argument proposed by Hegel could be summarized as follows. On the one hand, while the Enlightenment brought with it an emphasis on human subjectivity as individually contained in and of itself, it did so by hypostatizing that subjective individuality. In so doing, the fluid and relational aspects of self-actualization were lost, condemning to the level of utility the question of what ought to be.[22] Universal value was thus also derived as something extrinsic to the community, and universal ethicality could be established only by linking it to an arbitrary final point of a general will. 'What the Enlightenment sees is true, but *fatally partial*,' Taylor remarks.

> Thus it desacralizes, for it only sees the world as a heap of objects, open to human scrutiny and use; it does not see it also as manifestation, the emanation of reason ... All objects are seen as lying to hand. The dimension in which they are manifestation of something higher which would require an attitude of respect is occluded. Their only value must lie outside themselves, in their use for subjects, for men. Consequently, the universal category of value is an extrinsic one.[23]

This necessary debasement of the good, which for Hegel came to encompass only the partiality of utility, remained problematic on another level as well. Posing the will in terms of particularity meant that the content of that particularity had to be grounded in a notion of absolute freedom, either a notion that, itself remained meaningless unless one were either to forward a transcendental and a priori concept of the good or to accept as universal an accumulated set of particularized interests. But the former led to the posing of an already given 'truth' – hence begging the question entirely – while the latter led to a tyranny of majority, and, in the end, absolute terror.[24]

On the one hand, then, the radical autonomy of the moral subject, albeit fundamentally different from the earlier notions that linked morality (and subjectivity) to a normative ordering of some kind, would now be wholly dependent on human will. But that would imply having to pose a morality extrinsic to the social whole and hence not resolving the original problem posed by Hobbes and, later, Locke. Indeed, it would be unable to resolve the problem posed by all whom Hegel labelled as having accepted a partial, and hence 'utilitarian,' logic. On the other hand, by linking the radical autonomy of the moral subject wholly to human will, that which would be said to constitute the common good would subsequently be based on what could be seen only as an arbitrary collection of all the 'particularized wills' of society. Those particularized wills, taken together, would constitute, argued Hegel, an abstract majority based only on the proxy of representation, that is to say, one based on an abstract 'general will' of the people posed *as if* singular; *as if* universal; *as if*, therefore, representing the true.[25]

In the first case, then, one would be left with having to accept, as did Kant, the transcendental subject as the grounding for communal ethicality. In the second case, one would be left with having to accept, as Hegel accused Rousseau of accepting, the particular as if universal and, hence, as having to accept the *homogenization* of the social.[26] The one would lead to a formal but empty communal ethicality; the other, to the kind of levelling 'equality' exemplified, according to Hegel, in the brutal days of terror that followed the French Revolution. In his *Philosophy of Right*, Hegel thus remarked,

> [258]. ... Unfortunately, he [Rousseau] takes the will only in a determinate form as the individual will, and he regards the universal will not as the absolutely rational element in the will, but only as a 'general' will which proceeds out of this individual will as out of a conscious will. The result is that he reduces the union of individuals in the state to a contract and therefore to something based on their arbitrary wills, their opinion and their capriciously given express consent ... [Thus] the will of its refounders was to give it what they alleged was a purely rational basis, but it was only abstractions that were being used; the Idea was lacking; and the experiment ended in the maximum of frightfulness and terror.[27]

These two difficulties underscored a peculiar irony: if one were to follow through on the logic of modernity as founded on reason and diversity and, in so doing, push the principle of a radical autonomy of human participation and of the human will as the only meaningful way to accept and forward that proposition, it would seem that one would either be condemned to embrace a moral principle hoisted on the now vacuous terrain of equality or ultimately be reduced to accepting a civil society as nothing more than a sameness absolute in its destruction. In any event, this was, at least in part, what Hegel thought to be the problem, despite the glaring objections one might wish to take against this particular interpretation of Kant or Rousseau.[28]

But given this interpretation, it is worth investigating one of the ways in which Hegel chose to resolve the problem of grounding ethicality in relation to absolute freedom, for this resolution and, perhaps more to the point, the way in which Gramsci both acknowledges and rejects it set the backdrop for Gramsci's own development of the ethical, the political, and the democratic. Indeed, this resolution sets the backdrop for Gramsci's move 'beyond' the horizon of liberal theory and practice in general.

The Hegelian interpretation and attempted resolution of the impasse

In presenting his critique of Kant and Rousseau, Hegel took as a point of departure the posing of modernity as itself a fractured unity, a dialecticized unity of diverse and abstract elements held together by reason.[29] But, as noted earlier, equality of reason, at least as it had been proposed in the work of Hobbes and Locke, was not enough to create the social cement necessary to hold together civil society. It required, with all the pitfalls outlined already, an appeal to an extrinsic authority; it required a notion of obligation, in this case to the sovereign or to the state. In this way, social cohesion would not only be guaranteed, or at least attempted, but would be codified in a way that tried to relate the 'is' with the 'ought,' indeed, to present the 'is' as if it were the 'ought.'

The impasse encountered in the attempt to provide ethical content and cohesion necessary to a social order required for its resolution an incorporation of specificity *within* the social itself, without, at the same time, presenting that specificity as a distinct entity in and of itself. What Hegel found appealing in the radical rethinking of Kant and Rousseau, as distinct from that of other liberal 'utilitarians,' was, in part, the proposition that obligation itself ought to be drawn from the notion of the will – more particularly, the rational will – rather than having to be deduced from a 'duty' to the sovereign or the state, or both. By placing emphasis on the will in this way, a different conception of reason could be incorporated, one that could provide, at the very least, a criterion for the constitutive aspect of the social as entailing the specificity of human action. And it could do this, argued Hegel, without, at the same time, having to premise the meaning of that action on the calculation of 'means to an end.' As Hegel writes, '[258]. The state is absolutely rational inasmuch as it is the actuality of the substantial will which it possesses in the particular self-consciousness once that consciousness has been raised to consciousness of its universality. This substantial unity is an absolute unmoved end in itself, in which freedom comes into its supreme right. On the other hand this final end has supreme right against the individual, whose supreme duty is to be a member of the state.'[30]

Developing the concept of the will as a function of individual activity, without concomitantly positing an a priori truth, re-emphasized further the division between nature and culture. By underscoring the separation between nature and culture, and in so doing linking obligation to will, Hegel provided a view that could uphold the argument that there is no natural order to the social whole and, at the same time, begin to provide the theoretical tools necessary to deduce or establish individual morality and give content to communal ethicality.[31]

His resolution, as mentioned at the outset, was to begin to systematize reason in terms of a dialecticized *Geist*. By doing so, he neatly avoided all the traps thus far outlined: the trap of appealing to an external authority so as to give a functional ethicality and coherence to the social whole; the trap of appealing to an empty reason in order to give formal ethicality to the human participation and will; and, finally, the trap of appealing directly to this absolute humanity and hence requiring an arbitrary ethicality that would ultimately negate the diversity inherent in the social structures of modernity, producing in its place an abstract and generalized homogeneity of social life itself.

One of the reasons for his being able to avoid those dilemmas lay precisely in the distinction he designated between the moral subject and the ethical community, between, that is, *Moralität* and *Sittlichkeit*.[32] This distinction was neither formal nor arbitrary. It was rather one from which he planned to develop an ontology posing communal ethicality neither extrinsic to reality nor rooted in the particularity (and hence arbitrariness) of individual subjectivity. Indeed, it became one of the most basic distinctions necessary to give rational content to the ethical moment without, hoped Hegel, repeating the traps set out above.

As Hegel makes clear throughout his work, it would be impossible to achieve a result different from those already discussed unless one understood that morality could never be posed in and of itself. Instead, morality always had to be contextualized within, and as subject to, the dialectically constituted cosmological order. In this context, then, morality became for Hegel an inner or private aspect of life. However, it could only remain a meaningless abstraction unless cast in terms of (and hence linked with) its dialectical counterpoint, the public world, the community. For Hegel, then, Kant and Rousseau would never be able to resolve their respective errors: by remaining only at the level of a free will divorced from the greater cosmological whole, one whose unity was itself a synthesis, they would be able to produce only a vacuous morality, 'a pure aspiration, a pure ought to be [*Sollen*].'[33] This vacuous morality, this pure 'ought to be' could be avoided, argued Hegel in the *Philosophy of Right*, if one cast the individual as both moral subject and moral agent whose embodiment could be accomplished only in terms of the community. Without this complement of community, one would be able to deduce only an abstract 'duty for duty's sake.' Thus he writes: 'The particular subject is related to the good as to the essence of his will, and hence his will's obligation arises directly in this relation. Since particularity is distinct from the good and falls within the subjective will, the good is characterised to begin with only as the universal abstract essentiality of the will, ie, as duty. Since duty is thus abstract and universal in character, it should be done for duty's sake.'[34]

Conversely, given this complement of community, the criterion of what could be considered 'good' would thus be deduced without having to pose an a priori order or impose an external agency beyond reason itself. In that case, then, morality would embody the attempt to conform the individual's rational will with universal reason. Community would then become the ethical completion – indeed, the ethical substance – of that attempt. 'It is only as ontological reason,' confirms Taylor,

> which seeks its own embodiment in a community with a certain necessary structure, that rationality yields a criterion of the good. The content of the rational will is what this community requires of us. This then is our duty. It is not derived from formal reason, but from the nature of the community which alone can embody reason ... The demands on man as a bearer of rational will are thus that he live in a community which embodies reason, which is the fulfilled goal of reason. That is, what is implicit in the concept of man as a vehicle of rational will is only fully realised in such a community.[35]

For Hegel, then, this connection between morality and community grounds an otherwise vacuous 'ought' to the 'is'; and it is exactly this completion of morality in terms of the community as the bearer of ethical substance that forms the basis for Hegel's concept of *Sittlichkeit*. But since this concept is posed in terms of dialectical synthesis, *Sittlichkeit* is not simply the completion of *Moralität*. It is rather the constitutive unity of the 'is' and 'ought'; it is precisely their unified expression.

Given that *Sittlichkeit* is the synthesis of 'is' and 'ought,' it encompasses both reality, that is, existence, and the becoming of that existence, i.e., the making of 'what ought to be' into the 'what is.' In that sense, it becomes precisely the obligatory task that demands of the individual to bring into existence, to concretize, or to realize what it is that already exists. To clarify the matter, it is worth quoting Taylor at length:

> The crucial character of Sittlichkeit is that it enjoins us to bring about what already is. This is a paradoxical way of putting it, but in fact the common life which is the basis of my Sittlichkeit obligation is already there in existence. It is in virtue of its being an ongoing affair that I have these obligations; and my fulfillment of these obligations is what sustains it and keeps it in being. Hence, in Sittlichkeit there is no gap between what ought to be and what is, between Sollen and Sein.
>
> With Moralität, the opposite holds. Here we have an obligation to realise something which does not exist. What ought to be contrasts with what is. And connected with this, the obligation holds of me not in virtue of being part of a larger community life, but as an individual rational will.[36]

Relying, at least in part, on these distinctions, then, Hegel attempts to fight against both the homogenization of the social whole and the posing of a vacuous ethicality by re-enforcing a notion of the will as the embodiment of individual rationality while simultaneously attempting to ground that will in a universal ethicality. This is a universal ethicality that could act as a founding principle to the 'what ought to be' of a social whole. For, in posing the 'ought' in terms of a dialectically nuanced *Moralität* and *Sittlichkeit*, the former representing the private realm of civil society as the embodiment of the economic/utilitarian relations among men, and the latter representing the public realm of the state, as the highest expression of the ethical community, their linkage would be understood as a constitutive unity towards which society would unfold. Hence the social would itself become an expression of immanent movement whose ethicality would emerge in and of itself, rather than from the existence of a pregiven or externalized legitimizing truth.

But ultimately, and despite its profundity, the embodiment of ethicality in terms of a universal reason could not deliver on its promise to bring a better society to fruition. For as Marx and many others have challenged, Hegel's 'ethical society' had no strategic space available to negotiate the complex terrain of power relations. Nor, perhaps more to the point, did it have a space for registering the historicity of those power imbalances. Consequently, it was incapable of coming to terms with human misery and exploitation, except at the level of concept. Despite painstaking attempts to resolve the complex problem of ethicality while, simultaneously, encompassing a notion of diversity and the radical autonomy of the human subject, there was no room left for strategy, no room for tactics; indeed, there was no room left for politics: there was only the ethical ideal towards which society would immutably unfold.

In one sense then, we had bequeathed to us from Hegel a brilliant mapping of the ideal human condition, even a way to comprehend and ground the ethicality of life. On the other hand, the grounding of ethicality in an ontology of pure reason left one, at best, with only an ability to comprehend the world and not the means, both analytic and practical, to transform it. Idealist philosophy, however richly textured, necessarily lost sight of the political task, a blindness Marx had tersely criticized when he wrote, in the 'Theses on Feuerbach,' that 'throughout the ages the philosophers have only interpreted the world; the point is, however, to change it.'[37]

It is in this context – the context of attempting to fight for and establish a better society, one where ethicality is rooted in a modernity marked by its diversity and radical autonomy of the human subject without falling victim to the traps described earlier, without, that is to say, remaining in either a liberal or an idealist framework – where we can begin to situate the radical work of Antonio Gramsci. As we shall see, Gramsci's philosophy of praxis attempts to resolve the very dilemma we have been discussing, the dilemma that, as we saw, was impossible to resolve through the various liberalisms addressed above and had been wrongly resolved through idealism.

But more than this, Gramsci's radical reassessment attempts also to resolve the ethico-political predicament that some had claimed had struck at the very core of Marx's historicization of the hegelian dialectic. That is, the problem of articulating in analytic terms (as well as practical and strategic ones) a way to take seriously the profundity of placing history as the terrain upon which meaning, indeed reality itself, would be constituted, i.e., without hypostatizing a notion of the 'good' or, for that matter, accepting truth as an infinite and indistinguishable relativity.

As we shall see, Gramsci attempts to rework the marxist dialectic in such a way as to be able to acknowledge the importance of the will in not only providing a social cohesiveness to reality but, at the same time, becoming the vehicle for the creating and sustaining of the 'ought' of the ethico-political society. But, unlike Hegel, Gramsci attempts to ground the will in the ethico-political becoming of a specific social subject, revisioning subjectivity itself through the lens of a dialectic that has been radically historicized.

For as we shall examine, Gramsci was determined to clarify why the placing of history and reason as the direct expression of human life was so crucial for establishing what he called a 'real' democracy, a 'citizen democracy.' Moreover, he was determined to show how it was, in so emphasizing that placement of history and reason, that an ethical society could be produced, while not losing sight of – indeed, incorporating at a fundamental level – a fluid notion of strategy and tactics, and, in a word, politics.

He wanted to argue this point by maintaining that marxism was itself a 'philosophy' (of praxis) and, as such, was capable of holding to the tenet that both society and the individual were specific historical creations whose essence would be a function of that continual historical activity engaged in producing and reproducing social life. Yet, given that, he also intended to clarify the way in which the philosophy of praxis was a philosophy quite capable of showing how ethicality could itself be rooted in the radical autonomy of a human subjectivity neither homogeneous nor pre-established, nor posed as a 'natural' given. In fact, he wanted to show that that subjectivity was fundamentally heterogeneous, diverse, and fractured, though, at the same time and because of this heterogeneity, it would become the terrain upon which the 'ethico-political' society, i.e., the 'better' society, could be produced and maintained.

As Gramsci saw it, then, this clarification required, at the very least, lengthy discussions on the relationships between history and reason, and the ramifications that this conceptualization had for a notion of science, law, and, indeed, the marxist dialectic itself. Thus we find in the *Quaderni del carcere* extensive explications on the role and importance of these particular philosophical positions drawn from the texts of philosophers as diverse as Vico and Croce. Let us now turn to his reading of their work, for it is from their arguments, and the way in which Gramsci will interpret them, that we shall become better able to determine how Gramsci's prison notebooks represent a crucial contribution to a post-liberal democratic theory.

TWO

Gramsci's Epistemological Eclecticism:

What He Borrows from Vico and Croce, and Why

A systematic treatment of the philosophy of praxis cannot afford to neglect any of its constituent parts of the doctrine of its founder. But how
should this be understood? It should deal with all the general philosophical parts, and then should develop in a coherent fashion all the general
concepts of a methodology of history and politics and, in addition, of art,
economics and ethics, finding its place in the overall construction for a
theory of the natural sciences.[1]

That Gramsci chose to refer to marxism as the 'philosophy of praxis'
rather than to continually use the expression 'dialectical materialism'
– or even the term 'marxism' itself – has often been attributed to one of
two reasons, sometimes both.[2] The more common of the two dismisses the phrase as a strategic camouflage necessary to divert the censo-
rial gaze of the prison guards whose duty it was, should they have
found proof that Gramsci's mind was still functioning in any way, but
particulary in an anti-fascist, pro-left way, to end, and end abruptly, that
mental activity.[3] The other reason cited, almost as frequently and often
in conjunction with the first, is that, for Gramsci, whose intellectual
background was founded upon classical German and Italian philosophy, marxism could best be represented as a philosophy of 'action'
whose improvement was bound up with having to revitalize (in a
slightly refurbished form) its idealist and speculative roots. Still others
pointed to the direct links between Gramsci's work and a leninist praxis
par excellence and insisted the latter become the primary focus of
study.[4] Hence, on the one hand, long testimonials attesting to the dif-

ficulty of reading the correct meanings behind his strategically placed metaphor; hence, on the other, whole debates erupting over how marxist or hegelian (or crocean, gentilean, bergsonian, sorelian, even kantian) was the 'real' philosophy of the Gramsci prison notebooks.

There is another way of grasping the complexity of Gramsci's philosophy of praxis. And that is to accept that what Gramsci wrote is precisely what he meant. We shall discover that if we accept the development of his own arguments, which begin by dismissing notions of a philosophy 'in general,' of a human nature 'in general,' and, finally, of a 'general will,' Gramsci's rendering of the philosophy of praxis elaborates a richly historicized and profoundly dialectic conception of the social whose subjectivity, i.e., whose very meaning, is itself an 'active unity,' a constitutive expression nuanced by and, at the same time, forming the terrain upon which political struggle takes place.

By posing the social as entailing at its very core the fluidity of political movement, that is, by incorporating *contingency* as the primordial feature of the social, Gramsci attempts to detail in theoretical terms what constitutes the 'is.' As we shall discover, the acceptance of contingency has not only certain ramifications for the conceptualization of self, but also certain ramifications around the posing of the collective will, of collective consensus, and indeed of legitimation itself. But incorporating a dialectical/historical notion of contingency as a central feature of meaning and identity also allows Gramsci to posit an 'ought.' That is, it allows him to begin to articulate a notion of the 'better' society as one whose regulation, maintenance, and reproduction are based precisely on a vital, consensual link between the collective will of a specific 'the people' – a people immanent in their intellectual and creative self-development – and the government that becomes its expression.[5]

What might be intended by Gramsci's insistence on 'active' or 'constituent' unities, or even his emphasis on the notion of 'dialectical movement' in history, with its concomitant stress on the will and its relation to politics and philosophy, can best be understood by situating his remarks in the context of an entire group of thinkers whose projects might seem, or indeed were, contradictory to that of Marx or of Lenin. His remarks must be situated in the polemical writings and philosophical discussions of, in particular, Vico and Croce, and, to a lesser extent, that of Hegel and Kant, because Gramsci drew explicitly from their accounts in a number of ways, though always attempting, in so doing, to rid a borrowed concept of its metaphysical roots. Among the notions that we will assess in this chapter are those of science as probability, and of truth as an aesthetic; finally, we shall examine the incorporation of immanence or movement in terms of an ethico-political concept of history.

This is not to suggest exactly the reverse of what has been criticized at the outset of the chapter. There is no intent here to argue that Gramsci's work could best be understood as some peculiar version of a vichean or a crocean logic. It is simply to suggest that the richness and complexity of many of the concepts Gramsci incorporates from their work, as well as those he later develops (such as the notion of the will or the more familiar concept of hegemony, or even the concept of democracy itself), emerge from his own intellectual jousting with those whose speculative and idealist philosophies directly contradicted the philosophical underpinnings of those of Marx or Lenin. It in this context that we must pause first before examining Gramsci's work directly, and investigate, instead, some of the writings of Vico and Croce, assessing, in so doing, what Gramsci found useful in their arguments, and why.

Against 'external realities' or dualisms of any kind

Gramsci, like many political philosophers, often wrote on the question regarding the essence of what might be considered 'human,' or, as he put it, the 'practico-political problem of what is man.'[6] This question was rhetorical in the best sense of the word, for it allowed Gramsci to make the point over and again that philosophers from every epoch, in attempting to answer that question, have always carried the baggage of their own societal presence – with its prejudices peculiar to that time period – into their analyses detailing reality and a person's place in it. Indeed, and in the name of producing objective conditions for the safeguarding and reproducing of social systems based precisely, or at least in part, on a given concept of man, this question had often raised a multitude of issues. For Gramsci, it raised at least two.

The first had more to do with the general nature of meaning itself. For implicit in the question 'what is man?' was an underlying assumption that might accept 'meaning' and hence truth itself as if universal, standing apart from the everyday. Indeed, implicit in the question 'what is man?' was for Gramsci the entire polemic raised around philosophy and its relation to history – that is, the polemic dividing philosophy from history as if there might exist an 'objective' rationality external to human consciousness and devoid of any error or particularity; as if, that is to say, philosophy could be autonomous from the very beings who conceptualized it. To put it slightly differently, the one question concerning the nature of man brought with it another: whether it was possible to avoid the usual trap of maintaining a 'general philosophy about philosophy,' an externalized philosophy somehow existing apart from history, and from which a whole series of 'oughts' regarding truth, humanity, or even the social order could be deduced, ipso facto.

The second set of issues had a more narrow focus: in posing the question 'what is man?' could one reconcile – or better, resolve once and for all – the often wrongly made deduction that man himself could best be understood in terms of a series of paired oppositions invoked to describe, through counterpoint, the individual and his or her humanity? Would it be possible, instead, to establish a systematic philosophy that would no longer require that the 'humanity' of a social agent be established through the age-old *opposition* between man and nature or even between man and woman, or as posed as that which exists between spirit and matter or, in twentieth-century terms, posed as if an opposition between collective humanity, on the one hand, and a massified science and/or technology, on the other?

As Gramsci saw it, it was in the context of these seemingly 'self-evident' paired oppositions, whether between objectivity versus subjectivity, or history versus nature, and so on, that the whole weight of philosophical tradition tended against the assumption that these oppositions should or could be otherwise, or even dispensed with altogether. It was in this context, in other words, that the whole weight of philosophical tradition tended to grant to homo sapiens a generalized and natural essence distinct from (and therefore focused around) its counterpoint, be it nature, woman, God, or science. Hence, it was in this context too that when Gramsci asked 'In what sense can one identify politics with history and therefore all life with politics?'[8] he was, at least at one level, searching for a way to end the continual philosophical quest for the '"objectivity" of the "external world."' He was attempting systematically to rid philosophy of the tendency to grant the existence of a dual reality, of an 'objective' reality, knowable outside of human activity, and one from which a subjective-identity in counterdistinction to it had consistently – and wrongly – been deduced.[9]

If, as Gramsci rhetorically proposed, there could be no politics outside of history and no human activity outside of politics, how could this formulation be expressed systematically without, on the one hand, lapsing into some sort of subjectivist dualism or, on the other, appearing as if a self-evident 'truth' gleaned from Marx's eleven theses on Feuerbach?[10] In attempting to resolve that dilemma, Gramsci looked for, and found refuge among, a set of philosophical inquiries that seemed partly (in some cases, completely) at odds not only with each other's systematic assumptions, but with what Gramsci himself seemed anxious to develop. As noted at the outset, he turned to, among others, the philosophical proposals of Vico and Croce, particularly with regard to their systematizing of knowledge, science, and the aesthetic.

Attempting to 'cleanse' these concepts of their metaphysical and idealist content,[11] Gramsci began to incorporate them so as to clarify and make more precise some of the conceptualizations proposed by Labriola and Marx: that philosophical 'dualisms' must be routed in their entirety; that 'truth,' identity, indeed meaning itself, must be understood precisely as a constitutive unity fissured through political struggle; that history is no more (or less) than the practico-political activity of the individuals who constitute it; and that philosophy is no more or less than the historical methodology of that practico-political activity.[12] So that we do not fall into a series of self-evident platitudes or solipsisms of our own, it is important now to examine in more detail the philosophical route Gramsci traversed, what was at stake, and why.

The contribution of Vico: Science as knowledge as history

It must be said at the outset that Gramsci's interpretation of Vico's major accomplishment(s) in political theory was strikingly close to the reading made by Benedetto Croce, an interpretation worth discussing in some detail if we are to underscore what it might be that Gramsci attempts to glean from it. Croce's enthusiasm stemmed from the fact that Vico's *New Science*[13] broke with the 'self-confidence,' as Croce was to call it, of cartesian philosophy, replacing Descartes's ahistorical 'I think therefore I am' with *verum ipsum factum*, or 'the truth is what is done (created).'[14]

For Vico, the posing of *verum ipsum factum* rendered a specific meaning to knowledge (*scienza*), other than the more obvious one of reformulating 'truth' as a temporal moment of certainty. In the earlier versions of his work, that passage specifically created a basis with which to identify the knowledge of all things created or of all things to be created with a superior being ('God'), since, as he initially reasoned, only a superior being could have created, and thereby have access to, the omnipresent logic of the universe.[15]

This meant that for the homo sapiens, who clearly was not the creator of the entire universe, any knowledge produced in the temporal world could be understood only as something 'approaching' truth; that is, could be understood only as probability. In short, it meant that the

product of man's creativity could be identified, as Vico argues, only
with consciousness, and not with science, properly speaking. As he first
explains in an earlier edition of *The New Science* (1725), paragraphs 137
and 321 respectively:

> Men who do not know what is true of things take care to hold fast to
> what is certain, so that, if they cannot satisfy their intellects by knowl-
> edge [*scienza*], their wills at least may rest on consciousness [*coscienza*] ...
> The 'certain' in the laws is an obscurity of judgement backed only by
> authority so that we find them harsh in application, yet are obliged to
> apply them just because they are certain. In good Latin, *cerium* means
> particularised, or, as the schools say, individuated; so that, in over-ele-
> gant Latin, *cerium* and *commune*, the certain and the common are opposed
> to each other.[16]

Thus we find in the early formulation of his *Scienza Nuova*, that Vico
had promoted to the status of Truth a concept of truth as entailing a
singular logic based on, and indeed incorporating as its totality, both
objective and subjective reality. By incorporating notions of both objectivity and subjectivity, Vico further underscored a concept of truth as
made up of two distinct and counterposed entities (namely, the object
and subject), which were, at the same time, presented as entailing
'equal weight' in their distinction; that is, were assumed to be, and were
presented as if, equivalent to each other. Among other things, this
meant that truth entailed a particular logic that could, precisely because
it was a product of a rational ordering, be ascertained as such. Truth in
this sense was bound by (or entailed) certain fundamental and absolute
laws, the understanding of which, i.e., the very logic of that truth, was
named by Vico 'science.'

This interpretation gave a particular status of recognition to man's
own intellect, intuition, and reason, each now understood to be bound
also by the limitations of man himself.[17] But it did so by insisting that
knowledge must be divided into two distinct spheres – on the one side,
as the true; on the other side, the certain; on the one side, that is, by
making an appeal to a universal *authority* outside man; on the other
side, by making an appeal to a universal *reason* in man; on the one side,
as science; on the other, as history.[18]

It was in the third edition of the *New Science* that Vico reconsidered
the rigidity of this categorization and, as a consequence of following
through on his own logic, introduced a caveat: if one could argue that
the identity of the subject with its object was the completeness of truth
and hence a 'science,' it seemed reasonable to extend the logic to in-

clude raw human activity as foundational to 'reality.' It seemed reasonable, in other words, to change the position slightly and to ask why it should not be the case that the *certainty* of a reality humanly constructed be understood as anything less than 'truth' in itself and, therefore, as a 'science,' properly speaking. For if the reality of man, the reality that stood (given Vico's dualism) external to the natural order, was indeed a product of human activity in all its various manifestations, it would follow logically that human reality could be knowable in its entirety, and not simply as a close approximation to the truth.[19]

It would seem that if one followed through on the logic implied by *verum ipsum factum*, it could thus be deduced quite clearly that history – the very circumstance and product of human interaction – could be intelligible or, rather, would entail a particular rationality or logic that Vico now claimed also as knowledge, and more precisely as 'science.' That is, if *verum ipsum factum* meant, at least in part, that the reality of the natural world could be ascertained owing precisely to the logic of imposing an identity of objectivity with subjectivity – thus insisting on the intensity of the relation a social agent might have to what had been or might be created – a new concept of truth-as-science could be developed that would contain within it particularity. At its most simple and direct point, then, Vico drew the identity that history, inasmuch as it is a creation of man and ascertainable as such, is equal to science.[20]

The logical inconsistency inherent in the previous attempt to divide Truth (reality) into two distinct 'camps' of knowledge, the one being science, the other history, was now reconciled, not from a uniting of the two realms of knowledge into one reality, but from maintaining this division in terms of two sciences, i.e., the natural sciences, on the one hand, the social sciences, on the other.[21] This new and altered conception of knowledge, *despite the logical foundation for its existence still firmly ensconced in the dualist antagonism between man and nature*, provided for a dramatic rethinking of social relations and, indeed, of society itself. It established a distinct entity of logic called 'history,' but a history that was accessible to the producers and creators of history, that is, to mankind. History, as such, was now posed as fundamentally rational in the sense both of an intellectual intelligibility and of a science.

Albeit posing this newer reading still in terms of an appeal to an external authority against which a *universal* rightness or wrongness around the whole of truth could be deduced, the emphasis on history in terms of a science/knowledge meant that a notion of ethical and moral activity could now also be placed at the level of individual reason. That is, ethicality could be established in part as a product of the thought and action of all humanity.[22] And as this was done in the name of science, it could now be said that the entire knowledge (i.e., truth) of producing and comprehending *ethical* and *moral* reasoning entailed a logic, a philosophical methodology, which itself was rooted in the terrain of human activity and which by its very nature was rational.[23]

But more than this, the vichean identity between science, knowledge, and history (and the ramifications Croce and Gramsci would later make of it in terms of an ethico-political morality) endowed the concept of science with a new dimensionality. For if, as Vico proposed, 'the truth is what is created,' science would now include in its ranks relativity, probability and prediction, law of tendency, or, in a word, change.[24] That is, it now granted to humanity a fundamental access to history, for not only could it be said that humankind was now understood to be the creator of history, a creativity linked to rationality and logic, but, as living participants in that history, they were capable of changing it and, perhaps more to the point, were required to become involved.

This was a particularly seductive point both for Croce and for Gramsci.[25] In the case of the former, as we shall shortly examine, it meant that all that was or could be expressed in society – i.e., logic, poetry, feelings, intuition; indeed, language itself – must now also be considered as science, must be considered rational, real and necessary, rather than mystic, divine or arbitrary.[26] It meant for Croce a way to develop a basis for an idealist logic that incorporated a 'scientific' history as fundamental to the construction of an (ideal) real. Indeed, rather than maintain Vico's claim that 'knowledge is a form of doing,' it meant refashioning it into its speculative inverse, 'doing is a form of knowledge.'[27]

For Gramsci, it indicated a possible way to connect the notions of a 'law of tendency' or 'probability-as-truth,' even relativity, with the concepts of 'progress,' 'historical movement,' 'freedom and necessity,' and so forth. Indeed, it indicated a possible way to articulate the very notion of a 'political science' and the ethical reality to which that science might conform.[28] But before any serious conclusion can be drawn concerning Gramsci's usage, we must continue our philosophical investigation by turning to Croce's interpretation of, and subsequent attempts to mend, the vichean split between the knowledge known and created by man (reason) and that known and created in nature (God/authority).

For Benedetto Croce, who alternatively pitted himself against transcendental metaphysics, scepticism, positivism, and historical materialism, this identity served as an initial point with which to construct his moral, aesthetic, and political philosophy. But Croce was an idealist. And this meant, among other things, that however crucial the vichean identity 'history equals science' was for his establishing the 'Aesthetic' as 'science of expression,' Croce was not about to leave it in its dualist form. From the start, he proceeded to refashion this identity in terms of the arguments extracted from his own (peculiar) reading of hegelian philosophy.[29]

This meant, primarily, that Vico's commitment to a dual appropriation of knowledge would be amended to conform with the position that reality entails but one truth (spirit), one overall 'knowledge' of knowledge. Claiming, as he would so bluntly express it, 'there is no such thing as a general philosophy or history or science; there is no general theory of knowledge,'[30] this newer amendment to the meaning of reality did not mean that Croce now planned to produce an overall theory of knowledge. But neither did it mean a reduction of all things known (or created) to a one-dimensional science.[31] Rather, it was an attempt to posit the natural sciences in a definite relation with the social sciences, one of abstract to concrete, where knowledge, properly speaking, would be the name given to the dialectical synthesis – what Croce called the 'active unity' – of these two sciences.[32]

Croce named this synthesis 'Philosophy,' a category that no longer stood, claimed Croce, beyond or outside reality. Rather, this synthetic entity would now be understood as the constitutive and expressive *methodology* underwriting all of science and history. And since, as Vico had shown, all that could be known or understood by man fell either to science or to history, then Philosophy, for Croce, would become also the specific methodology of all knowledge (both concrete and abstract) and therefore of all reality.[33] To put it another way, philosophy was now to be understood as the science of all reality. It was the methodology required to comprehend fully the presence of man's thoughts and actions in the creation of history – a history that, although distinct from, could not be independent of, the 'physical or abstract' sciences, as Croce was inclined to call them.[34]

To what extent, however, did this seemingly endless rearranging of terms of identities and distinctions mark a significant advance on Vico's *verum ipsum factum*? Or, more to the point, was Croce simply providing us with albeit sophisticated identities, nevertheless tautological ones, based on seemingly well-reasoned but inevitably solipsistic musings about reality and a person's relation to it? Without committing ourselves to a lengthy study of Croce's philosophy of spirit, we need to investigate Croce's unquestionably peculiar reading of Hegel before we can satisfactorily answer that question.

It will be demonstrated below that it is precisely this 'peculiar' rendering of Hegel – what Croce refers to as the mere salvaging of 'living' concepts from the 'dead' and 'rotted' ones in the hegelian system[35] – that tends to prevent these identities from remaining at the level of descriptive abstraction useful only for ivory-towered sport. What becomes obvious as we wade through certain parts of Croce's logic is not only the fact Croce himself is convinced he has defeated the authority/reason dualism in Vico's theory of knowledge, but the fact he is convinced he has defeated all aspects of dualism: the splitting of theory from practice, thought from action; indeed, politics from history.[36]

But pointing out the salient features of Croce's rather clever (if not entirely successful) feat of recombining vichean dichotomies with hegelian dialectics serves a second function. It will become the basis upon which we will be able to discover how Gramsci planned his own attacks against dualisms that split into separate categories science-knowledge and nature-authority, and all that this splitting has implied. Indeed, by investigating this attempt by Croce to secure and blend vichean dichotomies with hegelian dialectics, it will become clearer how, minus its idealist shell, Croce's argument becomes quite useful for Gramsci's articulation of the philosophy of praxis itself.[37] Indeed, these attacks against dualism prove crucial for reaffirming not only the significance of what is meant by progress in the philosophy of praxis, but what might constitute at the theoretical level a people's democracy.

Why Croce

Croce's salvaging of living concepts from the land of the dead involved two specific conceptual moves. The more significant of the two (in Croce's estimation) had to do with an incorporation of Kant's a priori synthetic judgment into Hegel's dialectical ordering of the relations between history, philosophy, art, and religion.[38] The second had more to do with Croce's interpretation of equivalence, identity, opposition, and difference in the hegelian dialectic itself, an interpretation that, as we will find, brings him back full circle to the a priori synthetic unity already transcended in the work of Hegel.[39] But despite this so-called regression to kantianism, the reinstitution of an a priori synthetic unity allows Croce to deposit into his philosophical arsenal two crucial concepts upon which Gramsci would later rely: that is, the notion of distincts and the notion of degrees (or moments).[40]

Let us begin, then, with Croce's peculiar interpretation of Hegel, which attempted to render the very foundation of the hegelian dialectic into a triadic form, with 'being' as thesis, 'nothing' as antithesis, and 'becoming' as their synthesis. Croce understood this triad as equating a positive pole of existence entirely in terms of its negative pole (non-existence) where their self-identities could have no other concrete expression outside of becoming.[41] That is, becoming gave *meaning* to the otherwise empty abstractions of being and nothingness. From this somewhat narrow (others would say wrong) understanding of the complexity of the dialectic, Croce drew the conclusion that according to this method, any universal (concept) would necessarily be rendered into a direct and total equivalence with, rather than maintaining a difference from, its opposite prior to dialectical synthesis.[42]

Croce saw this deduction as incredibly illogical. On the one hand, it seemed to Croce that it would render what would have been understood as 'universal' (and hence fully determined) into mere abstraction awaiting synthesis; on the other hand, it would place the burden of constituting their difference (not to mention negation) entirely on a dialectical process of sameness. This conclusion gravely upset Croce for he saw this 'illogic' as an all too obvious gap in Hegel's reasoning and one not properly disposed of either by Hegel or by his critics alike. In his typically sarcastic style, Croce thus remarked,

> I do not see how anyone still succeeds in keeping his seat on it. It has been said: If being and nothing are *identical* (as Hegel proves or thinks he proves), how can they constitute becoming? Becoming in Hegel's theory must be a synthesis of *opposites*, not identities, of which there can be no synthesis. [For] a = a remains a, and does not become b. But being is identical with nothing only when being and nothing are thought badly, or are not thought truly. Only then does it happen that the one equals the other, not as a = a, but rather as $\emptyset = \emptyset$. For the thought which thinks them truly, being and nothing are not identical but precisely opposite, and in conflict with one another. And this conflict (which is also union, since wrestlers in order to wrestle, must lay hold of one another!) is becoming.[43]

For Croce, then, Hegel's appropriation of being and nothing represented a hurried attempt to underwrite a notion of becoming by losing sight of, or better, by slipping over, what made up the distinct concepts themselves, i.e, what constituted the individuality within each of the two (universal) concepts out of which becoming would constitute their unified expression. This was, for Croce, the 'essential flaw' of hegelian logic.[44] He wanted to argue, instead, that a 'true' concept, unlike a 'pseudo' one, is a fully realized concept, a concrete-universal that can never fall into the trap of being either a general or an abstract concept.[45] And he wanted to argue that it should be considered as a fully determined concrete-universal, not simply because universality implied 'oneness,' 'indivisibility,' or 'wholeness' but because the totality itself was *predicated* on two (and only two) distinct abstractions.[46]

This meant for Croce that should one attempt to divide a concrete-universal, one would necessarily reach two and only two distinct abstractions which would give to that universal its character or essence, beyond which there could be no concept. These two distinct abstractions would be either opposite abstractions (Croce's example: that of being and nothing) unified by an a priori synthesis to constitute the expression of the concrete-universal (Being); or these abstractions would be distinct but not necessarily opposite abstractions (like 'useful' and 'good') whose a priori synthetic unity would condition the existence of the concrete-universal (as, for example, in the case of the 'good,' as the condition for the universal/concrete concept of ethico-political morality).[47]

This did not mean that a true concrete concept would be posited as a thing-in-itself, for, in this (kantian) sense, thing-in-itself would imply a static notion of knowledge, a position Croce was fervently trying to uproot. Croce wished rather to demonstrate how thing-in-itself would imply an abstract knowledge always-already present and existing outside phenomena, and therefore, outside history. In other words, if one were to ignore the substantiality of concrete universals, and hence deny the existence of distincts, then one would have to take as a given a concept of knowledge that wholly existed a priori, that is, external to the concept. In this sense, subjectivity could be neither a part of the natural sciences nor a part of the social sciences nor, for that matter, a part of man's active creation. That position, of course, would lead to, among other things, the reliance on an analytic proposition directly in contradiction to the now well-established *verum ipsum factum.*

For Croce, a true concrete concept was necessarily formed by the unity of abstract oppositions or 'distincts.' This meant in part, and in keeping with Kant's *Critique of Judgement,* that Croce understood individual-aesthetic judgment as a synthetic (and a priori) unity of subject and predicate whose unity was precisely a condition *of* existence.[48] Croce then replanted this particular reading of the individual-aesthetic judgment into an idealist framework to argue that a true concept, as a concrete-universal, fully determined concept, would always and of necessity be predicated on the unity of specific abstract or distinct oppositions.[49] Thus, for example, the concrete-universal concept of beauty would not 'mistakenly' be understood (as he had accused Hegel of so doing) as being, at one and the same time, both an abstraction posed in *opposition* to the 'ugly' as well as a fully determined concrete-universal in identity with the 'ugly' where their difference – and hence, their meaning – could be ascertained only through dialectical synthesis.

Rather, in adopting Kant's a priori synthetic unity, Croce reasoned that beauty would now be understood as predicated on the synthetic unity of the abstract notion 'beautiful' plus its opposite (and also abstract) notion of 'ugliness.' Furthermore, it meant not only that these abstract but distinctly opposite notions structured the concept of beauty itself – so that, now, what would be considered as beauty would entail both a beautiful and an ugly moment in the unfolding of this concrete universal – but that beauty itself would take its place in the dialectical process as a fully determined concept. In this context, the notion of distincts allowed Croce, among other things, to incorporate 'within' the dialectic a particular, albeit abstract, condition of otherness as the very condition around which a universal concept could be expressed.

Given this predication and involvement of distincts, Croce reasoned that if the universal concept called beauty were to be posited as the first (positive) pole in the dialectical triad, in opposition to the second (negative) pole, it would not lose its identity, or, to use Croce's description, would not 'melt' into a meaningless sameness only to be disengaged in some 'miraculous' way by the third term of the dialectical triad. Rather, the beautiful and the ugly would retain their distinction (though made to be 'identical' through dialectical synthesis) precisely because they were, each one of them, complete concrete-universals predicated on the unity of two abstract terms prior to the dialectical process itself.

It is worth taking one more example to clarify exactly where Croce wished to lead us, and, more to the point, what Gramsci found important about this problem of distinction. Using the concept of the truth, for example, Croce would say that if the truth were a fully determined concrete-universal, as it was considered to be, it could not be 'demoted,' as he would put it, to the status of an abstraction now opposed to but equated with falsity or error, where their distinction could be drawn out only through dialectical synthesis. Rather, the truth would be understood as constituted by the incomplete abstractions of both truth and falsity, which, although opposites, would not cancel each other out. Instead they would create from their unity-in-distinction the universal essence of the two.[51]

Thus Croce would say that all truth is constituted by elements of truth and falsity (or error). As he would say, also, all beauty is constituted by both beautiful and ugly moments. He would say that all existence contains both life and death; that all reality is exhausted by the unity of thought and action. In short, he would argue that all true concrete-universals are always predicated on, and therefore constituted by, two abstract opposites or distinct moments, moments that, because they are so placed, would permit the concrete-universal to retain its distinction even when made equivalent to its opposite (also a concrete-universal) within the dialectical process.[52]

It should be mentioned at this point, however, that Croce developed the argument around distincts on a condition thus far omitted: that there must exist a particular order of one abstract distinction to the other. More important, not only was this order exact rather than arbitrary; the two moments must also stand in a relation of one to the other, as first degree to the second.[53] This was a logical – and not hierarchical – ordering. It meant not only that the two distinct elements that constituted a concrete-universal were unified prior to dialectical synthesis (as examined above), but that this unity had to be understood as an *active unity*. That is, it had to be understood in terms of a *linear progression from one step to the next*, rather than simply in terms of a dialectical movement from negation to synthesis.[54] More precisely, it meant that the first degree or moment in a universal unfolding of the concept stood as the condition upon which the second degree or moment would be predicated.

As typical of Croce's writings, he explained the importance of this point by relying on a descriptive example. In this case, he likened the specific ordering of distinctions within a fully determined concept as similar to the first and second rungs on a ladder or the first and second floors of a house.[55] Croce was trying to emphasize that the first degree (or, in the case the ladder, the first rung) was not more important than the rest; rather it was the logical condition without which the second degree (or rung) would be impossible to obtain.[56]

Thus Croce argued that in the concrete-universal 'thought,' the a priori synthetic unity of that universal would be constituted both by (pure) intuition, as the first moment or degree of thought, and by the (pure) concept as the refinement and, accordingly, second moment or gradation (or degree) of thought. [57] Intuition, as the first degree then, did not stand in opposition to the pure concept of thought, but was rather the very condition upon which the latter could be formed. There could be no thought without, at the minimum, this pure intuition, no logicality or making more coherent any expression without its antecedent being present.

In the concrete-universal 'action,' or what he modifies and renames as pure practical activity, the a priori synthetic unity would be constituted by its first moment, which for Croce would be the economic or 'pure' will, distinct from, but of course not devoid of, thought.[58] The second moment of pure practical activity would be categorized by

Croce as the (also pure) 'ethico-political moment,' which, because it would be cast as the second gradation or degree, would become precisely the moment of making more coherent the economic activity or the so-called will. In this context, the (pure) will would no longer stand in opposition to morality; it would, rather, simply be the condition upon which the ethico-political would become a reality, i.e., would become concrete. In the final analysis, then, this would mean that there would be a *definite and permanent* ordering – that of first degree to second – to the moments that constituted each concrete-universal, an ordering that would, ipso facto, produce a totalized and fully determined meaning.[59]

By thus relying on a somewhat altered kantian notion of the a priori synthetic unity, coupled with his own notions of distincts and degrees, Croce arrives at what he considers the only logical alternative to dualism. Indeed, he arrives at what he assumes to be the only logical way to remove from various identities (born out of opposition) all 'empty' abstractionism and thus make more meaningful the equivalences earlier stated around philosophy, history, science, and, now, the aesthetic. This meant, furthermore, a positing of the notion of spirit (in this context meaning all ideal reality) as the *total expression* of the a priori synthetic unity of 'knowing' and 'doing,' or, as Croce put it, as the expression of the 'theoretical' and 'practical' act, firmly rooted in the now renovated hegelian system.[60]

For Gramsci's purposes, several consequences could be drawn from this move. But for Croce, it meant, first, that reality, as a system of knowledge, would be wholly constituted by the theoretical and the practical, outside of which there could be no meaningful conception of thought or action. To put it slightly differently, the theoretical and the practical were possible only within the context of the real (e.g., the Idea or Spirit), outside of which they would be 'impossible,' 'nonsensical,' or 'meaningless.' And as this was an a priori synthetic unity of theory and praxis, this meant, as we have seen, that intellectual activity constituted the first moment of Absolute Spirit, distinct from, but not a negation of, practical activity.[61] Accordingly, then, the will would no longer be identified with or based on 'feelings' or 'whim,' nor would it fall 'outside' of thought, since it too would be constituted, in part, by reason. As such, the will would directly be a part of the (ideal) expression of the intellect; indeed, it would be directly rational. Thus we find Croce writing,

Freed from the equivocal term, which is feeling, and now passing to the problem of the relation between the theoretical and the practical activity enunciated, we must in the first place declare the thesis that the *practical activity presupposes the theoretical*. Will is impossible without knowledge; as is knowledge, so is the will ... In recognizing this precedence of knowledge to will, we do not wish to posit as thinkable a theoretical man or a theoretical moment altogether deprived of will. This would be an unreal abstraction, inadmissible in philosophy ... [For the] forms of the spirit are distinct and not separate, and when the spirit is found in one of its forms, or is *explicit* in it, the other forms are also in it, but *implicit*, or, as is also said, *concomitant*.[62]

Given this argument, then, Croce thus deduces that morality itself could not be conceived outside of man's practical and theoretical activity.[63] In fact, any type of 'praxis' would now be inconceivable without thought. Simply stated, Croce arrives at the conclusion that the absolute spirit must be understood as an active *progression* of the four distincts; namely, the will with its counterpoint, ethico-morality; and the intuition with its counterpoint, the intellect. The first unified pair (will/ethico-morality) constitutes the whole of practical activity; the second pair (intuition/intellect) constitutes the whole of thought. Both pairs taken together form the whole of (pure) reality, understood as representing and necessarily inscribing the 'twofold degree.'[64] Thus, what one is confronted with is an 'active progression' that would have on the one side a pure practical activity whose 'second' moment or degree would be its more coherent expression of will (i.e., posed now in terms of an ethico-political morality). But this category of the practical would remain an empty abstraction unless, continuing in the dialectic relation, theoretic activity would be posed in distinction to – indeed, as the condition of – the practical. Intuition clarified by its second degree (intellect) would complete the whole of the theoretic, and the union of both theoretic and practical would thus constitute the whole of (pure) reality.

With all this in place, Croce was now able to turn his attention towards the original problem encountered with Vico's previously sketched reformulation of science and knowledge and the dualism this had required. Croce suggested that given the position where all of human creation, that is, all theoretical and practical activity (which taken together exhausted the whole of reality and constituted its essence), was now to be understood as science and, second, given that philosophy was now held to be the methodology of that science, he was ready to argue that the first moment (or degree) of philosophy would be named aesthetic, the science of expression, while its second moment (or degree) would be called logic, the science of pure concept. The economic would constitute the science of the will, and history, the science of ethico-political morality.[65]

Thus, whereas Kant posed the aesthetic as the point of arrival, for Croce it became the point of *departure*. Whereas Hegel posed philosophy as the synthesis of the dialectical opposites art and religion, for Croce it was now to be equated with history, where history was to be understood as the highest moment or 'expression' of philosophy.[66] Thus, too, it was history for Croce – and not kantian aesthetics or hegelian philosophy – that was posited in the development of absolute spirit (i.e., in the development of an ideal reality), as the point of *arrival*. Indeed, this premiss led Croce to argue that not only could there be no plausible conception of history outside of reality (spirit), *but the creation of history itself would always imply an active progression*. As a bonus to the argument, it would always imply a *knowledge* of that progress as one that would, a priori, be accessible to human comprehension – accessible precisely since it was conceived as the expression of man's creative presence, i.e., as the first degree in the unfolding of Absolute Spirit.

Essentially for Croce, then, four consequences at once became both obvious and crucial. First, reasoned Croce, if history were now to be identified with philosophy (history being its highest moment or expression), logically, then, ideal philosophy could not be condemned (as it had been by his detractors, among them Gramsci) as being anti-historical or 'abstract.' Because there could not be, by definition, any 'meaning' outside spirit, there could be no general, abstract, or arbitrary logic to reality, no general 'philosophy' of philosophy, indeed, no philosophy outside praxis.[68] Applauding the novelty of his own work, Croce thus congratulates himself, writing:

> The richness of reality, of facts, of experience, which seemed to be withdrawn from the pure concept and so from philosophy, is on the contrary, restored to and recognised in philosophy, not in the diminished and improper form which is that of empirical science, but in a total and integral manner. This is effected by means of the connection, which is unity between Philosophy and History – a *unity* obtained by making clear and profoundly studying, the nature of the concept and the logical a priori synthesis ... Finally, the doctrines and the presuppositions of formalist logic are refuted in a precise manner. The autonomy of the logical form is asserted and consequently the effort to contain its determinations are declared in vain. [The words or expressive forms] are certainly necessary, but obey, not the laws of logic, but that of the aesthetic spirit.[69]

What followed then for Croce was a specific notion of history as tel-eologically unfolding towards an ethical ideal. That is, since history could now be placed in an idealized dialectical form, it always involved an *immanence* of some kind, a 'developing,' 'progressing' – in short, a 'becoming' – and did so in a definite, necessary order of first degree to second within the distinct moments of spirit itself. Moreover, and since, as Croce examined, the dialectic established meaning wholly unto it-self, it thus removed the possibility of posing any 'truth,' particularly an ethical truth, as if transcendental in the kantian sense.[70] Indeed, giv-en this understanding of both progress and ethical reality, the so-called story of history for Croce would always be considered identical/equiv-alent to the 'story of liberty,' where liberty emerged precisely in the immanent unfolding of the pure, logically ordered movements of spir-it.[71] Finally, since the ethico-political was both a distinct element in this universal unfolding and, as well, the 'highest expression' of it, then the meaning, or rather 'aim' of progress would always be situated at the (ideal) ethico-political moment, which, for Croce, was located at the lev-el of 'culture.' In that sense, progress could never occur, claimed Croce, at the more 'primitive' moment (to use his own wording), of the eco-nomic-juridical, the level at which he accused the communist militants of remaining, having adjusted their sights 'too low.'[72]

For Croce, then, the unfolding of history, with its concomitant 'sto-ry of liberty,' not only produced a conception of social ethicality quite unlike anything Hegel or Kant may have proposed; it also presented a critique of the kind of abstract generalities regarding the nature of the individual and his or her relation to the social whole found in hobbes-ian or lockean liberalism. Dismissing both Hobbes and Locke as posi-tivist philosophers devoid of any sense of negativity or error,[73] Croce argued instead that if one were to take seriously the problem of truth as being constituted wholly within reality and as a direct expression of the specificities of truth-error, then not only could there be no such entity as a 'philosophy-in-general,' but neither could there be a 'man-in-general,' a 'society-in-general,' and so forth. Logically there could be only a historically rooted humanity with an essence immanent in its development, an essence developed by the individual, lived by the individual, and representing at every ideal turn a *rational, real,* and *nec-essary* movement/progress of that human development.

In Croce's systemization, this ideal historicization of human devel-opment consequently held that all people were first 'artists' (since the aesthetic was the first degree and expression of reality) and, as creative and intuitive artists, intellectual; and, as intellectual, then wilful; and, as wilful, then ethical and moral. As we will shortly discuss, Gramsci stands this notion on its head, as it were, claiming, instead, that all people are, first and foremost, 'intellectuals,' and, as intellectuals, capable of creative judgments and a sharpening of the will, and, therewith, capable of inventing, maintaining, and reproducing the ethico-political society.[74]

But, for Croce, the realm of freedom would emerge from (yet remain linked to) an ideal realm of necessity; that is, it would emerge from the rationally inscribed movement of history, teleologically unfolding towards its ethical ideal. The site for this freedom was the ethico-political moment of culture; its content, an immanent, creative unfolding of an (idealized) history; an immanent, creative unfolding of the (idealized) artist-intellectual-philosopher, who could comprehend, participate in, and therefore help create, that development called progress.[75]

In short, Croce presented a logically inscribed, self-contained, indivisible yet immanent history, an 'active' idealism, an active conception of reality/praxis constituted by the unity-in-distinction of thought and action, truth and error, science and philosophy. These distinct but inseparable entities spelled for Croce the downfall of dualist, transcendentalist, positivist – even what he considered to be abstract-idealist – conceptions of reality (and, hence, knowledge). And they did so, claimed Croce, by squarely placing an idealized history at centre stage.[76] Historical materialism, in this context, came to mean nothing other than an abstract economic science attempting to account for all human activity at the level of generalities. It became nothing other than a hysterical and threadbare excuse to bring back pre-cartesian and pre-kantian philosophy.[77]

Given the hardened caricature this rethinking of Vico and Hegel seemed to produce, it might be well worth asking now what might conceivably have been useful – or even slightly appealing – for Gramsci in this crocean revision and subsequent systematizing of philosophy, history, and science, not to mention 'progress' itself. For it must be said that Gramsci forwarded several major criticisms. The most obvious one was that Croce's idealizing of history collapsed onto real historical events a conceptually rigorous and logical ordering pregiven to the actual moment, despite claims to the contrary.[78] Thus, despite Croce's attempt to make theoretically coherent the claim that history would be a continual process of development, there could be no conceptual space for understanding why or in what way politics entered into the making of a society, let alone whether or not that society might be 'better.' There was no way, in other words, to incorporate as a necessary moment in the constituting of that process of development any form of political struggle.[79]

In this light, Croce's notion of the rational or of the real and necessary aspects of human/societal development was considered by Gramsci as ideological and arbitrary speculation, in the most narrow sense
of the word – what other critics have dismissed as 'banal common
sense.'[80] Indeed, what Croce's theorization of the rational and real
would amount to, argued Gramsci, would be that *all* history – that is,
any part of historical life, including torture chambers of every description and oriental satrapies – would be for Croce an a priori and constitutive moment of liberty in the unfolding of spirit.[81] There could be no
way to distinguish regressive from progressive moments in history, for
everything in life would be an essential component necessary for the
creation of a liberty/progress, a 'realm of freedom' that would, ipso
facto, be considered 'ethico-political.' 'This becomes clearer,' writes
Gramsci,

> if one examines the concept of history around which the book *Storia
> d'Italia* centers, that is [in terms of] the concept of 'liberty.' Croce, contra-
> dicting himself, confuses liberty as a philosophical principle, or specula-
> tive concept [i.e., as 'ethico-political'], with liberty as an ideology ... [For
> him] 'liberty' as an historical concept is the dialectical process of history
> itself and can have no distinct, identifiable 'representatives.' [Hence] his-
> tory is liberty even in the oriental satrapies.[82]

This slippage, then, between representation and event, now emphasizing the theoretical aspects, and then, when politically opportune,
emphasizing historical ones, was, for Gramsci, a philosophy that, in the
final analysis, *depoliticized* any notion of real progress and change. Indeed, at best, it simply led to a validation of the status quo, a point
Gramsci underscored with a particular note of sarcasm:

> Someone in an article in *Critica fascista* made the astute observation that
> when Croce sees the last twenty years in perspective, he will find an his-
> torical justification for the present process of 'liberty' [i.e., the fascist
> movement]. If you keep in mind what I wrote you earlier about Croce's
> position in wartime, his standpoint will become clearer to you. As the
> high priest of contemporary historicist religion, Croce loves the thesis
> and anti-thesis of the historical process, emphasizing now one, now the
> other, for 'practical reasons,' since he sees the future in the present and
> is just as concerned with it. Everyone must play his part: the high priests'
> duty is to safeguard the future. Truly a strong dose of moral cynicism
> goes to make up this 'ethico-political' conception, today's version of
> Machiavellianism.[83]

In Gramsci's estimation, then, not only did Croce represent a particular kind of liberalism, but he was also, given the contemporary situation in Italy, the intellectual bearer of fascism. Croce's work, Gramsci
argued, lent a philosophical credibility to the emergence of the fascist
regime, since by positing liberty as the unfolding of history, Mussolini
and his blackshirts could be posited as the necessary (read: 'progressive') development in the unfolding of the 'story of liberty' for twentieth-century Italy.[84] And even though Croce vigorously denied the
charge,[85] Gramsci was fond of pointing out that Croce remained quite
free under Mussolini's government to publish, lecture, and score philosophical debating points on such topics as political morality, liberty,
and freedom of 'expression,' while others in opposition to the regime
tended to find themselves exiled, imprisoned, tortured, or worse.

This being the case, then, one is forced to come back to the question
earlier posed: What is it that Gramsci found appealing, indeed crucial,
in Croce's philosophy? For, clearly, Gramsci was opposed to any phil-
osophical/political theory that tended to legitimate a fascist state. And
yet Gramsci did 'borrow' from Croce, often prefacing his remarks with
such statements as: 'It seems to me that Croce's view of history must be
defined as "speculative" and "philosophical" rather than as "ethical-
political". This view is the opposite of historical materialism because it
is "speculative," not because it is "ethical-political."'[86]

What Gramsci thought might be crucial for a philosophy of praxis
could be narrowed essentially to three points: i / that the concept of
science and philosophy must be intimately connected to the question
of an immanence or a becoming (hence raising also the concept of distincts on the one hand, and the immediate incorporation of negativity
or error as fundamental to any truth, on the other); ii / that the concept
of the will be understood as fundamental to the philosophy of praxis,
and that that will be posed as a *rational* expression, that is, as an 'active'
expression of theoretical/intellectual and practical activity in which
both moments formed the constitutive unity of that will and conditioned the emergence of an ethico-political society; and iii / that the
ethico-political itself be incorporated, in all its profundity, as the site of
struggle, the point of arrival, as it were, for progress and change.[87]

To clarify these three main points, one of the tasks Gramsci took on
was precisely that of showing *why and how*, in marxism, the fundamental relation between 'science' and 'praxis' had been established in such
a way as to incorporate Vico's dictum (and Croce's interpretation of it)
at its very core. But Gramsci was also prepared to show why it was
important to maintain this insistence on science and truth as 'historical'
error; i.e., that truth and ethics were neither neutral, nor already pre-

scribed. Indeed, he was prepared to show that this non-neutrality and
irreducible contingency were not only fundamental components of
radical politics per se but utterly connected with reproducing the 'what
is' and, more to the point, creating the 'what ought to be' out of the very
fluidity and specificity of politics itself. Thus he writes:

> *Statement of the problem*: Production of a new Weltanschauungen to ferti-
> lize and nourish the culture of an historical epoch, and philosophically
> directed production according to the original Weltanschauungen. Marx
> is the creator of a Weltanschauung. But what is Ilich [Lenin]'s position?
> Is it purely subordinate and subaltern? The explanation is to be found in
> marxism itself as both science and action, [i.e.,] the passage from utopia
> to science and from science to action.[88]

As we shall see, Gramsci intends, first, to 'rid' these concepts of their
metaphysical trappings; that is, he intends, with Marx, to 'ground' the
concept of politics in the very notion of historical error. But to do this
effectively requires, according to Gramsci, a rethinking of the marxist
dialectic itself. This 'rethinking' and the consequences that follow from
it form the basis for the discussions in the next chapter.

THREE

Science, Immanence, and the 'Real' Dialectic:

A Question of the Political

It has to be said that the author [Bukharin] fails to grasp the very concept of metaphysics, just as he fails to grasp the concepts of historical movement, of becoming and, therefore, of the dialectic itself ... [Instead, the] author falls headlong into dogmatism and therefore into a form, though a naive one, of metaphysics ... He does not succeed in elaborating the concept of philosophy of praxis as 'historical methodology', and of that in turn as 'philosophy', as the only concrete philosophy. That is to say, he does not succeed in posing and resolving, from the point of view of the real dialectic, the problem which Croce has posed and has attempted to resolve from the speculative point of view.[1]

In criticizing Bukharin's marxism as a representative sampling of 'naive metaphysics,'[2] Gramsci insisted that a philosophy unable to account analytically for creativity and intellectual growth as fundamental to a concept of the real would, ipso facto, be unable to account for diversity and change, except by invoking dogma or superstition, or both. Indeed, Gramsci was willing to go farther than this. In contrast to Bukharin and others, he was to argue that a 'real' philosophy of praxis not only took explicit account of creative and intellectual activity at an analytic level, but placed this activity as the central, practical aspect to building what Gramsci called 'a substantive democracy,' a citizen democracy, one that would be based on and express the will of the people.[3]

Moreover, and as we shall discuss in some detail, for Gramsci this primary emphasis on intellectual and creative potentiality not only was seen to be a necessary basis for the overthrow of an oppressive system, but was considered a requirement for the founding of a new and more open social order. His argument posited a notion of absolute necessity drawn from historical/political struggle and, thus, understood necessity itself as something imbued with 'error' or particularity. To put it slightly differently, this reposing of absolute necessity as linked to and expressing intellectual and creative activity meant also that the truth of the 'what is' entailed an always-already contingent and fluid dynamism specifically rooted in historical circumstance. More important, it also meant that the truth of the 'what ought to be' – that is, the ethical imperative connected with the founding of a new social order – also entailed an always-already contingent or 'impure' truth, itself hammered out in the process of political struggle.[4] In this sense, then, ethics and morality – indeed, any kind of universal 'ought' – were for Gramsci wholly inconceivable without the political moment. At the same time, the political was wholly inconceivable without intellectual and creative reason.

But the problem thus far was that the way in which the political seemed to enter the ethical and the will, indeed history itself, might be open to similar criticisms launched against Croce's idealist attempts at placing a 'fluidity' or 'dynamism' into history as a direct function of creative/intellectual logos. As we noted earlier, Croce's position tended either, at best, to reinforce banal common sense or, worse, to give theoretical and practical support to the emergence of a fascist regime.

In one sense, then, the problem that began to surface for Gramsci was precisely that of showing how elements like the ethical-political or the will or notions of immanence and contingency were already central to marxist theory. In other words, the problem seemed to be, at least at one level, to show how these concepts were analytically central to a philosophy of praxis, and indeed how they had already been incorporated – at least implicitly – in a way that neither vindicated the status quo nor became a purely academic exercise on the whys and wherefores of societal power and change. But at another level, the problem as Gramsci saw it was to clarify the fact that, in having already taken as a given the entire problematic of a contingent truth, i.e., a truth imbued with historical specificity, Marx had radically altered not only the concept of the historical/materialist dialectic itself but the concept (and centrality) of the political.[5]

One of the tasks in the *Quaderni*, then, was to clarify not only how, in a philosophy of praxis, political activity would be understood in the practical sense as something fundamental to creating, changing, or maintaining a societal structure, but that, in emphasizing the fluid or dynamic nature of history, the concept of the 'political' would itself be understood in terms of its specificity, that is, in terms of its 'error,' its 'particularity,' and, hence, its contingency. It was a way of posing the concept of the political as *if* a 'moment,' that is, as a process that could both build momentum towards creating a coherent unity and, as well, provide a terrain upon which that unity could be maintained. Bringing in error or contingency in terms of the political was also, hoped Gramsci, a way to develop analytic space for resolving the questions around 'what ought to be' without invoking an a priori truth or an a priori ethicality.

As Gramsci reasoned, this distinction cast the political not only as the first moment of a societal system, but, to use Gramsci's terms directly, as the first moment of philosophy. 'In a philosophy of praxis,' Gramsci wrote, 'the distinction will certainly not be between the moments of absolute spirit, but ... will be that of establishing a dialectical position of political activity (and of a corresponding science) ... One might say, as a first schematic approximation, that political activity is precisely the first moment or first level.' [6]

In direct contrast to Croce's assessment, which, as we saw, put the political as a 'final moment' of spirit, as a point of arrival in the unfolding of the dialectic, the political moment would, instead, be understood as *the point of departure*, the first moment, as it were, in the making of history. On the other hand, and somewhat similar to Croce's argument earlier discussed, this moment would entail a logical and not hierarchical ordering of, in this case, politics to history. It was not meant to privilege the concept of politics above and beyond that of history. Rather, the political moment would itself be understood as a constitutive unity, one that was both a heterogeneous and a concrete 'starting-point.'[7] Since this conceptual clarification by Gramsci bears profound implications both strategically and analytically for a philosophy of praxis, it is worth examining the way in which Gramsci developed the political as a 'first moment' of marxist theory itself.

The 'political' moment

To begin, then, Gramsci's insistence that the political moment must be understood as a point of departure was an initial attempt to incorporate the contingent nature of 'truth.' But it was a way of doing so by emphasizing that that truth could be understood only as entailing objectively concrete content. Without being able to incorporate the real in this way – that is, without being able to incorporate it as 'concrete' –

ethicality would remain, as had been the trap in crocean idealism, hypostatized as an a priori unfolding of a scientific and rational (read: predictable) progress.[8] And yet, it was also a way to come at the whole question of change itself: not only to ask, at both an analytic and a practical level, the question 'what are we fighting for?' but to demonstrate how, in that fight, one could best incorporate real possibility and real change in a vital way, i.e., in a way that would bring to fruition, and institutionalize on a permanently dynamic basis, better living conditions as such and for whom.

On the one hand, then, posing the political as a point of departure was precisely the way in which Gramsci intended to 'take history seriously'; it was, as Gramsci would call it, an 'absolute historicism.'[9] It meant incorporating into history an active and immanent conception of politics – to use Gramsci's specific rewrite of a crocean Hegel – while maintaining their equivalence at the level of an 'identity-in-distinction.'[10] On the other hand, it also meant incorporating at a theoretical level the by now clichéd machiavellian insight that politics was 'the art of the possible,' that is, the strategic understanding of, and the possibility of implementing, progress and development. Implicit within such an understanding was a coming to terms analytically with a concept of change that entailed historical specificity and rational necessity.[11] In this sense, then, change would not be cast simply as something different from before; nor would it be posed as something arbitrary, accidental, or misguided. Change would express (and be linked to) a rational terrain, that is, the necessary predicaments of a specific historical moment. Indeed, it would include, in and of itself, a kind of logical internality expressing that necessity.

These two aspects of the political moment, the one bearing on social truth, the other on social strategy, were considered by Gramsci to express and, at the same time, constitute 'reality,' outside of which there could be no meaning.[12] This reality – a concrete, and hence necessary, reality – was one constituted by the dialectical synthesis of social truth/social strategy, which, taken together, articulated and expressed historicized totality. It not only gave conceptual space for the notion of politics but, as Gramsci would reiterate throughout the *Quaderni*, indicated the way in which the marxist dialectic would be able to conceptualize as concrete, fluid, and rooted to societal needs the very notion of progress and, thereby, of possibility itself. [13]

Moreover, it was a way, argued Gramsci, to defeat the earlier transcendental and positivist notions of conceptualizing change as that which must entail an a priori constitutive unity permanently embraced in a teleological unfolding of an absolute ethical idea. As we will see, by focusing on a conception of reality as absolute history, i.e., as a totalized expressive unity of practical and theoretical activity, Gramsci insisted instead that the notion of progress would also take on an analytic specificity; indeed, it too would be understood as an 'ethical' struggle, a political struggle par excellence to create the 'what ought to be.'[14] That is, this new ethico-political society and the morality appropriate to it would not be conceived in terms of a logical, self-contained attribution of philosophical reason, dialectical or otherwise.[15,] Its relational existence and hence its 'meaning,' would not be conceived by definition, but rather as rooted in the consequences of social life itself. 'Morality should not be a question of a *hierarchy* of ends,' Gramsci explained, 'but of a gradation of the ends to be attained, granted that what one wants to "moralise" is not just each individual taken singly but a whole society of individuals.'[16]

What constituted, analytically, the meaning of ethicality and progress would, instead, be that which was specifically produced in, and on the terrain of, history. 'Meaning', in any sense, be it linguistic/grammatical or ethico-political, was for Gramsci an active elaboration and reconstruction of the dialectic in terms of the social agent's theoretical and practical activity, drawn from and rooted in the realm of necessity.[17] Theoretical and practical activity would be understood as a synthetic, constitutive unity, where those elements constituting that synthesis could now be posed as something other than predetermined or homogeneously contained unities.[18]

Gramsci wanted to press the argument that these constitutive unities were, in themselves, a product and a process of politics, that is, something mediated by, contingently forged from, and resulting from political struggle. Such was true not only of morality, but of all forms of truth, science included.[19] Indeed, this refocus meant, for Gramsci, not only that a broader conceptualization of history and philosophy must be contextualized as an aspect of the political, but that any philosophical/historical discourse must be understood as expressing a 'politics' of some kind; that is, as expressing a dynamic movement that, as such, could *never maintain itself as a completely closed entity*. In this respect, science, too, as 'system,' was precisely 'political.'[20]

Relying on politics as meaning 'political moment,' a moment that was to be taken as a point of departure, implied something quite different from a fixed or immutable politics or one concerned only with strategic and tactical organization. It was suggestive of a *discursive* cluster arising from *specific* circumstances derived from specific relations between people living in and acting upon a particular society. Hence we find, for example, following this line of reasoning, Gramsci's reading of Machiavelli's *Discourses* and *The Prince* as being theoretical arguments that put forward not abstract suppositions about a 'general' people and a 'general' society, but particular historical/political positions. Machiavelli's positions attempted, as Gramsci saw it, to speak to those 'not in the know,' i.e., to the rising bourgeois classes and their role in the formation of a specific society (in this case, emergent liberalism).[21]

A similar point could be, and indeed was, made by Gramsci regarding the theoretical suppositions of Hegel or Croce, Vico, Rousseau, Voltaire, and so forth: that their philosophical and literary works, taken as a whole, elaborated a specific, though not necessarily unitary or homogeneous, conception of 'what is man' and 'what is society' or, more to the point, what they 'ought' to become. In fact, this was a point Gramsci would emphasize throughout the *Quaderni*: that the work of Marx and Engels, Labriola, and Lenin – and even those who claimed to be progressive, but whose positions he found naïve or vulgar – taken as a whole, initiated or at least contributed to a specific theoretical/practical discourse on the left, which attempted to articulate the 'what ought to be' of politics and of life, of progress and of change, as something different from (and better than) that of the status quo.

And yet, on the other hand, it was also Gramsci's contention that this 'different and specific' emergent theoretical/practical discourse of the left had often tended to promote, at least in certain instances, a set of political tactics and strategies based on formalistic and what he considered to be utterly misleading appropriations of marxist-leninist theory/praxis. In being formalistic, one section of the left took as a given the phrase 'law of capitalist development' to mean an 'iron-clad,' flat, or empirical fact, which, ipso facto, seemed capable of producing only already-given agendas around political organization, leadership, and the role of 'the people.' Indeed, it presented classes, and the class struggle itself, as if already fully homogeneous and constituted entities.[23] For Gramsci, these formalistic theories – however much passionately held – could produce only stillborn reaction, or, worse, provide an avenue for the consolidation of opposite and reactionary forces: 'if we continue to take up the formalistic positions which we have taken up hitherto … we shall obtain the opposite result to the one we want.'[24]

This formalism was incapable of acknowledging what for Gramsci was absolutely the central feature of marxism: that history represented the 'expression' of a diverse and fractured historico-political terrain made coherent, that is, unified, only through struggle, i.e., only through the political moment. It was in this sense that history was mediated through the political, or, to put it slightly differently, that all of history, truth, and, hence, all reality was, itself, 'political.'[25] It was thus in this sense, too, that for Gramsci, the concept of history was both identical to and *made* equivalent with politics, or, as Gramsci would usually phrase it, 'history = politics.'[26]

Formalism, even though of a leftist variety, could not account for this kind of mediated unity (and therewith, of politics) any better than the formalism of idealist philosophy. So similar was the trap to which this myopic formal reasoning led that the critique of the latter could often be applied to the former. As Gramsci remarked: 'Nor, yet, has the faculty of reason or of spirit created unity and cannot be recognised as a unitary fact ["unitary" in the sense of establishing a concrete principle of unity], since it represents a purely formal and categorical concept. It is not "thought" but what people actually think that unites or differentiates mankind.'[27]

At a very general level, then, Gramsci attributed the lack of incorporating 'real life' into a concept of truth as having arisen from an attempt to search for (and find) in Marx's work a correspondingly correct 'formula' or 'key' to the interpretation of marxism. It was precisely the problem of accepting historical 'fact' as if a dogma or a rule rather than posing the 'what is' as that which is always, of necessity, contingent.

And yet, given this critique, the question that emerged for Gramsci was to ask why this seemingly profound misreading of the philosophy of praxis (as entailing a static, homogeneous and 'objective' truth rather than a fluid political moment) had not only become a leading interpretation within certain sectors of the left, but had provided a whole series of (wrong-headed) strategies and tactics. His answer, at least analytically speaking, was twofold. On the one hand, reasoned Gramsci, there seemed to be a problem with the way in which science had been conceived and the importance science would have, not only for a fuller conception of political struggle, but also for possible change. On the other hand, and quite connected to this problem of science, was the way in which the dialectic in historical materialism had been understood, and, more to the point, the seemingly complete misrecognition or disacknowledgment of the importance that that concept had for a marxist appropriation of other concepts such as becoming or immanence, as well as mediation, contradiction, and negation.

If we turn now to the *Quaderni* directly and guide our attention in terms of these two specific areas, we shall observe quite readily how Gramsci, in drawing upon the work of both Marx and Engels, and to a lesser extent that of Labriola, was able to detail the 'specificity of the political'[28] and how that specificity (history/error/difference) tried to ground the notions of will, the ethico-political, and 'progress' as marxist expressions.[29]

The problem (and importance) of science

For Croce, as we have seen, science meant, above all, 'methodology,' and in that context, a 'rational,' that is distinct and predictable, methodology, capable of underwriting the logic inherent in 'pure' concrete-universal reality, outside of which there could be no meaningful concept or knowledge. He named that methodology 'philosophy,' the science of all pure expression, with the logical proviso written in that this philosophy did not mean a 'philosophy-in-general' or a 'science-in-general' but always entailed the specificity of the (pure/idealized) historical moment. Indeed, speculative philosophy was precisely its 'expression.'

But as Gramsci had recognized, Croce's formulation was a mechanical teleology of prediction/evolution, which presented as ethico-political an always-already made progress neatly unfolding in, and against, history. And yet Gramsci was not averse to the point Croce was attempting to make and resolve 'from the speculative point of view': i.e., that the concept of progress/development was something 'rational,' and hence understandable, 'scientific,' and therefore in some way both predictable and within the realm of possibility, that is, 'obtainable.'[30]

On the other hand, Gramsci was also not averse to the discussions on science as raised by either the scientific marxists or the utopian socialists, although he found both sets of discussions quite problematic. The one group, according to Gramsci, conflated the natural sciences with that of the social, and thereby gave credence to the somewhat unfortunate metaphor of the economy as the 'anatomy' or 'backbone' of society.[31] This metaphor was unfortunate for a number of reasons, chief among them being that the social was now posed as a homogeneous and anthropomorphized entity internally speared with a 'backbone' against which all difference had to be muted. The other group tended to conflate the concept of science with that of an absolute and value-free 'truth,' thus coming to the unfortunate position critiqued throughout these pages, namely, that society could be established *sui generis*.

Under the general rubric of scientific marxists, Gramsci lumped together writers as diverse as Bernstein and Kautsky, Plekhanov, even Loria; that is, those who interpreted historical materialism as reducible to an 'economic science.'[32] Bernstein and Kautsky, for example, while rejecting as simplistic the 'inevitability arguments' around the fall of capitalism nevertheless rejected that position, argued Gramsci, by maintaining a very narrow definition of class (and of class struggle) as that which would be determined solely by the economic contradiction in capitalist relations of production.[33] As Gramsci saw it, the problem with this position was that it led to the assumption, among other things, that a victorious class struggle could 'erupt' only when the full development of the antagonisms between the two classes under capitalism had become a reality. And this meant, on a practical level, that until that full development became a reality, the revolution, such as it was, could be waged only passively and within the so-called democratic institutions already established.[34] Moreover, it led to the conclusion that the state that emerged during that period must be a direct and intentional result of ruling-class interest.

On the other hand, and as Gramsci mentioned throughout the notebooks, Loria's 'economic science' was even more threadbare.[35] In Loria's interpretation of Marx's historical materialism, all phenomena would simply be reduced to an abstract economic principle. By so reducing it, class struggle, its organization and strategy, would be conflated, ipso facto, with the impossible task of predicting the 'exact moment' when capitalism would fall. And yet, the impossibility of this task seemed not at all to bother Loria. Indeed, attacking those who would seek to organize and protest before that infamous moment had arrived – thereby wasting their energy and everyone else's – Loria thus perpetuated the myth of the 'exact moment' in the following way:

> If, as the new apostles of force contend, the proletariat masses can at any moment annihilate the prevailing economic order, why do they not rise against the capitalism they detest, and replace it with the cooperative commonwealth for which they long? Why is it that after so much noisy organization, the utmost they are able to do is tear up a few yards of railway track or to smash a street lamp? Do we not find here an irrefutable demonstration that force is not realizable at any given moment, but only in the historic hour when evolution shall have prepared the inevitable fall of the dominant economic system?[36]

To this crude form of economic reductionism, Gramsci gave the name 'lorianismo.'[37] Dismissing it as a vulgar attempt to equate the complex of material social relations with a one-dimensional and abstract notion of class, Gramsci argued that *lorianismo* could provide only a concept of class struggle as a 'technical instrument'; that is, as a vacant category that somehow would entail meaning outside of the historical process to which it was a part.[38] Understanding class struggle as a technical instrument to be employed at some historic hour led to an understanding of political organization and struggle as something that always-already existed as such, whose class victory was as inevitable as the total annihilation of the capitalists the *lorianistas* had so self-assuredly predicted. That the infamous historic hour never arrived was due, in part, argued Gramsci, to the fact that classes were conceived of as already constituted. Hence, the very concept of class struggle itself had been conflated with an *abstract* theoretical notion of class. In the process, strategy and tactics were, ipso facto, deduced from a given dogma, pure and simple.

At best, the insistence on the 'inevitable fall of capitalism' with its concomitant victory to the working classes was, for Gramsci, a political move best reserved as a form of sloganeering, implemented in order to 'keep up the faith' or to 'rally the troops' when the odds seemed particularly insurmountable. 'When you don't have the initiative in the struggle and the struggle itself comes eventually to be identified with a series of defeats,' Gramsci solemnly observed,

> mechanical determinism becomes a tremendous force of moral resist-
> ance, of cohesion and of patient and obstinate perseverance. 'I have been
> defeated for the moment, but the tide of history is working for me in the
> long term', etc. Real will takes on the garments of an act of faith … [In this
> sense] the mechanical conception has been a religion of the subaltern …
> and continues to be a 'necessity', a necessary form taken by the will of the
> popular masses, and a specific way of rationalising the world and real
> life, which provided the general framework for real political activity.[39]

But taken as a point of principle, leftist 'lorianism' represented, among other things, the name for both political passivity par excellence and a kind of political blindness, which, sadly ironic, often found as its target left-wing organizations and supporters rather than those of the status quo. Indeed it became the expression for all those who, like Loria, showed outright indignation for any group that might organize against a repressive system in ways other than already given organizational principles derived from a set of abstract theorizations. It was the kind of reductionism that allowed no possibility for posing classes as the historical products of complex socio-economic relations, and, thereby, as the expression of a political struggle and of a history-in-the-making; it was the kind of reductionism that spoke loftily of progress and truth, all in the name of a (leftist) science *sui generis*.

However pathetic lorianism might have been, there was one last form of 'scientific' economic reductionism that Gramsci identified as even more problematic. Best contextualized in his attack on Plekhanov's *Fundamental Principles of Marxism*, and characterized by Gramsci as 'the so-called "orthodox" tendency,' this approach relied heavily on positivist logic, so much so that it effectively removed any notion of creativity from the production of social relations.[40] In the *Fundamental Principles*, Gramsci argued, Plekhanov presented the notion of orthodox marxism as precisely the 'pure science of the real.' Dismissed by Gramsci as a 'relapse into vulgar materialism ... typical of the positivist method, demonstrating only his meager speculative and historicgraphical ability,' this kind of marxism generally brandished a superficial form of economics.[41] By superficial, Gramsci meant that the logic inherent in this economic science took as a given the (incorrect) deduction not only that society split rigidly along two, and only two, 'scientifically determined' class axes, but that the strategies to overcome, or better, overthrow, that persistent split could best be calculated 'with the precision of the natural sciences,' that is, according to carefully outlined predictions regarding the immanent collapse of capital exchange, circulation and what was considered to be an inherent 'bourgeois-decadent' lifestyle.

The utopian socialists fared just as poorly in Gramsci's estimation. For, even though the writings of Robert Owen, François Fourier, the Saint-Simonists, and others were clearly not ignorant of, or antagonistic to, the ongoing debates around science and its relation to leftist political practice, their essential flaw had to do with the way in which concepts dealing with or incorporating the 'what ought to be' had been posed. Gramsci argued that possibility and freedom, indeed the very notions of what ought to be understood as 'better,' were always predicated on an already established notion of the ethical good as neutral or value free and, in that sense, as absolute and pure. Here one would find the conflation of a totalized knowledge with that of an absolute science, so that, for a utopian socialist, a better society was one that could be perfected as such – in the same way one might prune a rose-bush to make it flourish.[42]

This equating, then, of an absolute science with a factual or bounded (closed) totality of truth, i.e., an absolute knowledge, committed the twin error of regenerating in more contemporary terms the pre-vichean, or, at best, neo-kantian, assumptions around the appropriation of a knowledge somehow existing outside of history.[43] At the same time, it advanced as 'progressive' the argument that a value-free society, that is, one based on 'scientific certainty' seemingly devoid of any historical specificity or 'bias,' could exist – in fact, *ought* to exist – as the aim of democratic struggle. In the name of scientific/technological objectivity, the rigid class reductionism of 'scientific marxism' was exchanged, mixed metaphors and all, for the empty abstractionism of a philosophy-science and society *sui generis*.

Apart from a variety of difficulties with the logic of this position, the kind of political strategy it seemed to produce was one that saw change as simply a 'technical adjustment' of society at large, as though power and the relations inscribed by it existed merely as descriptive categories representing – and, therewith, entrenching – no real interests of any one particular group over another. It belied a strategy to change power imbalances as one based on the simple exchange of, at best, more sophisticated debate. Indeed, it was precisely the posing of radical change 'as if' an activity that could emerge without the 'impure' political element that brought Marx to respond:

> Do not say that social movement excludes political movement. There is never a political movement which is not at the same time social [and vice versa]. It is only [when] there are no more classes and class antagonisms that *social evolutions* will cease to be *political revolutions*. Till then, on the eve of every general reshuffling of society, the last word of social science will always be: Le combat ou le mort; la lutte sanguinaire ou le néant. C'est ainsi que la question est invinciblement posée.[44]

And yet, despite the major difficulties inherent in both economic reductionism and utopian socialism, there was one other appropriation of science that Gramsci held out as the contemporary embodiment of the worst aspects of the two thus far discussed. This was the scientism of what Gramsci called quite simply, 'naive metaphysics,' best represented in Bukharin's *Popular Manual*, and categorized accordingly as 'vulgar sociology.'[45] It was a scientism that posed society as a system, system as a science, and science as the search for laws of causality, i.e., for the 'eternal truths,' or the single 'Big Truth' – the age old search for God.[46] As Gramsci put it, Bukharin's *Popular Manual* becomes 'one of the most blatant traces of old-fashioned metaphysics ... the attempt to reduce everything to a single ultimate or final cause. One could reconstruct the history of the problem of the single ultimate cause and demonstrate that it is the manifestation of the "search for God." In opposition to this dogmatism recall once again the two letters of Engels' published in the *Social Akademiker.'*[47]

On a theoretical level, these assumptions led to a separating of, and posing at distinctly opposite poles of, a philosophical materialism at the one end – which Bukharin variously categorized as the only 'true' philosophy – and, at the other end, a philosophy of praxis or as Bukharin was inclined to call it, a 'subjectivist sociology.'[48] This subjectivist sociology was precisely, for Gramsci, an upside-down idealism 'in the sense that the speculative categories are replaced by empirical concepts and classifications which are no less abstract and anti-historical.'[49]

In Gramsci's estimation, this meant that in combining the worst aspects of scientific and utopian marxism and neatly packaging the result for popular consumption, Bukharin was able to incorporate into the so-called iron-clad law of historical movement not only a formal positivistic logic as 'truth,' but the equally seductive notion that society could be made value free and representative of a pregiven human nature. Moreover, it led to the strategic/organizational conclusion that if society operated according to a series of permanent rules, i.e., according to a 'science' in a one-dimensional and formalistic sense, then the tasks involved with changing society would become strictly a mechanical matter, and revolution would become, as mentioned earlier, merely an awkward 'technical difficulty.' Thus Gramsci, surmises,

> the philosophy implicit in the *Popular Manual* could be called positivistic Aristotelianism, an adaption of formal logic to the methods of physical and natural science. *The historical dialectic is replaced by the law of causality and the search for regularity, normality and uniformity.* But how can one derive from this way of seeing things, the overcoming, the 'overthrow' of praxis? In mechanical terms, the effect can never transcend the cause or the system of causes, and therefore can have no development other than the flat vulgar development of evolutionism.[50]

The main flaw, then, with Bukharin's attempt to wed formalistic science to utopian socialism was the conflation of 'revolution' with 'evolution,' or, more to the point, the impossibility of revolutionary politics – indeed, the impossibility of any politics or, for that matter, any history.[51] And yet this particular kind of scientism, despite its collapse of the political, was quite seductive for a number of those on both the left and the right of the political spectrum. Such was the case in part because that position held out the promise of being able to 'predict' future possibilities, as if they, too, could somehow be deduced from a naturalistic 'law' of social change.[52] 'Since it appears by a strange inversion of the perspective that the natural sciences provide us with the ability to foresee the evolution of natural processes,' Gramsci wryly observed, 'historical methodology is "scientifically" conceived [by Bukharin] only if and in so far as it permits one "abstractly" to foresee the future of society. Hence the search of essential causes, indeed, for the "first" cause, for the "cause of causes."'[53]

Gramsci wanted to clarify instead how, in the philosophy of praxis, the use of science could never be appropriated as an exact measurement or way to 'predict' future events, or as a logic necessary to illuminate as fixed or causal the entire 'chain of human history.' Neither could it become a 'technology' in the sense of promising a value-free future. To think otherwise was, for Gramsci, 'a strange delusion which has little to do with science.'[54] 'Theses on Feuerbach' had already criticised in advance this simplistic conception. In reality one can "scientifically" foresee only the struggle, but not the concrete moments of the struggle, which cannot but be the result of opposing forces in continuous movement.'[55]

In pointing to the 'Theses on Feuerbach,' Gramsci insisted on resituating science as the 'historical methodology' of the philosophy of praxis.[56] At first glance, this position may not have appeared altogether different from the preceding positions he was challenging. His use of science, for example, similar to that of Croce and others, also focused on the 'rational,' on the notion of a 'law' of historical movement, on 'economic science,' even 'truth.' However, and as we will explore in more detail below, the difference lay in the manner in which he tried to clarify (and some would argue, alter) Marx's renovation of the hegelian rational and real, and, therewith, the dialectic their unity expressed. That is, the difference lay precisely in the way Gramsci posed the unity of the contingent, be it logic, truth, economics, law, movement, or whatever.

For Gramsci, this contingency had to be understood in terms of a dialectic between history, philosophy, and politics – a unity he named, borrowing in part from Vico, 'the *new science*.'[57] Gramsci wanted to insist on the point that science and 'life' were identities, although entailing their own distinction, which, taken together, constituted and expressed reality. That is, he wanted to argue that these were abstract distinctions which, taken together, constituted a unity (of opposites) whose meaning would not be drawn from an external variable or archimedean point 'beyond' the (totalized) terrain of history. Meaning would be established, maintained, or changed precisely in terms of, and hence bounded by, this terrain. In this context, the 'rational' and the 'real' would become one.[58]

As we will see, this insistence on the unity of the rational and the real was not simply an apparent redefinition of Hegel (or, even earlier still, that of Vico), nor was it simply a rewrite of Croce's insistence on history as the 'expression' of an ideal science and practical activity, naming philosophy as the methodology of that science. Indeed, Gramsci took great pains to differentiate his posing of history as an expression of 'science/philosophy' from that of Croce. As well, he took great pains to differentiate his re-posing of 'rational/real' from that of Hegel. For Gramsci, the only way to resolve the idealism of either was to ground the identity (of science and philosophy or of the rational and the real) in the political moment, itself a dialectical synthesis of, and yet constituted by, the terrain of history.[59] As he put it, the philosophy of praxis 'is "mutilated" if it does not also include the identity of history with politics [and make that identity] also equal to the identity of politics and philosophy.'[60]

In trying to make dynamic and real the identity of science and philosophy, Gramsci insisted on a grounding of history, which was itself a dialectically constituted unity of political practice. This linking of, or making equivalent, science with philosophy was precisely the identity-in-distinction spoken of earlier: each term maintained its own meaning, even when expressed as a constitutive element of the dialectical synthesis, a synthesis that was meaningful precisely because it was the expression of the political and, therewith, of the historical moment. Thus he writes:

> The idea that the Hegelian dialectic has been the last reflection of those great historical nexuses, and that the dialectic ... should become, with the disappearance of these contradictions, a pure conceptual dialectic, would appear to be at the root of those recent philosophies, like that of Croce, which have a utopistic basis ... [Rather it should be understood that] everything is political, even philosophy or philosophies and the only 'philosophy' is history in action, that is, life itself.[61]

But given these identities and distinctions, it might be said that Gramsci, despite his sustained and angry critiques to the contrary, still did no better than to present, if not an idealism 'upside down,' then perhaps one that might be 'inside out.' What Gramsci needed to clarify was how the dialectic he was incorporating was, indeed, an historical-materialist one. Moreover, he needed to clarify why that dialectical reasoning defeated the logical inconsistencies he had accused others of having assumed or maintained. It is to his posing of the 'real' dialectic and its emphasis on the political that we now must turn, for this is precisely the route Gramsci takes to resolve that particular dilemma.

Rational and real in the 'real' dialectic

In posing the problem of dialectical methodology, Gramsci had argued that the dialectic of the philosophy of praxis would be 'mutilated' if it were not carefully contextualized in terms of the political moment, in terms, that is to say, that incorporated as fundamental the concrete unity of the rational and the real. 'If the environment is the educator,' reflected Gramsci,

> it too must in turn be educated, but [Bukharin's *Popular*] *Manual* does not understand this revolutionary dialectic. The source of all the errors of the *Manual*, and of its author ... consists precisely in this pretension to divide the philosophy of praxis into two parts: a 'sociology' and a systematic philosophy. [But as we have seen] separated from the theory of history and politics, philosophy cannot be other than metaphysics, whereas the great conquest in the history of modern thought, represented by the philosophy of praxis, is precisely the concrete historicisation of philosophy and its identification with history.[62]

But despite Gramsci's immediate nod to Marx, his development of the dialectic seems to have relied on a somewhat unconventional reconstruction of the rational and real. On the one hand, the rational appropriately entailed theoretical activity, which, for Gramsci, included both intuitive/common sense as well as intellectual reasoning, a position that appears not too far distant from Croce's posing of the theoretic as constituted by the twofold degree (of intuition and logic). Moreover, this 'rational' was a conception also closely allied to Ricardo's wellknown approach of deducing a position from the exigencies of a given context within real life, i.e., his strategy of 'supposing that ... '[63] On the other hand, the 'real' embodied the concept of practical activity as expressed in the first thesis of Marx's 'Theses on Feuerbach' (i.e., the 'sensuous, objective [*gegenstandliche*] activity'),[64] and, as such, contained within it intellectual activity.

In this context, the real formed the condition or basis – the first moment, as it were – upon which the rational could be constructed. In paraphrasing Engels's rewrite of Hegel, this aspect of the real meant for Gramsci that 'all that is rational is real and [that] the real is rational,' i.e., that the rational and the real could not be separated from each other, except at the level of abstraction.[65] Indeed, it was the dialectical nexus of the rational/real unity that Gramsci designated as the embodiment of a certain 'necessity,' a necessity created out of the people's will and intellectual activity. As such, it would be capable of becoming an expression of life itself.[66] In this sense, then, the realm of necessity would become precisely the fertile terrain out of which possibility and change, indeed freedom itself, could be obtained. 'In other words,' as Gramsci remarked, 'it is the point at which the conception of the world, ie contemplation, philosophy, becomes 'real', since they now aim to modify the world and revolutionise praxis. One could say therefore that this is the central nexus of the philosophy of praxis, the point at which it becomes actual and lives historically (that is socially and no longer just in the brains of individuals), when it ceases to be arbitrary and becomes necessary-rational-real.'[67]

To put it slightly differently, then, misrepresenting the relation between the rational and the real as something outside of a dialectical nexus and not bound to history was, for Gramsci, the central deficiency in those debates that had erupted between naturalism, scientism, and positivism, and that, in having incorrectly posed the rational and the real, ended by 'seeing whether nature and history proceeded by leaps or only by gradual and progressive evolutionism.' And yet, he found these debates quite significant precisely because, in wrongly posing the relationship of the rational and real (and, hence, trying to figure out which way history might 'proceed'), they expressed the common-sense thinking of the time, a common sense that entailed a specificity and materiality of its own; that is, they expressed a political viewpoint, with concomitant ethico-political assumptions about future possibilities and present strategies employed to ensure that future. Thus Gramsci surmised, ' ... the theoretical significance of this debate seems to me to consist in this: that it marks the "logical" point at which every conception of the world makes the passage to the morality appropriate to it, when contemplation becomes action and every philosophy becomes the political actions dependent on it.'[68]

In contrast to those debates, by dialectically linking theoretical/practical activity to the rational and the real, Gramsci was trying to underscore the importance of that identity as itself a 'practical' act, a conscious act that implied, at its very core, political movement. In this light, it was an obvious link to Marx's 'Theses on Feuerbach' and an attempt to concentrate on the ontological question of grounding truth on the 'is' and deducing from that reality the 'what ought to be.' Thus, he drew the conclusion that

> the identification of theory and practice is a critical act, through which practice is demonstrated ... This is why the problem of the identity of theory and practice is realised especially in the so-called transition moments of history ... for it is then that the practical forces unleashed really demand justification in order to become more efficient and expansive; and that theoretical programmes multiply in number, and demand in their turn to be realistically justified to the extent that they prove themselves assimilatable into practical movements, thereby making the latter yet more 'practical' and 'real'.[69]

By combining the theoretical and the practical in this way, the rational implied for Gramsci a 'science' with a small 's'; while the real implied a 'history' with a small 'h.' That is to say, there could be no 'general' Science of science or an overarching History of life. There was only a unity, a dialectical unity of the relation between the real and the rational that expressed both reason and method, a common-sense and an ethico-political morality, all of which was rooted in the terrain of history, however fractured and multiplicitous.

In this sense, and very similar to Croce's use of 'distincts,' Gramsci extended the argument to suggest that the rational and the real were distinct entities that, taken together, would exhaust the whole of history. In so doing, the real would form the logical premiss for the rational, without which the latter would be unable to provide any concrete meaning. To paraphrase Gramsci, the rational and the real would form 'the distincts of "science and life", [or] of "philosophy and history."'[70] Their dialectical unity would form a contingent, 'active unity'; the nexus would itself become the social terrain or structure. Moreover, by being rooted to, and expressing this structure, one could 'become conscious of their situation, and fight it out.'

> Without having understood this relationship [between the rational and the real], it seems that one cannot understand the philosophy of praxis, its position in comparison with idealism and with mechanical materialism ... It is not exact, as Croce maintains, to say that in philosophy of praxis the Hegelian 'idea' has been replaced by the 'concept' of structure. The Hegelian 'idea' has been resolved both in the structure and in the superstructures and the whole way of conceiving philosophy has been 'historicized'; that is to say, a whole new way of philosophising which is more concrete and historical than what went before has begun to come into existence.[71]

On one level, then, the unity of the rational and real, posed also as a relation between philosophy, politics, and history, was precisely 'science,' inasmuch as it represented the complex body of knowledge that was itself a dynamic, changing unity. It was a science/knowledge that attempted to avoid the pitfalls of either a science-in-general or an overarching Philosophy of philosophy. It was the notion of a science as a specific methodology of history/politics, a politics-as-science, that is, a 'political science,' the methodology of philosophical/political activity or, more precisely, of praxis.[72] Out of this unity, a concept of the philosophy of praxis emerged that represented a 'coronation of modern culture,' to use Gramsci's description, and as such was 'impure in the most profane sense of the term.'[73] Indeed, to ignore the threefold 'terrain' out of which marxism had emerged was to remain blind to the essential ingredients of marxism itself: that, as the constitutive expression of French materialism, German idealism, and English political economy, marxism was an historical product; it was their 'expression' in the most profound sense of the word. 'These three cultural movements,' Gramsci remarked,

> are at the origin of the philosophy of praxis. But in what sense is this affirmation to be understood? That each of these movements has contributed respectively to the elaboration of the philosophy, the economics and the politics of the philosophy of praxis? [Isn't it] rather, that the philosophy of praxis has synthesized the three movements, that is the entire culture of the age, and that in the new synthesis, whichever 'moment' one is examining, the theoretical, the economic or the political, one will find each of the three movements present as a preparatory 'moment'? This is what seems to me to be the case. One could say in a sense, I think, that the philosophy of praxis equals Hegel plus David Ricardo.[74]

In this sense, and from his having situated the rational and real *within* history, as a *part* of history as well as an *expression* of history itself, Gramsci reasoned that theoretical/practical activity was always 'manmade' and, hence, entailed political specificity. Moreover, and given political specificity as the core nexus to the rational/real, this positioning led Gramsci to conclude, in part, that there could be no omnipotent truth devoid of human activity, nor could there be an underlying, arbitrary, or general logic to knowledge or scientific methodology. It allowed him to argue that there could be no science-in-general and that, in this context, *scienza* (science/knowledge) would be 'political' inasmuch as it 'transforms men and makes them different from what they were before.'[75]

To put it slightly differently, Gramsci argued that there could be no such thing as 'orthodoxy,' unless by orthodoxy one were to mean nothing less than the recognition that the philosophy of praxis was itself a *synthesis*, an immanent expression of the three most important progressive philosophies already mentioned.[76] In this sense, orthodoxy could be used not only to underscore the dynamic nature of marxism, but to emphasize that this new synthesis represented a radically altered conception of the world, one that was, 'sufficient unto itself,' that is to say, 'total.' Without this kind of orthodoxy, without this kind of self-sufficiency or totality, a philosophy, Gramsci concluded, could never become revolutionary.

Orthodoxy is not to be looked for in this or that adherents of the philosophy of praxis, or in this or that tendency connected with currents extraneous to the original doctrine, but in the fundamental concept that the philosophy of praxis is 'sufficient unto itself', that it contains in itself all the fundamental elements needed to construct a total and integral conception of the world, a total philosophy and theory of natural science. [It includes] ... everything that is needed to give life to an integral practical origination of society; that is, to become a total civilization. The concept of orthodoxy, thus renewed, helps to give a better definition to the attribution 'revolutionary' [itself].[77]

Posing orthodoxy as both an expression of history, i.e., an expression of *specificity*, and, at the same time, one that was totalizing, that is, universal, was yet another way for Gramsci to emphasize, and equate as fundamental to a philosophy of praxis, the argument around truth/ science we have been discussing: that it always entails some kind of historical contingency or fluidity.[78] But it also meant, since objective truth, to paraphrase Gramsci, could only ever be 'humanly objective,'[79] that universality itself was always-already 'subjective,' that is, 'impure' or meaningful only on the *condition* of its specificity. In the eleventh notebook, Gramsci amplified the point: '[Objectivity corresponds] exactly to "historically subjective": in other words, objective would mean "universal subjective". Man knows objectively in so far as knowledge is real for the whole human race *historically* unified in a single unitary cultural system ... There exists therefore a struggle for the cultural unification of the human race.'[80]

What makes truth *real*, that is, what gives it any meaning, would thus be for Gramsci precisely its subjectivity, i.e., its historical 'error.'[81] But putting forward the concept of historical error not only allowed Gramsci to incorporate into a concept of universality the problem of subjectivity, it also allowed him to underscore once again the political, i.e., contingent, nature of that subjectivity. For, if it could be argued that universality existed only in and on the terrain of history (understood as a 'terrain' precisely because 'history' would itself be a constitutive moment, always in a process of synthesis or unity), then the political moment, as an element of that synthetic unity, must always be present. And given that presence (of subjectivity, contingency), there could thus be no concrete universality that existed beyond or 'outside' history; that is, there could be no external objectivity to reality, only the dialectical expression of the rational and real-in-the-making whose unity would constitute the substance or grounding of 'objectivity.'

But to reason as he did – that is, to acknowledge and emphasize universality or truth as 'rooted' in a contingent history – was not yet enough to divorce Gramsci's philosophy of praxis from the difficulties encountered in a crocean idealism or kantian transcendentalism. Neither was it enough to separate it from the vulgar evolutionism of mechanistic or reductionist materialism. For, given the various identities of politics = science = philosophy = history, and so forth, the obvious question would still be lingering: If everything, including truth, were to be considered 'political,' how would Gramsci avoid what he acknowledged could become a series of 'wearisome and tautological platitudes'?[82] More important, how would Gramsci be able to ascribe ethicality to his argument as something other than 'that which is created as such' or as something ethical by definition?[83] For, although he strenuously attempted to clarify and sustain those sets of equivalences, basing them in part on whether (and in what way) a constitutive unity might be linked to the 'realm of necessity,' the charge could be made that Gramsci's reading of a philosophy of praxis might still appear hopelessly ensconced in an idealist appropriation of history.

What was needed to separate the philosophy of praxis from these so-called philosophical errors, and, more to the point, what Gramsci argued would prevent it from lapsing into either simple tautological reasonings or speculative logics, was a serious re-examination (and reaffirmation) of the historical materialist dialectic itself. For Gramsci this meant, in particular, a clarification of the way in which that dialectic was utterly rooted in, and unintelligible without, the concept of an (historicized) 'immanence.'[84]

Gramsci argued that a realist form of immanence had often been neglected in the discussions of marxist theory, in part because of a tendency to overemphasize the 'materialist' side of the historical materialist dialectic at the expense of its 'historical' component.[85] That tendency had its roots, as we saw, in the various kinds of scientism discussed earlier, where the rational and the real where hypostatized outside the political moment; where, that is to say, 'truth' was presented 'as if' already given, as if static and external to the circumstance to which it was a part. Indeed, it was a tendency Marx himself had already criticized and dismissed in his first thesis on Feuerbach: 'The chief defect of all hitherto existing materialism – that of Feuerbach included – is that the thing [*Gegenstand*], reality, sensuousness, is conceived only in the form of the object [*Objekt*] or of contemplation [*Anschauung*], but not as human sensuous activity, practice, ie not subjectively.'[86]

On the contrary, Gramsci reasoned that, since the concept of science in a philosophy of praxis meant both creativity/discovery and the methodology of that creation, i.e., the methodology of history-in-the-making, one must proceed with a notion of science that incorporated a particular concept of movement or 'becoming.' One must proceed with a notion that incorporated both specificity (history) and the possibility (the ought) of that specificity. Indeed in this context, movement or immanence was precisely the unified expression of the 'is' and the 'ought,' i.e., the 'organic unity of history, politics and economics,' or, as Gramsci would put it, the unified expression of the rational and real, outside of which there could exist no meaningful concept or knowledge.[87]

Moreover, and as we also detailed, since the philosophy of praxis was precisely the unitary moment of the three political philosophies of French materialism, German idealism, and English classical economics – indeed, since it was their (dialectical) 'expression' – the philosophy of praxis, as such, was, for Gramsci, precisely the embodiment of this 'historical immanence.' It was the 'inversion' of the hegelian dialectic, without expelling from its ranks the concept of movement or becoming, 'in order to construct the synthesis of dialectical unity, (and put it, instead, as) the "man walking on his feet."'[88] As Gramsci wrote: 'It seems to me that the unitary "moment" of synthesis is to be identified in the concept of immanence, which has been translated from the speculative form, as put forward by classical German philosophy, into an historicized form with the aid of French politics and English classical economics.'[89]

But, on another level, emphasizing the concept of an historicized immanence – indeed, insisting that this immanence was what marked the core of marxism itself – meant for Gramsci simply recognizing the point Marx had earlier underscored in his third thesis on Feuerbach when raising the question of who educates the educator.[90] That point was simply that history entailed a 'fluidity' that could never be considered neutral or devoid of meaning, or as something formed arbitrarily. Indeed, that 'fluidity' was, for Gramsci, precisely and at its core, articulating a concept of immanence that could never exist without the political moment, itself contingent and forged through struggle. For Gramsci, this point was perhaps one of the most profound and radical arguments put forward by Marx: that there was no such thing as a value-free immanence, if, that is to say, immanence or 'becoming' were posed in terms of a rational/real dialectical unity.[91]

Characterized as 'a master–pupil relationship, one between the philosopher and the cultural environment,' one that exemplified the 'unity of science and life, [a unity which] was precisely an active unity, in which alone liberty of thought could be realised,' the question of becoming was posed as the synthetic unity, internal to, and yet encompassing the relationship between philosophy and history.[92] It was the nuanced 'ought' connected to and yet folding back to shape the 'is.' Thus, unlike Croce's story of liberty or, for that matter, Hegel's *Sittlichkeit* – both of which had presupposed an ethicality attributable to the logic of the Idea (and, hence, a 'becoming' that could represent only an abstract teleology) – for Gramsci, 'historicized immanence' pointed directly to a specific, and ethical, 'what ought to be,' born from, and constituted by, the fluidity of *political* struggle, immanent in its identity: 'For the relationship between master and disciple in the general sense referred to above is only realised where this political condition exists, and only then do we get the "historical" realism of a new type of philosopher, whom we would call a "democratic philosopher."'[93]

With this notion of 'historicized becoming,' it could be said, then, that not only would a concept of the universal subjective be developed that attempted to go beyond the abstractionism of speculative logic and, at the same time, give content to a social ethicality, but a concept of the individual could be forwarded that was neither abstract nor devoid of an 'ought.' For, given that there could be no such thing as an objective truth free from error, no truth external to history, no 'thing-in-itself' set above or beyond negativity, the meaning of human nature itself must be understood as a product of political struggle, i.e., a product of this subjectivized immanence.[94] And since subjectivity was itself an expression of specific historical circumstance, by extension, then, there could never exist a 'neutral' concept of what ought to be.

> Reflecting on it, we can see that in putting the question 'what is man?' what we really mean is: what can man become? That is, can man dominate his own destiny, can he 'make himself', can he create his own life? We maintain therefore that man is a process, and more exactly, the process of his actions. [For] if you think about it, the question itself 'what is man?' is not an abstract or 'objective' question. It is born of our reflection about ourselves and about others, and we want to know, in relation to what we have thought and seen, what we are and what we can become; whether we really are, and if so to what extent, 'makers of our own selves', of our life and of our destiny. And we want to know this 'today', in the given conditions of today, the conditions of our daily life, not of any life or of any man.[95]

In other words, for Gramsci, the meaning of 'what is man?' and 'what could man become?,' like the concepts of philosophy or science, was also always subjected to and, at the same time, would become a subject of history. Human nature was precisely that which was historically created, that could 'change with changes in the circumstances,' that which expressed the 'synthesized' unitary moment of theoretical and practical activity, that which embodied both the exigency of the past and the presence of the future. It was always, consequently, a process of movement, an expression of a synthesized unity:

> That 'human nature' is the 'complex of social relations' is the most satisfactory answer, because it includes the idea of becoming (man 'becomes', he changes continuously with the changing of social relations) and because it denies 'man-in-general'. Indeed social relations are expressed by various groups as of men which each presuppose the other and whose unity is dialectical, not formal ... One could say that the nature of man is [therefore] 'history', and, in this sense, given history is equal to 'spirit', that the nature of man is 'spirit' [too] if one gives to history precisely this significance of 'becoming' which takes place in a *concordia discors*, which does not start from unity, but contains in itself the reasons for a possible unity.[96]

Not only did Gramsci thus insist on the point that the meaning of human nature is an historical creation and, therewith, at its very core, 'political,' but he stressed that the very notion of meaning entailed its own specificity as a product and expression of becoming.[97] In this sense, meaning itself could never be neutral. It implied 'discovery,' 'invention,' 'possibility,' and 'change' – but not of an arbitrary kind. It was, instead, rooted in the dialectical unity of the rational and the real; it 'changed with changes in the circumstances.' In this sense, the 'is' and the 'ought' were both constructed out of the realm of necessity and the realm of the not-yet-existing, where necessity would not be opposed to possibility, but rather would become the condition without which the realm of possibility simply could not exist.

> Possibility is not reality: but it is in itself a [kind of] reality, [for] whether a man can or cannot do a thing has its importance in evaluating what is done in reality. 'Possibility' means 'freedom'. [And that] measure of freedom enters into the concept of man. That objective possibilities exist for people not to die of hunger, and that people do die of hunger has its importance, or so one would have thought. But the evidence of 'objective' conditions, of possibilities or of freedom is not yet enough: it is necessary to 'know' them, and to know how to use them. And to want to use them.[98]

Two conclusions were thus deduced directly. On the one hand, the marxist dialectic would have to be understood exactly as the embodiment of substantive and rational immanence.[99] On the other hand, the ethicality to which this immanence pointed could not be seen as relative or drawn in and of itself. Rather, it would be bounded by the experience and 'truth' of history, itself premised on and expressing a kind of negativity: the negativity of the 'not-yet' (but potentially obtainable) real. For Gramsci, the comprehension of the 'what ought to be' and the making of it into an existing better society would thus be both the expression of necessity *and* its condition of possibility. Moreover, the process of creating that condition would be precisely the 'critical act,' the making more coherent the rational and real. It was, in short, the return to the terrain of the political, the first, the last, and mediating moment of real life.

If, as Marx already concluded in 'Theses on Feuerbach,' the 'critical act' was the politics of creating, out of the unity of theoretical and practical activity, changes in the social circumstance, then politics would become also, to quote Gramsci's reference to Machiavelli and sleight-of-hand with regard to Croce, the 'art of the possible,' that is, the creating of an ethical positionality. Indeed, as we noted earlier, this notion of politics as contouring or referencing the possible – and, more to the point, the negative dialectic to which it pointed – became a corner-stone for Gramsci's attack against the 'flat, vulgar evolutionism' of mechanical materialism and the 'pure historical movement/progress' of scientific-idealism. But, as we also saw, it was a way of infusing into ethicality a universal subjectivity, a 'truth' that would be profoundly historical, i.e., one that expressed the synthetic totality of the specific circumstances to which it was a part.

By insisting on the concept of an historicized immanence as absolutely central to the philosophy of praxis – indeed, as synonymous with it – Gramsci tried to make concrete the rational dialectic, as Marx would call it. It was a rationality that radically re-posed knowledge and circumstance and possibililty as a (dialectical) function and process of politics. In not having understood the importance of error and immanence to what Gramsci renamed as the 'real' dialectic, 'the uneducated and crude environment [was left to dominate] the educator, rather than the other way around. [But] if the environment is the educator, it too, must be educated, but the *Manual* does not understand this revolutionary dialectic.'[100]

To be absolutely clear about Gramsci's point, what was so 'revolutionary' about the real dialectic was precisely the argument that not only must change or possibility, indeed society itself, be understood as 'linked' to necessity (i.e., historically specific conditions) but its meaning – its very subjectivity – would be constituted by the impurities of truth. That is, they would be constituted precisely by the political moment, always in a process of being established 'as such.' In that sense, then, there would be no essence or absolute meaning to history. But also, truth created as such could never be understood as 'neutral' or value free, or 'good' in and of itself; it could never stand outside of an ethico-political reality. In presenting society as a totalized unitary moment, a synthesis, conditioned, as it were, by its distinct 'preparatory moments,' meant, then, that the struggle around potentiality, around the 'what ought to be,' would be one that embodied precisely the relations, experience, and cultural precepts of the social groups from which it was born.

Creating a new possibility, a new society, was thus, for Gramsci, a struggle to 'make more coherent' what at the moment would exist only as splintered, fragmentary, and negative, a struggle that involved grounding itself on the concrete will of a specific people. That making 'more coherent' the synthetic unitary moment – which, as we have seen, would always be understood as actively political and not divorced from history – would mark the passage from the old society to the new. Indeed, this passage from the old to the new was for Gramsci the 'cathartic moment' par excellence. It was the expression of an immanent unity whose process of formation would be forged in the political battles to transform society; it was an immanent unity whose realization would be established precisely in the passage 'from the realm of the purely economic (egoistic passional) to the realm of the ethico-political moment.'[101]

In characterizing the attempt to make concrete what at the moment could exist only as possibility, Gramsci thus envisioned a complex and complete change in both the structure of reality and its superstructural component, neither of which could exist as value free, static, or as always-already given. Indeed, as we have seen, it was a complete reassessment of the concept of the social terrain itself, now posed as fluid and entailing both experience and negation:

> Structure ceases to be an external force which crushes man, assimilates him to itself and makes him passive ... [Structure] is transformed into a means of freedom, an instrument to create a new ethico-political form and new sources of initiative. To establish the 'cathartic' moment becomes, therefore it seems to me, the starting point for all the philosophy of praxis, and the cathartic process coincides with the chain of syntheses which have resulted from the evolution of the dialectic.[102]

What we find, then, for Gramsci is that the *concept* of the philosophy of praxis is itself the science of the historicized dialectic, both absolute and immanent in its expression. It is the complete denial of a dual reality, the complete historicization of the rational and the real, the posing as 'active' the synthesis of their unity, an activity nothing less than political – indeed, nothing less than ethical.

But still there remained a problem with Gramsci's absolute historicism. As we will see in the next chapter, it had to do with his clarifying the way in which social and political 'ethicality' could be based on a specific 'the people' without, in the end, privileging a pregiven social agent. For Gramsci, this issue would partly be resolved by incorporating directly the question of the will, now contextualized in terms of a subjective universalism or totalizing and historically immanent truth. Let us now turn to the question of the will to determine exactly what was at stake, and why.

FOUR

The Understated Importance of the Concept of the Will

Gramsci, in reflecting on the fascist victories in Italy and elsewhere, recast his impressions of that victory in the following way: 'the State had been conceived of as something abstract by the collectivity of citizens, as an eternal father who was supposed to have thought of everything, foreseen everything, etc. Hence the absence of a "real" democracy, of a real collective will, and hence, as a result of the passivity of individuals the need for a despotism more or less disguised as a bureaucracy.'[1]

This passage holds several key propositions, but in particular, the suggestion that a 'real' democracy would entail something both organic to and in some way expressive of a 'real' collective will. In other sections of the *Quaderni*, Gramsci would push the argument much farther than this. As we will detail here, for Gramsci, not only did a radical democracy have to include a socio-political institution that in some way encompassed the will of the people, but, he argued, only from the structural terrain of a collective will made 'coherent and homogeneous,' as he would say, by organized political struggle, could the possibility of establishing a progressive and democratic society exist and be reproduced as such. Indeed, democracy would be the logical and ethico-political expression of that will.[2]

But given its central importance to Gramsci's work, the notion of the will has had a peculiar reception by scholars and political activists alike.[3] In many of the ensuing commentaries attempting to explicate and popularize his work, the meaning of what this 'will' entails and the subsequent processes it implies in relation to the creation of a new state representing that will have often been contextualized in other terms or concepts (such as the party, the organic intellectual, even hegemony), which are themselves products of the very process they are expected to clarify.[4] Even the well-known phrase 'pessimism of the intelligence, optimism of the will,'[5] which has become more or less synonymous with the very core of Gramsci's political writings, is often dismissed as a spirited rallying cry with no real significance for the philosophy of praxis, except perhaps to underscore and, in a sense, romanticize Gramsci's constant 'struggle despite all odds' against the rising tide of fascism.[6]

In short, the vast array of analyses directly relating to the conception and use of both 'will' and the 'collective will' has been surprisingly superficial and, more often than not, is omitted entirely from a general assessment of his work. As with other concepts Gramsci employed that were not traditionally considered a part of marxist theory, the general omission of the will may stem, in part, from a reluctance to follow Gramsci's own recommendations regarding the incorporation of methodological or conceptual aspects of other philosophical systems that may seem directly at odds with a philosophy of praxis.

The problem is certainly exacerbated by Gramsci's own ambiguities in the notebooks, with remarks often containing obscure reference points or sarcastically appropriating the notion of the will as a way to criticize the fascist theorists using their own terms.[7] For it hardly need be said that Gramsci was writing at a time when the word 'will' was not only frequently used as a political rallying point by the *camicie nere* (the fascist blackshirts), but heatedly discussed and given priority by thinkers as varied as Giovanni Gentile (in his *Origins and Doctrine of Fascism*)[8] and Henri Bergson (in his *Creative Evolution*, among other works).[9] Indeed, as is well known, Mussolini, Hitler, and others stressed the importance of establishing a new and so-called progressive state that would be based on the movement, and maintained by the triumph, of the will.[10]

It should be underscored at this point, then, that Gramsci was quite aware of those debates and circumstances, all the more so since much of the intellectual reading material not censored by his fascist prison guards was precisely that which was, for obvious reasons, selected because it conformed in substance and in form to the dictates of Mussolini's regime. In some sense, it could also be suggested that Gramsci's choice to focus on the will and its 'transcendence' to an ethico-political state could be seen, at least in part, as a way to criticize the contemporary fascist thinkers, using the weapon of their own rationality.

In any event, what we will find is that Gramsci's posing of a will, and in particular a 'national-popular collective will,' is not just a way for

Gramsci to criticize the fascists per se or to give a cosmetic treatment to the problem (and requirement) of social consensus as the logical foundation for a democratic state. Even less is it to be understood as a militant rallying cry. Rather, we will find that the posing of the will in terms of the real dialectic (as outlined in the previous chapter) provided a way for Gramsci to give historical specificity, i.e., concrete substance, to the concept of the ethico-political itself. More to the point, by detailing how content could indeed be assigned to (social) ethicality, this relationship of the dialecticized will to the ethico-political allowed Gramsci room to say whether the new society being advanced could be considered 'progressive' or 'better' than that of the status quo, and why that must be the case. In this sense, too, Gramsci was able to tackle the problem raised in the first chapter: how to posit the social 'ought,' the *Sittlichkeit*, without relapsing into hegelian dialectics or liberalist semantics.

To put it somewhat differently, then, for Gramsci, this posing of a collective will was a kind of historicized 'inversion' of the hegelian *Sittlichkeit/Moralität*. As such, it could be seen, at least in part, as a way to fuse the best areas of the liberal-democratic tradition with the most fundamental aspects of a philosophy of praxis. Given this kind of fusion, the case could then be made that the intellectual and creative reform, and the fluid possibilities that that reform would imply, would necessarily become the fundamental principle upon which a post-liberal-democratic theory could be articulated.

But to make this claim stick, several points within Gramsci's argument should be examined. First, it must be established that Gramsci's rendering of the will was neither transhistorical nor psychological, nor was it arbitrarily relativistic or caught in the fatal nihilistic rationalism into which some detractors have accused him of having (inadvertently) fallen. His rendering of the will, it shall alternatively be suggested, was a specific denotation of a *politics/knowledge terrain*, a grounding often posed in the notebooks as the 'operative awareness of historical necessity,' or, in a phrase, conscious will-power. This will-power construction, which was established by Gramsci through a complex reworking of the marxist dialectic, shall then serve, second, as a basis with which to assess Gramsci's ethico-political hegemony, a hegemony, as we shall also note, that becomes the active expression of an intellectual/moral reform somewhat refurbished through the lens of a machiavellian marxist.

By posing the will in this manner, that is, on the one hand, as a will-power terrain, and, on the other, as linked to the ethico-political, two points will become clearer. The first is that Gramsci's concept of will, steeped as it is in terms of an absolute historicism, must be understood in a radically non-essentialist manner. In so doing, it will become quite clear how this relational concept answers directly the dilemmas outlined in chapter 1. But, second, it shall also be added that this radical non-essentialist rendering takes Gramsci to a precipice over which he himself cannot leap (and perhaps, neither can we). For as we shall observe, it seems to bring us full circle to the same positions against which Gramsci had so adamantly fought. That is, it seems to take us to the level of strategies as opposed to theory; description as opposed to analysis; teleology as opposed to politics, properly speaking.

By relying on the will as a 'will-power' terrain, it would seem, in other words, that Gramsci is able to avoid posing an abstract ethicality only at the expense of having to construct a teleological, a priori, and, hence, abstract concept of the working class itself. As we shall see by the conclusion of this chapter, he recognizes what seems to be the 'fatal flaw' of the argument, and proceeds to resolve it directly. What becomes important for us in this chapter, then, is not only to show the way in which the 'will' itself becomes a central feature of the philosophy of praxis despite the trap, but to analyze the way in which Gramsci proceeds in order to counter and resolve it.

Will as the basis of a philosophy of praxis

In an initial proposition, Gramsci tossed out a claim that, at first sight, might appear dramatically idealist in nature: 'Per sfuggire al solipsismo ... occorre porre la questione "storicistamente" e nello stesso tempo porre a base della filosofia la "volonta" [In order to avoid solipsism, we must put the question "historically" and at the same time put at the base of philosophy the "will"].'[11]

Without repeating the whole of the argument discussed in chapter 2, compare how similar his initial proposition might seem to Croce's 'practical will' established in his *Aesthetic* and *Philosophy of the Practical* and briefly summarized as follows: The theoretic form of pure spirit, which is, at one and the same time, a distinct and concrete universal of that spirit, is itself constituted by (the pure form of) intellectual and intuitive knowledge.[12] Now, as we noted earlier, this intuitive and intellectual knowledge, which exhausted all aspects of the theoretic form of spirit, remained in the speculative (pure) realm of the Idea and could not be understood concretely unless, according to Croce, a relation was established with the only other form of spirit, that form being called the practical.[13]

Similar to that of its counterpart (the theoretic, whose first moment was intuition), the crocean practical was itself constituted by two moments, the will, on the one hand, and morality, on the other. Here the will was called upon by Croce to act as the foundation, that is, as the first moment or degree of practical activity. Following this schematic reasoning, morality would then be posed as the second moment (or degree) of the practical, a morality that was conditioned by, and could only remain abstract without, the vitality of the will.[14] For Croce, then, this meant that with intuition and reasoned logic we would be able to understand (pure) reality; with the will (tempered with morality) we would be able to change it.[15] In other words, the will, in Croce's context, was precisely the ability 'to do' (or resist doing); it was action or activity.

Developed in this way, Croce thus attempted to give content or meaning to the will. Moreover, given that it existed as the first moment of practical activity, the will would thus also become the first moment of *all* knowledge. Hence, it was both 'rational' (i.e., the embodiment of 'thought in activity') and as well not neutral or arbitrary; that is, it was 'specific.'[16] It is worth repeating in part Croce's explanation: 'with one [we] appropriate the universe, with the other [we] create it. But the first form [i.e., the practical] is the basis of the second [the theoretic]; and the relation of the *double* degree ([will/morality] = Practical; [intuition/intellectual] = Theoretic), which we have already found existing between aesthetic and logical activity is repeated between these two on a larger scale.'[17]

In the final analysis, then, the will, for Croce, was a *condition* of knowledge and, at the same time, was non-existent without thought. But implicit also was the notion that thought/knowledge must pre-exist the will, and indeed, pre-exist history. 'Knowledge independent of the will,' concluded Croce, 'is thinkable; will independent of knowledge, unthinkable.'[18] As remarked in chapter 2, this particular rendering of the will and its relation to 'doing' and 'knowing' allowed Gramsci to make an obvious critique, without, however, dismissing the problem entirely. '"To do" here has [for Croce] a particular meaning, so particular in fact that it finally means nothing more than "to know" and the phrase resolves itself into a tautology ... [Even so] this conception should be considered in relation to the philosophy of praxis.'[19]

Like Croce, in certain respects, Gramsci also argued that the will ought to be considered as the basis, the foundation, of knowledge.[20] Like Croce, too, Gramsci argued that the will was not to be conceived of as arbitrary or based upon (or understood as) intuition, fantasy, even drive. That is, the will was neither psychological nor metaphysical. It was instead a political expression in the strongest sense of the word 'political.' And herein lay the initial, and profound, difference between the two: the will, for Gramsci, was a conceptual category denoting the combined ability to 'think' of the real and begin to work towards the 'possible' of that which did not yet exist. In some ways an early formulation of what in contemporary terms has been called the 'political imaginary,' the will for Gramsci was precisely the *creative component* of practical/political activity. But, at the same time, the will marked the terrain or boundary of that practical/political activity, a terrain made coherent or unified precisely through political struggle.

Gramsci arrived at this particular repositing of the will by insisting on the primacy of the real dialectic, a primacy that, as we saw in chapter 3, underscored two main principles: first, that the dialectical unity of the theoretic and practical posed by Croce was inside out, inverted, as it were, since it refashioned reality as knowledge above all else, and thereby took pure knowledge as the premiss or explanatory category for detailing reality and all that could be said to be in it. As we saw, though, for Gramsci, the 'real dialectic' was, instead, an active unity of the theoretical and the practical, an active unity that privileged the actual material conditions of reality above all, and hence took historical circumstance as its point of departure. But, second, since these material conditions were themselves the synthesis of an active unity, i.e., were themselves a 'praxis' that entailed both negation and positivity, history was always immanent, always imbued with the possibility of change, while at the same time becoming the constant terrain upon which the battle to institutionalize or make permanent that change could occur. The will, in this sense, could be understood as both process and strategy.

From those two points, Gramsci's posing of will could in no way become a parallel structure to Croce's notion of the will as the basis or first moment of all knowledge. It was rather a fundamental *nexus* of practical/political activity, the creative point of departure, as it were, for the philosophy of praxis. And as this was a 'synthesized' will, i.e., constituted dialectically as an 'expression,' not only was it to be cast as the initial point of departure, but that point of departure would itself be indicative of a relation, an open process of, as Gramsci would put it, 'relating means to ends.'[21] In this context, the will, for Gramsci, became precisely a *strategy of power*, that is, the political act of creating in reality what, at that moment, might exist only as 'possibility.' But it did so by remaining grounded in – and indeed linked to – the terrain of 'effective reality,' or, in a word, history. That is, it was the act of transforming the 'what ought to be' into the 'what is,' but doing so by 'accurately identifying the fundamental and permanent elements of the process.'[22]

By casting the will in these terms, as both a creative act *and* an awareness rooted in historical circumstance,[23] Gramsci began to contextualize the will both as a practical act of knowing one's circumstances and as that which was involved with the process of envisioning a future possibility. This vision would be considered 'utopia' inasmuch as it was not yet reality, *but* could also fall within the realm of freedom inasmuch as it might be connected to necessity and hence would have a concrete potential to be realized. One could say, then, that if Gramsci's rendering of historicized immanence (or 'becoming') was the 'science' of politics, the will was its 'art,' the so-called art of politics.

Indeed it could be said that the art of trying to articulate and, more to the point, create real possibilities or real alternatives – the 'what ought to be' of science and of life – would, in this context, be understood as the political act par excellence.[24] For the forging of a collective will would embody the rational and intellectual aspects of practical activity; but, posed as such, it would also become a strategy of power and, as well, the terrain upon which that strategy could be effected. To put it slightly differently, then, effective or 'real' change could come about and be institutionalized as such only to the degree to which the vision of a future possibility was to be based on actual social conditions – conditions that might exist *en potentia* but would require some coherence in order that it be directed towards particular ends. Thus, as Gramsci often repeated, mankind must always set for itself only such tasks as it has the means to resolve so that those 'tasks *become* duty, will *becomes* free.'[25]

Since real will for Gramsci was thus always 'political will,'[26] infused with and born out of this intellectual and creative power/knowledge terrain, and since this will was also the analytic term for transforming the 'ought' into the 'is,' Gramsci concluded that those who attempted to make concrete, i.e., envision and attempt to put into practice, a new philosophy, a new *Weltanschauung*, must be considered political scientists; indeed, they would be active politicians par excellence. For not only were they political inasmuch as they were 'practical romantics,' capable of dreaming of a utopia based on the real necessities of life and hence responsible in part for forging a new history, but, in so becoming 'practical romantics,' their projects would express a politics itself, since those projects would specifically be designed to enhance certain living conditions over others. Indeed, this was precisely how Gramsci cast the important contributions of Machiavelli and his work in general. In his thirteenth notebook, Gramsci concluded:

Machiavelli is not merely a scientist: he is a partisan, a man of powerful passions, an active politician, who wishes to create a new balance of forces and therefore cannot help concerning himself with 'what ought to be'

... [But the question becomes one] of seeing whether 'what ought to be' is arbitrary or necessary: whether it is concrete will on the one hand or idle fancy, yearning or daydream on the other. For the active politician is a creator, an initiator; but he neither creates from nothing nor does he move in the turbid void of his own desires and dreams. He bases himself on effective reality ... but does so in order to dominate and transcend it (or contribute to this). What 'ought to be' is therefore concrete; indeed, it is the only realistic and historicist interpretation of reality. It alone is history in the making and philosophy in the making; it alone is politics.[27]

By placing the will at the 'base' of philosophy, where philosophy would thus be understood as the richly complex dialectical synthesis of politics/history, Gramsci tried systematically to elaborate the difference between utopian visions based on arbitrary speculation or, as he would put it, 'pure thought,' and those based on historical 'necessity.' The former simply represented, as he would say, 'fairy tales and idle daydream,' the latter, a 'concrete political act.'[28] For 'necessity' itself would become a constraint whose boundaries would be established in part by this will-power terrain. And as a boundary, it would delimit the possible routes that might be taken to effect real change. This point was, for Gramsci, a serious strategic and analytic one that most political scientists tended to miss. 'Political science abstracts the element of the "will,"' claimed Gramsci, 'and does not take account of the ends to which it is applied ... [whereas] ... the attribute "utopian" ought not to apply to political will in general but [only] to [those] specific wills that are incapable of relating means to ends and hence, are not [really] even wills, but idle dreams, whims, longings, etc.'[29]

Unlike Croce, then, for whom the intellectual and intuitive existed outside the will, for Gramsci, they were *unthinkable* without the will, without this 'operative awareness,' to use Gramsci's expression, 'of historical necessity.'[30] As one can see, then, Gramsci was not merely interested in writing an 'anti-Croce' similar in form to Engels's 'anti-Dühring' (although he does insist throughout the notebooks that this is, in part, what he wishes to accomplish).[31] The critiquing of Croce's positing of the will and the attempt to re-present this will in historicist/immanent terms as the 'first moment' of the philosophy of praxis was, rather, a way to situate, analytically, the question of bringing to fruition a 'better' society, as such and for whom. That is, it was an attempt to infuse the will with historical error, i.e., with its own specificity, which, ipso facto, entailed an 'ought' posed discursively rather than in a priori or transhistorical/universalistic terms. In contrast, this was an 'ought' brought into existence only by, at the very least, accounting for the will-power terrain, the actual practical/political matrix that itself was produced by way of a 'suturing' or 'making more coherent' this terrain.[31]

By entailing conceptual space for both the 'ought' and the 'is,' this historically and politically nuanced concept of the will became, for Gramsci, a systematic attempt at articulating the importance and fluidity of the structure or terrain as, itself, a 'ground' – a fractured, diverse, i.e., discursively ontological 'ground' – of social ethicality. It also became a systematic attempt at articulating theoretically and practically the way in which direct participation could and must contribute to making the 'impossible' real. To put it in the philosophical terms Gramsci always used, one had to grasp that the social structure was itself the embodiment of movement from the 'realm of necessity' to the 'realm of freedom' in order to concretize the latter into the former, a movement made possible only with the direct participation of the people.[33] And it was an attempt to do so by using Croce, and indeed Hegel, against themselves.

Given that 'thinking about' and 'acting upon' real possibilities (the 'what ought to be') was precisely a political act, the outcome of the rational and intellectual aspects of practical activity, the will became for Gramsci, in the final analysis, both a strategy and a matrix of power. But it also became the practical terrain, the 'horizon' if you will, upon which that strategy could be effected. It formed both the 'given' (the parameter) and the possible direction; it was a discursive terrain whose boundaries would be constituted out of 'necessity' but, at the same time, would be constrained by that necessity. Posed as such, the will entailed a kind of 'diversity' or 'heterogeneity,' one that at a fundamental level could express, or at least account for, a changing consciousness, and, indeed, a changing consent.[34] By posing the will in this way, that is, as an immanent knowledge/power terrain, Gramsci thus attempted to account, analytically, for the movement from the 'realm of necessity' to the 'realm of freedom.'[35] But he tried also to account for the fundamental *legitimacy* of that particularly fluid 'freedom,' and therewith to account for a flexible or open consent of the people as the prima facie ingredient in founding and maintaining a 'better' society.

'Ethico-political' as an expression of collective will

Were this to be the main contribution of Gramsci's repositing of the will as a creative matrix, the so-called art of politics in the real dialectic, we should already have gained quite a bit, in terms of both political philosophy and the possible routings or strategies that might be said to ensue. But Gramsci did not terminate his theoretical and practical forays at this point. Instead he used them to make more meaningful the concept of a 'collective' will and, therewith, the very concept of social ethicality and, indeed, of democracy itself.

He did this, in part, by suggesting that what was at stake in creating a democracy was making sure that the political system itself reflected an ongoing – that is to say, fluid – 'organic unity' between the intellectuals and the people-nation, between leaders and led, between 'theory and practice,' and so forth.[36] Moreover, he stressed that this 'organic unity,' in order to be 'truly representative,' must itself be based on, and fundamentally expressive of, the will of the people. And as this will, as we noted earlier, could be contextualized only in terms of a power/knowledge terrain, it was a will that not only would delimit a boundary or trajectory but would also always be posed in terms of a discrete and fractured process of 'becoming,' representing the actuality of a synthetic, dialecticized nexus of specific circumstance or reality.[37]

But as society did not 'unfold' in some kind of predetermined way, this will could never be understood as an always-already given or continuous thread existing a priori or external to the social whole. Rather, it had to become directed or focused if possibility were to become 'real' or progress were to be made permanent. Accordingly, it had be channelled into a single collective will, produced and performed, as Gramsci would phrase it, by a 'single collective man.'[38] Indeed, it would have to 'presuppose the attainment of a cultural-social *unity*,' concluded Gramsci, 'through which a multiplicity of dispersed wills with heterogeneous aims are *welded* together within a *single* aim on the basis of [one] equal and common concept of the world.'[39]

This unified terrain was precisely forged through political struggle rather than some form of arbitrary happenstance or dictatorial enforcement. This 'welding' was precisely, to put it in more familiar terms, *a process of hegemony*, a fluid and ongoing relational *fusion* between the 'what ought to be' and the 'what is.' It was a unified welding that bespoke of a 'process' that itself was neither arbitrary nor continuous, but whose continuity had to be created and sustained in order to provide the grounds upon which a new political arena could emerge.

As a result of its having been forged from specific and diverse social networks, this new political arena would, moreover, not only contain the seeds for a new state, but would forward, ipso facto, a specific ethical component, itself inherently 'political' with all the layered nuances that this concept of political necessarily entailed.[40] Hegemony in this sense would both be the cathartic moment, i.e., the practical *result* of having welded dispersed wills together in order to form a 'coherent' collective will (and thus an ethico-political whole), and be understood as the philosophical linking of the impossible 'what ought to be' with concrete political action. 'From this, it follows,' Gramsci neatly surmised,

> that the theoretical-practical principle of hegemony has also epistemolog-
> ical significance, and it is here that Ilich [Lenin]'s greatest theoretical
> contribution to the philosophy of praxis should be sought. In these terms
> one could say that Ilich advanced philosophy as philosophy in so far as
> he advanced political doctrine and practice. The realization of a hege-
> monic apparatus, in so far as it creates a new ideological terrain, deter-
> mines a reform of consciousness and methods of knowledge: it is a fact
> of knowledge, a philosophical fact. In Crocean terms: when one succeeds
> in introducing a new morality in conformity with a new conception of
> the world, one finishes by introducing the conception as well; in other
> words, one determines a reform of the whole of philosophy.[41]

In one sense, then, we have before us a particularly original resolution to the problem raised at the outset of chapter 1: how to give content to social ethicality without posing an 'external' archimedean point
or resurrecting the idealism of a hegelian *Sittlichkeit.* By posing the will
as a synthetic and dialecticized terrain, a knowledge/power terrain
that would contain within it an immanent coupling of the 'is' and the
'ought,' Gramsci began to construct the specificity for socio-ethical
content itself. It was to be one that, by necessity, would be rooted in the
practical/political will of a people, themselves immanent in their
subjectivity.[42] Moreover, since the will could be made 'real' only when
linked to the social ought, will/morality could become 'universal' only
when forged into a unity through the hegemonic process of the ethico-
political, itself (historically) immanent in its formation and linked to
necessity. From this it could be said that *a radical democracy would be
precisely the 'expression' of ethico-political hegemony,* i.e., one that, ipso
facto, ground its 'truth' in the historicism of a collective will, hegemonic
in its legitimation.[43]

And yet, in posing the question of the collective will in terms of organic unities, synthetic totalities, and the like, two new problems immediately begin to surface. On the one hand, it could appear as though
Gramsci was simply transferring, despite his meticulous rethinking of
the will in terms of an historicized dialectic or process of hegemony, a
whole series of definitional propositions, which in the end no more

resolved the problem of ascribing ethical content than did that of the hegelian *Sittlichkeit*. On the other hand, and perhaps as a more serious charge, it might appear that Gramsci had fallen into a trap against which he himself had so steadfastly fought: the rendering to a single logic or closed totality notions of society, of state, and of man. For, if we stopped the analysis at this point, Gramsci might appear as if he could be in agreement, possibly in substance but definitely in form, with, ironically enough, the philosophic basis of fascism.[44] Indeed, it could be argued that given Gramsci's insistence on the notion of an historicized will immanent in its expression and given that his notion of the will was to become the point of departure for the theorization (and legitimation) of the democratic state, then, read as such, the will could thus be seen as a totalizing entity *in and of itself*, capable of – and indeed pressed into – reshaping society into a single, homogeneous and closed oneness.[45]

To see if this charge might hold, let us compare Gramsci's position with, for example, the arguments by Giovanni Gentile, one of the leading fascist philosophers in Italy and founder of what came to be labelled as 'actual idealism.'[46] Presented in two of his more popular essays, the first entitled 'The Totalitarian Nature of Fascist Doctrine,' the second, 'The Fascist State as a Democratic State' (both found in his 1934 *Origins and Doctrine of Fascism*), Gentile writes in part:

> Any analysis that does not always presuppose the oneness of things leads not to clarification but to the destruction of the ideas ... : a proof that men cannot be considered in fragments, but only as one and indivisible. So we have established the first point in defining Fascism: the totalitarian nature of its doctrine which is concerned not only with the political order and management of a nation, but with its will ... So the Fascist state, unlike the nationalist state, is a purely spiritual creation. [But it is also] a national state because, from the Fascist standpoint, the nation itself is realized in the spirit and not as a mere pre-supposition ... it achieves its reality in the very consciousness and will of the individual.[47]

Here Gentile was clearly putting forward the principle of a closed totality whereby the state would become the collective personality of the people, a 'personality' constituted by a funnelled, unified, collective will of the citizenry. Moreover, the individual would be a constitutive subject of that state, standing neither outside or above it, nor below it. Not only do we have a vulgarized rendition of Croce, for, in Gentile's estimation, there could be no private arena or, for that matter, no political or civil society (there would exist only the state as the embodiment of will), we also have a vulgarized restatement of the classical hobbesian man who, in order to avoid the chaotic and embattled state of nature, must become a cohesive element in the body politic, *sans* the social contract.

Given that for Gentile there would be but chaos which lay beyond the state (since there could be no rational order 'outside' of the state), there could, likewise, be no meaning for the citizen beyond the state – and should this citizen attempt to find meaning elsewhere, coercion must become the order of the day. To do otherwise, according to Gentile, would both block the 'true' function of spirit and corrupt the homogeneity of the will from whence that spirit might spring. Indeed, it is towards the state-as-embodied-spirit, Gentile reminds us, that the 'citizen' ought, indeed must, direct his or her energies.

'What ought to be,' in fascistic logic, would come to mean, in other words, nothing more than 'what is.' Not only would this identity/equivalence of 'is' and 'ought' sabotage any notion of possibility, error, freedom, creativity, and so forth, it would mean the exact opposite: coercion rather than consent, rule rather than law, a despotism disguised as bureaucracy, etc. For 'what ought to be' would come to express an always-already fully constituted will and society, indeed, the citizen itself. As Gramsci rightly commented in a rejection of that position: 'For Gentile history is entirely State history ... hegemony and dictatorship are indistinguishable; force and consent are simply equivalent; one cannot distinguish political society from civil society; only the State, and of course, the State-as-government, exists.'[48]

This kind of theoretical and political totalitarianism was exactly the kind of 'totalizing' Gramsci intended to defeat, that is, the appeal to an ontological grounding based on a *fully closed* and hence *circular* oneness of the social whole itself.[49] As we have seen, Gramsci sought to get beyond this idealized notion of history as if a fully sutured product of thought teleologically unfolding towards an abstract ethical proposition. He did this in part by rethinking the social whole in terms of the concept of a will, which entailed, at its very core, diversity and immanence – or, to put it slightly differently, one that entailed an otherness that could never be fully recuperated. But however much this particular rendering of the will might have indicated a way in which fluidity and openness could methodologically (and strategically) be incorporated without presupposing a formal and continuous totalizing process, this concept was, at the moment anyway, sadly lacking in substance: Gramsci still needed to show *why* this power/knowledge 'will,' this will-as-fluxed-terrain, was ethically 'better,' *why* incorporating openness at the root of a society would necessarily pave the way towards a radical, that is to say progressive democracy.

Responding to this particular dimension of the problem, Gramsci set the parameter of his discussions in a very direct and, indeed, urgent way. In some sense, one might say he began by stating the obvious. Casting about for a means to 'ground' this heterogeneous vision of the 'what ought to be' – and why it ought to be so – as well as a way to critique the fascists on their own terms, Gramsci calmly reminded his readers that any social theory 'worth its salt' must in some way provide an answer for the well-worn question 'what is man?' as earlier detailed. But it must also account for the fact that the very essence of humanity reflected within it *both* the circumstances of its history *and* the conscious efforts to change that history. That is, radical social theory needed to incorporate at a fundamental level the fact not only that people have changed over time – or, indeed, that change is both subjected to and in some way a *sine qua non* for life – but that the social itself must be understood as a direct expression of a rational and political will always in the process of being constituted as such. To think otherwise, that is, to pose the question of the will as if fully sutured and homogeneous rather than as an immanent, open strategy (and horizon) of the possible, would mean simply the return to an even poorer form of metaphysical materialism.[50]

A playfully sarcastic Gramsci put it this way: '[If man is "only what he eats"], then the determining matrix of history would be the kitchen and revolutions would coincide with radical changes in the diet of the masses.'[51] If there were no 'remainder,' no 'error,' no 'specificity' – if, that is, everything were to be understood as 'recuperable' and thus able to be fully totalized – then not only could there be no room for change, there could be no accounting for it when it occurs.[52]

Incorporating a changing, subjective will as something 'internal' to reality, as something created without the use of 'genius' or 'vanguard' or 'accidental' happenstance, was precisely something Gentile's fascism could not provide. For given Gentile's posing of a closed totality and the resultant emergence of the state as the 'ethical' embodiment of rational will, Gentile would have to accept, ipso facto, an already given, that is, 'fixed,' identity of the people themselves and, therewith, a fixed or homogeneous notion of their collective will. Indeed, this is precisely what a fascist logic would want to accept: a closed and neatly presented categorization of immutable identities and fixed notions of what is 'good' and 'healthy.' As Gentile himself wrote, 'The healthy man [is precisely one who] believes in God and in the freedom of Spirit,' a premiss that prompted Gramsci to retort:

In just two propositions of Gentile's, we find: 1. an extra-historical 'human nature' which one can't see quite what it is; 2. the human nature of the healthy man; 3. the common sense of the healthy man and therefore, [4.] the common sense of the non-healthy. But what is meant by 'healthy man?' Physically healthy or not mad? Or someone who thinks in a 'healthy way', right-thinking, philistine, etc ... [In reality] the problem of what is man is always the so-called problem of 'human nature' or the so-called [problem] of 'man-in-general'. But is 'man' a starting point or a point of arrival ... ? [Isn't the] whole attempt in so far as it posits the human as a starting point [simply reflecting] a theological or metaphysical residue.[53]

For Gramsci, then, it was incontrovertible that a human being would entail a fixed nature or essence, for as we noted much earlier, to accept an always-already ordered nature would be to deny the profoundly political, and no less historical specificity of life itself. 'Man is the precis of all of the past reflected in the present,' as Gramsci would phrase it, the 'unity of science and life in which alone liberty of thought can be realised.'[54] So, if what it were to be human was precisely 'the synthesis not only of existing relations but of the history of those relations,'[55] it would be no less the case that a social theory that accepted a total 'fixity' of human nature, and hence its homogenization, would be incapable of articulating a progressive conception of life. This was precisely the defensive charge Gramsci levelled against Gentile and others.

Man does not enter into relations with the natural world just by being himself part of the natural world, but actively, by means of work and technique. Further: these relations are not mechanical. They are active and conscious. So one could say that each one of us changes himself, modifies himself to the extent that he changes and modifies the complex relations of which he is the hub ... In this sense, knowledge is power ...
   ... [But, given this, it] is necessary to elaborate a doctrine in which these relations are seen as active and in movement, establishing quite clearly that the source of that activity is the consciousness of the individual man who conceives of himself not as isolated but rich in the possibilities offered him by other men and by the society of things of which he cannot help having a certain knowledge.[56]

By taking seriously the claim that we are a synthesis of the past, and hence are social beings immersed in, and expressing, an historicized immanence, that is, by accepting the profoundly political character – and hence historical specificity – of all meaning, including that which describes 'human nature,' Gramsci attempted, as we saw, to divest the concept of the social whole of any residue of a homogenized abstraction. Moreover, he attempted to do so by establishing the theoretical (and practical) importance of creating a collective will, one that was radically non-essentialist but nevertheless linked to a specific social subject, history, and circumstance. As such, it would become the strategic force for realizing and maintaining a people's democracy and, as well, the horizon that would delimit that democracy. To put it slightly differently, the social 'ought' would be born out of a political battle, a battle to 'reform the intellectual and moral climate' – a battle, that is, of hegemony. Its ontological core would be established simply and precisely as a (political) synthetic unity forged by the act of constituting the subject as such, and linking that unity to the practico-political terrain of the will.[57]

In this sense, then, the ethical community would be a civil society that, albeit channelled, focused – in short, synthesized into a 'wholeness' or 'totality' – would remain unsutured, open, continually 'immanent' in its creation. In utter contradistinction to a fascist rendering of the ethical state, for Gramsci, this residual, open and immanent, and subjective social whole was the crux of democracy itself: the realization of an ethico-political hegemony born out of and constituted by the willpower terrain of a people whose subjectivity would itself remain fluid, active, and creative.[58] At its most profound point, then, civil society, the arena where the collective will was forged and instituted as such, would become, precisely, a kind of ethico-political state without accepting a fixed notion of state; it would be precisely an historicized *Sittlichkeit*, immanent in its expression.

To understand totality then as complete homogenization would imply, as Gramsci put it, that

> we are still on the terrain of the identification of State and government – an identification which is precisely a representation of the economic-corporate form, in other words of the confusion between civil society and political society ... [But] it is possible to imagine the coercive element of the State withering away by degrees, as ever-more conspicuous elements of regulated society (or ethical State or civil society) make their appearance. The expressions of 'ethical State' or 'civil society' would thus mean that this [progressive] 'image' of a State without a State was present to the greatest political and legal thinkers, in so far as they placed themselves on the terrain of pure science (pure utopia, since based on the premise that all men are really equal and hence equally rational and moral, ie capable of accepting the law spontaneously, freely, and not

through coercion, as imposed by another class, as something external to consciousness).[59]

The dilemma of a 'totalized social' immanent in its expression

Gramsci was not just saying that the 'better' society would be forged out of an immanent strategy of a collective will shaped by – and shaping – historical necessity. He was also insisting that the establishing of a progressive unity must be done in such a way as to institutionalize an 'organic' connection between the will of the people and the intellectuals who lead.[60] Moreover, he was insisting that the philosophy of praxis had already addressed this link when it raised the question of specificity/error in the formation of the collective will and the essential role the will had in the founding of a new social order. For it was through this fundamental connection of a specific 'the people' that consent could be registered and remain a part of the construction and legitimation of a new 'historic bloc.'[61] Indeed, it was through this organic link, produced in an immanent society, that the avenue for real and direct representation was provided. 'If the relationship between intellectuals and people-nation, between leaders and led, the rulers and the ruled is provided by an organic cohesion in which feeling-passion becomes understanding and thence knowledge (not mechanically but in a way which is alive),' Gramsci thus surmised in the eleventh notebook, '*then and only then is the relationship one of representation*. Only then can there take place an exchange of individual elements between rulers and ruled, leaders and led, and can the shared life be realised which is a social force – with the creation of the "historic bloc."'[62]

By insisting on this relationship, Gramsci was attempting to provide a specific and yet, at the same time, historically universalized ethicality to the social vision. In other words, not only was he saying that the establishing of a new society based on the organic connection between the will of the people and the intellectuals who lead *must* occur in order to form the basis for an open consent, but he wanted to argue that that open consent was in itself *good*. He wanted to say that *that* cohesion would spawn a more progressive society, a more progressive state; indeed, would spawn a democracy. As Gramsci envisioned it:

We have said that the word 'democracy' must not be used only in the 'lay' or 'secular' sense, but can also be used in its 'catholic' and, if you like, reactionary sense. What matters is that a bond is being sought with the people, the nation, and that one considers necessary not a servile unity resulting from passive obedience, but an active unity, a life-unity, whatever the content of this life may be. It is precisely this living unity, irrespective of content, which has been missing in Italy, or there has not been enough of it to make it into an historical fact.[63]

What befit the democratic struggle for Gramsci, then, was the forging of a collective will that would act as a living unity between leaders and led. What befit the democratic struggle was, at the very least, the 'taking as given' the non-essential heterogeneity of the social. What had to be incorporated into a theorization of radical democracy was precisely the concept of diversity itself, a diversity constituted by the collective will of a people historically immanent in their subjectivity. This, for Gramsci, was a 'battle,' a battle of hegemony, the practico-political problem of attempting to institutionalize and make permanent a *Sittlichkeit* continually engaged in a process of 'becoming,' i.e., continually fluid, and yet, at the same time, totalizing inasmuch as it was 'real.' It was the creation of an 'ought,' that is, the creation of an ethical political community constituted by the collective will of a people historically immanent in their subjectivity.

It could be concluded, then, at one level, that, by posing the ethical society as a heterogeneous entity, he neatly avoided the trap of an absolute freedom and hence an absolute tyranny, as had been concluded by Hegel.[64] At the same time, by contextualizing the entire problematic in terms of a dialecticized 'will,' a will-power terrain connected to the social 'ought,' Gramsci escaped the pitfalls of privileging individual freedom above all else, a position that, as we saw in chapter 1, fostered an absolute weakness of the social system itself. Finally, by contextualizing the entire problematic in terms of an immanent rather than closed notion of totality and oneness, Gramsci defeated a fascistic rendering of ethical truth. Moreover, in so defeating that logic, Gramsci began to tease out the fundamental principles for a progressive and democratic society.

But despite the profundity of all these contributions, Gramsci still had to resolve a serious dilemma; in fact, he had to resolve two. And it could be said that the remedy of the first would become for Gramsci the irreparable flaw of the second. The main dilemma was simply this: in order to advance the concept of an historically immanent, 'fluxed' social totality, indeed any form of totality, Gramsci still had to posit an a priori 'first cause' to social truth, to ethicality. That is, in order for Gramsci to escape what could appear to be a relativist nihilism inherent in a position that forwarded ethicality as that which was created as such (even if linked to the terrain of the social body, itself born out of a hegemonic struggle), Gramsci still had to somehow 'ground' his ethical ontology. And since he was more than willing to ground that ontology in terms of the working class itself, he had to somehow explain why this particular set of 'the people' would, ipso facto, become the ethical embodiment and bearer of that progress, particularly and in spite of the fact that a crushing fascism had overtaken much of the movement.

To ignore the details of this discussion would open Gramsci to the charge that he might be promoting – however unintentionally and despite his many attempts to do precisely the reverse – a kind of socialist darwinism or evolutionary ethics. If that were the case, it could easily be concluded that Gramsci may well have defeated Gentile's 'totalizing' fascism only to have exchanged it for a bastardized (but friendlier) version of Croce's – namely, the positing of the 'story of democracy' as the history/anti-history antagonism (of the working classes) teleologically unfolding towards an 'impure' ethical ideal. In that case, as Gramsci himself noted previously, but with respect to Croce's 'story of liberty,' 'history would be liberty even in the oriental satrapies.'[65]

Given this dilemma, there were two completely different routes Gramsci might have taken in order to have met that challenge and to have disarmed it. The first was a radicalizing of the notion of hegemony and, therewith, the very concept of social totality; the second, a radicalizing of the notion of the structure and, therewith, the very internality of the social totality itself. Either route could have been drawn as a direct consequence of following through on his own logic thus far established around synthetic unities, the autonomy of politics, and the importance of the will. But no matter which way the logic were to be extended, both paths involved a serious set of difficulties.

The first path (radicalizing hegemony) seemed to insist on a relativity so extreme that, when taken to its logical conclusion, the ethical moment might seem as though it could be understood only as upholding the age-old (and obviously very problematic) 'everything that "is" is "good"' maxim; a maxim that implied, conversely, the upholding of a nothingness so absolute as to create the 'impossibility' of the ethical itself.[66] On the other hand, radicalizing the notion of structure within the social whole seemed to require the setting up of an already established and fully constituted ethicality created out of a privileging of 'experience,' based on the subject positionalities of (in this case) the working classes, whose exploitation and, hence, oppression emerged in direct relation to the means of production. Apart from other problems, the social 'ought' in this case, and indeed 'subjectivity' itself, might be understood instead to be that which was constituted directly from an abstract and teleological 'unfolding' of the antagonism (between worker and capitalist), rather than from a direct and necessary political struggle.

We had, on the one hand, then, a path that seemed to lead – however useful and important the notion of a radical hegemony might be for the concept of politics or, indeed, for the concept of history – invariably towards the seemingly vacuous realm of the 'impossible' rather than to the promised land of the 'possible.' On the other hand, the second path seemed to incorporate some form of an essentialist logic that, ipso facto, posited the working classes as the bearer of an ethical truth.

In one sense, and despite this glaring difficulty, the second conceptual path was the obvious choice for Gramsci, if for no other reason than for the fact that he was a machiavellian strategist and 'artist' par excellence – and there was a battle going on, with the successful outcome very much in doubt for those 'not in the know.' 'That objective possibilities exist for people not to die of hunger,' a practical Gramsci would often remind his readers, 'and that people *do* die of hunger has its importance, or so one would have thought.'[67] But, in another sense, it can be argued that Gramsci never even contemplated a radicalizing of the notion of hegemony, *except in terms of, or within,* the social totality itself (and not as a remedy against the problem of 'totalizing'), since it appeared that he equated it with the problems inherent in Croce's work and left it at that. In this context, he really 'saw' only the second path and proceeded to correct its limitations.

To be clear, then, radicalizing the notion of totality was a conceptual move that was invoked to 'correct' the problem of relying on any a priori notion of ethicality or an ethical community, while at the same time attempting to ground that ethicality in a 'non-essentialist' posing of the people as, ipso facto, the working class. The stakes were high: for, once the historico-universalism of an immanent communal ethicality could be established, a whole series of positions could be read back into the theorizing of the 'better society,' devoid, ironically enough, of any essentialist trappings.

Unfortunately, and as we shall detail in the following chapter, the radicalizing of the structure, and, therewith, of totality, in the final analysis led Gramsci to a precipice over which he could not leap. But, despite this – or perhaps because of it – his 'error' becomes the very terrain upon which we can continue the conceptual advancement of post-liberal-democratic theory. It is to that particular resolution, then, and the variety of analytic distinctions that follow, that we now must turn our attention.

FIVE

Investigating the Base/Superstructure Dilemma and What Gramsci Does to Change It

In a comment aimed at Marx but that could, equally well, have been applied to Gramsci, Croce once wrote that the author of *Das Kapital* never posed economics nor mode of production as the ultimate explanation of reality or the political configurations that could be said to emerge.[1] Indeed, Marx never posed any 'hidden God' to explain the phenomenal world. 'His philosophy was not that cheap,' Croce flatly acknowledged; Marx 'had not flirted in vain with the hegelian dialectic to go then in search for ultimate causes.'[2] This remark was neither innocent nor unknown to Gramsci, and, in a lengthy fragment attacking Bukharin, Gramsci quoted it directly as a way to counter the ill-thought-out practice of posing 'mode of production' as though it were a 'technical instrument' capable of revealing the hidden truth or underlying structure of reality.[3]

Attacking economism (and the instrumental logic on which it was premised) in terms of this veiled reference to Marx's 'flirtation' with Hegel – further contextualizing that attack along similar lines to Croce's unity-in-distinction – provided a way for Gramsci to situate the whole paradox he himself now faced: the paradox of rejecting an absolute truth without lapsing into absolute idealism in order to ground the analysis, fundamentally, in an absolute historicism. This was a paradox, as we saw from the preceding chapters, Gramsci had tried initially to resolve in terms of several intimately connected analytic propositions around science and the dialectic, indeed politics itself; and later still, around concepts such as the will and the ethico-political possibilities necessary for an open society. Moreover, it was a paradox whose reso-

lution necessitated, as we noted also, a radicalizing of dialectical totality, underscoring, in so doing, the notion of reality as itself an immanent
expression of two moments (i.e., the theoretic and the practical) outside
of which there could be no meaning.

But as we also saw, his attempted resolution brought Gramsci to an
epistemological crossroads which, for the moment, seemed to indicate
that an a priori ethicality was necessary in order to proceed with the
task at hand: that of taking seriously Marx's proposition that history
must be conceived as a social terrain upon which the working class
would become conscious of its struggle, would 'fight it out' and ultimately (no matter how difficult) would 'win and win decisively.'[4]

Gramsci, in attempting to resolve the twin problems of economism
and formal logic on the one hand, while, on the other, attempting to
remove the idealism from the concept of 'unity-in-distinction,' returned
to the marxist dialectic. In so doing, he sought to clarify and elaborate
Marx's posing of the social in terms of the well-known distinction between structure and superstructure. As Gramsci argued, each must be
understood in its distinction and yet posed as an historicized and dialectical unity that formed the totality of the social, outside of which
there could be only abstraction.[5] Similar to the reading of the practical
and theoretic moments, where neither could be privileged over the
other, but where the practical formed, in a philosophy of praxis, the
'point of departure' for analytic and practical strategy, Gramsci cast the
structure and the superstructure as two moments of reality, positing
them in a similar (but historicized) fashion as Croce had done with the
concept of totality as a twofold degree. In that sense one could say that
the structure was to the superstructure very much as one degree or moment to another, i.e., as relational and constitutive concepts, neither
predicated on an already given meaning or pre-established order of
importance. In this case, the structure would constitute the first moment of the real dialectic, though it be understood as 'first' simply in a
logical and not hierarchical or value-oriented sense.[6] Given this ar-
rangement, the superstructure would be unthinkable without structure;
conversely, structure would be unthinkable without superstructure.
Each concept taken by itself would simply constitute an empty analytic
expression, meaningless without its antithetical counterpoint.[7] 'Without having understood this relationship,' Gramsci thus surmised,

> it seems that one cannot understand the philosophy of praxis, its position
> in comparison with idealism and with mechanical materialism, the im-
> portance and significance of the doctrine of the superstructures. [For] it
> is not exact, as Croce maintains, to say that in the philosophy of praxis

the Hegelian 'idea' has been replaced by the 'concept' of structure. The Hegelian 'idea' has been resolved both in the structure and in the super-structures and the whole way of conceiving philosophy has been 'histor-icised', that is to say, a new way of philosophising which is more concrete and historical than what went before it has come into existence.'[8]

In this sense, and as we will discuss in more detail, Gramsci became neither the 'theoretician of the superstructures,' nor, for that matter, the theoretician of the structure; he privileged neither over the other. But in reworking their relationship, what we do find is that Gramsci sub-stantially reworked the notion of *structure-as-economic* and, in so doing, incorporated within the concept of economics not only the political moment and, therewith, historicized immanence, but the very notion of the will.[9] Moreover, this conceptual reworking attempted to locate change and, more important, the processes around forging a new or progressive civil society (and the state that would become its expres-sion) as an *integral* process of the structural moment itself, a process that could not be separated from, or understood 'outside' of, its superstruc-tural counterpoint.

It could be said, then, that this reworking of the notion of structure/superstructure was, and indeed remained, particularly insightful, for it allowed Gramsci tremendous analytic latitude in reformulating the concepts of economy and class, of the state and civil society, of legiti-mation and consensus, even the party structure itself – indeed, it al-lowed him tremendous latitude in conceptualizing the social contradic-tions, institutions, and forces in any given social formation. But, as we also examined, this reformulation was not entirely successful at resolv-ing the paradox mentioned already: the problem of theoretically estab-lishing the 'better' society, as such and for whom, without relying on a pregiven ethicality. To underscore the depth of this contribution and at the same time confront the paradox directly, let us continue by exam-ining, first, the dilemma Gramsci noted in terms of the base/super-structural shorthand posed by Marx and Engels and, then, how Gram-sci, in noting that dilemma, proposed to resolve it.

The 'base' versus the 'structure' dilemma

It is almost commonplace now to acknowledge, as did Gramsci, that the base/superstructure metaphor, posed by Marx and Engels to un-derscore the intimate and complex connections of politics and ideolo-gy to the economic foundation of society, turned out to be such an unfortunate expression.[10] It was an unfortunate choice for several reasons, but chief among them had to do with the one-dimensional positivism it implied by (seemingly) posing the economic relations of production as an 'underlying' foundation of reality, 'on top' of which politics and ideology could be situated as its superstructural expression. While it is true that Marx and, later, Engels angrily denounced this reading of their work,[11] it is no less the case that this general interpretation could be, and indeed was, drawn on the very basis of their own writings.[12]

Consider, for example, the passage in Marx's well-known 'Preface to The Critique of Political Economy,' often approvingly cited by Gramsci. At first glance it might well appear that Marx forwarded a one-dimensional interpretation based on a rigid distinction between economic and social reality. For example, Marx stated:

> The general result at which I arrived and which, once won, served as a guiding thread for my studies, can briefly be formulated as follows: In the social production of their life, men enter into definite relations that are indispensable and independent of their will, relations of production which correspond to a definite stage in the development of their material forces. *The sum total of these relations of production constitutes the economic structure of society, the real foundation, on which rises a legal and political superstructure and to which corresponds definite forms of social consciousness.* With the changes of the economic foundations, the entire immense superstructure is more or less rapidly transformed.[13]

Given this position, it could be suggested that the base/superstructure metaphor and the overarching but stillborn importance it seemed to attach to economic relations would become not only an entirely appropriate shorthand description, but the very corner-stone of marxism itself. However, Marx tempered this passage with what other scholars have dismissed as an unfortunate residue left over from his earlier studies in hegelian philosophy.[14] It was, of course, precisely this 'residue' that Gramsci incorporated directly (and often) in his attempt to make more meaningful the concept of the base (and of class), and remove from it an economic reductionist or, conversely, a metaphysical interpretation.[15] 'In considering such transformations,' Marx continued,

> no social order ever perishes before all the productive forces for which there is room in it have developed, and new, higher relations of production never appear before the material conditions of their existence have matured in the old society itself. Therefore, mankind always sets for itself only such tasks as it can solve; since, looking at the matter more

closely, it will always be found that the task itself arises only when the
material conditions for its solution already exist or are at least in the process of formation.[16]

Without getting side-tracked by the variety of interpretations one can
make of this and other passages in Marx and Engels's writings, we
know already from chapters 3 and 4 why Gramsci saw this passage as
one of the most profound and central propositions for the philosophy
of praxis: it allowed him to draw into sharper focus the complex layers
of the marxist dialectic itself and cast it in terms of an immanent historico-political practice. But it also allowed him to clarify, and in so doing
make more meaningful, the base/superstructure distinction in a way
that expressed directly the dialectical complexity of historicized immanence. As we shall detail shortly, it consequently allowed Gramsci to
articulate, both analytically and in practico-political terms, how fundamental historical change could emerge and be made permanent.

And yet, as it had often been posed thus far, that is, as entirely unrelated to an historicized immanence, the base/superstructure shorthand
tended to promote not just a rigid and linear economic reductionism.
It also tended to promote a notion of consciousness as either 'true' or
'false,' depending upon the degree to which one could 'know' one's
place and resolve (or not resolve) to change it.[17] Moreover, it tended to
obscure the notion of classes as if pregiven and fully constituted entities rather than as processes in formation, always established at the
point of struggle.[18] Indeed, it tended to suggest that power, and more
to the point, state power, was always 'already given,' albeit, in this context, as that which was understood to be a particularized (but still an
ahistoricized) appendage of the bourgeoisie. And while that reading
may have been an improvement over the universal ethicality that Hegel had ascribed to the state, it still suggested that state power was
neither a relational entity nor a process, but was rather always something 'contained,' always something existing within proscribed boundaries. Power, posed as such, often led to the 'obvious solution' around
the revoking of a social imbalance; that is, it always implied a strategy
of 'frontal attack,' assuming in so doing that that power could be neatly
excised (along with the capitalists themselves) in a direct overthrow of
the capitalist state.[19]

Given that reading of power, then, there was no room to account for
the differences in social formations with a strong civil society that not
only did not collapse under direct attack by one group over another,
but often absorbed the attack and, in some cases, was strengthened by

it. For Gramsci, a static reading of power often produced brutal miscalculations, and the tactical decisions drawn from it often proved fatally inappropriate. 'In Russia, the State was everything,' Gramsci wrote, 'civil society was primordial and gelatinous [thus frontal attack/war of position an obvious strategy]; but in the West, there was a proper relation between State and civil society, and when the State trembled a sturdy structure of civil society was at once revealed. The State was only an outer ditch, behind which there stood a powerful system of fortresses and earthworks.'[20]

In short, the base/superstructure metaphor tended to promote a caricature of marxist theory, of ideology, class struggle, and the state, where politics could be nothing other than a dogma properly speaking and society only the battleground of conflicting (but self-contained) power blocs. If nothing else, the sobering reality of fascist imprisonment reminded Gramsci just how inadequate and even misleading the base/superstructure shorthand had become. 'There is no doubt,' Gramsci reflected as he dismissed this formulaic reductionism, 'that all this is just an infantile deviation of the philosophy of praxis generated by the baroque conviction that the more one goes back to "material" objects, the more orthodox one must be.'[21] The tragedy was exacerbated, lamented Gramsci, in that, by upholding this baroque conviction, philosophers, politicians, indeed political militants themselves, would wrongly search for the 'one key' that would supposedly unlock an already fully articulated freedom. Thus, continued Gramsci, until the time when that one key might be found, repression would continue as if some sort of simple conjuring trick:

the philosophy of praxis loses a great part of its capacity for cultural expansion among the top layer of intellectuals, however much it may gain among the popular masses and second rate intellectuals, who do not intend to overtax their brains but still wish to know everything, etc. As Engels wrote, many people find it very convenient to think that they can have the whole of history and all political and philosophical wisdom in their pockets and at little cost and no trouble, concentrated in a few short formulae. They forget that the thesis which asserts that men become conscious of fundamental conflicts on the level of ideology is not psychological or moralistic in character, but structural and epistemological; and they form the habit of considering politics and hence history, as a continuous *marché de dupes*, a competition in conjuring and sleight of hand. 'Critical' activity is [thus] reduced to the exposure of swindles, to creating scandals, and to prying into the pockets of political figures.[22]

To rectify this (and other dilemmas), Gramsci resorted to incorporating into the structure a very particular conceptual manoeuvre. But the difficulty in assessing both the merits as well as the actual meaning of that manoeuvre cannot be overestimated. For one is faced with a myriad of obscure and, at points, seemingly conflictual comments scattered throughout the notebooks that sometimes make the base/superstructure shorthand appear absolutely unproblematic by comparison.[23] None the less, what we find is that Gramsci did more than simply redress the problem of economic reductionism by posing structure against superstructure as distinct analytic concepts, which, as was mentioned earlier, have no concrete meaning outside of the dialectical relation of which both concepts are a part. Perhaps more important, he fundamentally challenged the notion of 'economics' itself, and, therewith, the concepts of both class and consciousness. Given its centrality, it is to Gramsci's redressing of the economic moment as structure that we now must turn.

The 'economic' as 'structure' (or the so-called problem of 'quantity')

By following Marx's posing of the economic base as structure, Gramsci did more than simply reinstitute the dialectic. He was attempting to clarify an essential point he had understood Marx to be making in both the 'Preface to *The Critique*' and 'Theses on Feuerbach': that quantitative relations of production as such could never be the determining feature of a social system, much less the basis for establishing class formation. That is, structure could never be pared down simply to a set of verifiable data concerning productivity and exchange, from which a series of conclusions around class antagonisms and the material forces of production could then be deduced.

Clearly, this did not mean that Gramsci was rejecting quantitative statistical analysis per se, but rather, on the contrary, that quantity itself must be understood in a more fluid, and in a sense, 'political,' manner.[24] As he saw it, there could be no model or boundary that could be invoked 'with the precision of the natural sciences' in order to determine class structure or when a class could be said to exist, grow larger, maintain itself, or dissolve. Neither was there a 'fixed proportion' of wage rates or productivity levels to the organic composition of capital in order to deduce the well-being (or 'inevitable' decline) of the system per se. To insist otherwise, argued Gramsci, would be to fall victim to an abstract determinism or, at the very least, to remain wedded to the kind of 'individual fancies and arbitrary speculation' previously dismissed; that is, to insist on the privileging of either form over content or content over form.[25]

Gramsci suggested, instead, that the usefulness of this kind of quantitative analysis lay precisely in its 'schematic and metaphoric value,' accordingly applied

> to clarify, and bring out the general applicability of, many propositions concerning the science of organizations (the study of the administrative apparatuses, of demographic composition, etc.) and also concerning general politics (in analyses of situations or of relations of force, in the problems of the intellectuals, etc.) ... In other words, it cannot be applied mechanically, since in human collectivities, the qualitative element is predominant, and this cannot be measured mathematically.[26]

This particularly static and in a sense 'mathematical' notion of quantity had an important, albeit limited, usefulness, if, for no other reason, as Gramsci was fond of reiterating from Marx, the material circumstance of history were itself the expression or ensemble of all forces and relations of production involved in the reproducing of society. This expression would include not only the relation between capitalist and worker, but all aspects of culture, religion, race, sexual division, and so forth. As such, the 'real' foundation of society would be precisely the 'full ensemble of the material forces of production,' no less than 'and at the same time, a crystallization of all past history and the basis of the present and future history: it is both a document and an active and actual propulsive force.'[27] In this sense a non-static concept of quantity was required to underscore the actual structure of the social and, at the same time, to account for the very terrain out of which that social emerged.

This meant then, for Gramsci, that the structure and the material circumstance or terrain to which it gave shape could never be reduced to, or become, simply a 'base' in the positivistic, flat, or empirical sense of the word. It was, rather, always something incorporating, expressing, and being changed by human activity: 'Is structure therefore [to be] viewed as something immovable and absolute,' Gramsci rhetorically asked, '[or rather] on the contrary, as reality itself in motion; and doesn't the assertion put forward in the "Theses on Feuerbach" that the "educator must be educated" pose a necessary relation of active, reaction by man on the structure, which is an affirmation of the unity of the process of reality?'[28]

But Gramsci was saying more than this, too. Not only was he suggesting that the structure was 'greater than the sum of its component parts'; he was also insisting that so, too, was economics.[29] For the problem of 'economic determinism' or 'economic reductionism' was not simply that economics had been singled out as the explanatory feature of a society, but that, in so doing, economics had itself been 'reduced' to only one of its constituent facets, namely, a one-dimensional and stillborn notion of quantity.

For Gramsci, quantity was a *relational* concept appropriated 'in a special sense ... not to be confused with its meaning in arithmetic.'[30] This 'special sense' had more to do with 'degrees of homogeneity, coherence, logicality, etc.' of the social system than with 'numbers,' properly speaking. Indeed, it had more to do, as so many of the concepts Gramsci explicated in his texts, with dialectical reasoning, 'special' in the sense that it could only be understood in the context of the dialectic to which it was a part.

The difference was, however, that this time, in situating the concept of quantity in terms of dialectics, Gramsci was to draw explicitly from hegelian law 'another of those knotty theoretical problems' that had already been explicated best, as far as Gramsci was concerned, in the first volume of *Das Kapital*.[31] That knotty problem was precisely the elaboration of the notion of quantity as always connected to, albeit distinct from, its counterpart, quality – inseparable from it, except at the level of abstraction.

This did not mean, of course, that it would be impossible to articulate or make sense of each distinct entity. In fact, it meant precisely the reverse: one could describe in remarkable and thorough detail both areas of concern. But that discussion could only remain taxonomic and descriptive; that is, it could only remain as a distinct abstraction severed from the larger context to which it was intrinsically connected, since, as Gramsci would put it, 'there cannot exist quantity without quality or quality without quantity (economy without culture, practical activity without intelligence and vice versa).'[32] More precisely then, and to put it in philosophical terms directly, 'quantity,' separated as such, would thus become simply the analytic expression of the abstract moments of quantity/quality.[33]

Gramsci thus argued that only in the posing of the synthetic unity of quantity/quality would one be able to give meaning to each of those distinct and opposing abstractions; their unity (or nexus, as Gramsci referred to it) would completely exhaust the entire terrain (i.e., the concrete form and content) of the historico-political moment.[34] So crucial was it to understand the profundity of that quantity/quality nexus that Gramsci heralded it as perhaps marxism's most important contribution:

In the case of man, who is this external agent? In the factory it is the division of labour, etc., conditions created by man himself. In society it is the ensemble of productive forces. But the author of the *Manual* has not considered that, if every social aggregate is something more (and different) than the sum of its components, this must mean that the law or principle which explains the development of society cannot be a physical law, since in physics one does not get out of the quantitative sphere except metaphorically. However, in the philosophy of praxis, quality is also connected to quantity and this connection is perhaps its most fertile contribution. Idealism hypostatizes this mysterious something else known as quality, it makes it into an entity of its own, 'spirit', just as religion had done with the idea of divinity. [On the other hand] [By contrast] ... the same is true in the case of vulgar materialism, which 'divinises' a hypostasis of matter.[35]

On the one hand, then, the insistence on this quantity/quality dialectic could be seen, quite clearly, as an attack against vulgar materialism, which created, to use Gramsci's phraseology, a 'deity out of matter.' As well, it was clearly an attack against speculative idealism, which did the same, but with respect to spirit. But beyond its critical usefulness, the quantity/quality unity was also a way for Gramsci to clarify analytically the concept of quantity itself, and to pose it in that context as a 'distinction.'

On the other hand, and as we will investigate in more detail below, Gramsci used that notion of quantity-as-distinction in terms of a *foundational* unity. That is, he used it in terms of a (constitutive) grounding or terrain made equal to necessity, but, as such, as one counterposed to the (also constitutively) unified concept of quality. To put it slightly differently, then, quantity/necessity was always to be counterposed to quality/possibility, or, in a word, freedom.[36]

Before continuing, it might be advisable to consider the obvious question: Why all the hair-splitting and seemingly unfortunate attraction to Croce's notion of distincts? Wouldn't this simply force Gramsci into an unwarranted relapse of idealist taxonomy, except this time at the so-called concrete level of the concept? These were not idle worries; and even Gramsci confessed to being on tentative ground here, unsure as to whether or not this may have been the best approach:

Can one introduce the criterion of distinction into the structure too? How is structure to be understood? How, in the system of social relations, will one be able to distinguish the element 'technique', 'work', 'class', etc., understood in an historical and not metaphysical sense? Critique of

Croce's position; for polemical ends he represents the structure as a 'hidden god', a 'noumenon', in contrast to the 'appearances' of the superstructure.[37]

One can only surmise that one of the reasons for having put forward a logic that introduced into the structure the criterion of distinction had more to do with Gramsci's intent on resolving the question of how a situation, a society – indeed, life itself – *changed* and how new historical formations would arise in place of the old.[38] For as we know already, Gramsci was clearly concerned not just with the 'what and why' of change, but with the practicality of the 'how'; and he was interested in strategizing without having to inject an external element or pregiven agency into that account. For unless one were to embrace a kind of 'conspiracy theory' that posed historical movement or social passion as if, as the fascists had so characterized it, *schmutzig judisch* (a 'dirty Jewish' conspiracy); or unless one were to avoid the voluntarist notion that mass movements could burst 'spontaneously' onto the scene or erupt as if some kind of innate 'élan vital' as Bergson would have it, there seemed to be no analytic method available to take seriously Marx's claim that history constituted the very materiality of transformation and creativity within all social formations.[39] To put it in Gramsci's terms directly, there had to be a way to account for the fact that history formed the *substantive* foundation of 'quantity' itself. 'In the passage from economics to general history,' Gramsci thus noted, 'the concept of quantity is integrated with that of quality and [with] the dialectic quality-that-becomes-quality.'[40]

Without introducing some kind of logic of distinction into quantity itself, there was no way – at least as far as Gramsci could see it and as ironic as it might appear – to reject the familiar accusations of 'left-wing hegelian utopianism' flung at Marx's 'Preface' and, on the contrary, be thus able to take seriously the profundity of Marx's claim that no social order ever changes unless the conditions for that change are already present within the very foundation of the old society itself. By tentatively, cautiously, suggesting that the structure may usefully be divided into disparate but connected moments, Gramsci attempted, however weakly, to create an analytic category for change at the very level of the economic relations of production. 'Only on this basis,' he somberly remarked, 'can all mechanism and every trace of the [inherently] superstitious "miraculous" be eliminated, and should the problem of the formation of active political groups, and in the last analysis, even the problem of the historical function of great personalities be posed.'[41]

Bringing in distincts could be seen as an attempt, then, to incorporate possibility and change at the level of a structure rather than 'banishing' either to a superstructural moment. Indeed, it would allow Gramsci the conceptual space to discuss how the 'realm of freedom' would be located precisely within the material conditions of social life and, in that sense, would allow him to rethink history as equivalent to but distinct from economics. Indeed, it would allow him to locate the political moment at the level of economics.

But by introducing a kind of marxist logic of distinction into the structure, Gramsci re-emphasized something else as well: the concept that *human intervention* as 'practical activity' could also be located at the level of structure. That is, by relying on the complexity of distinction in the context of the quantity/quality nexus, and posing this nexus as itself constitutive of the structural moment the so-called first moment of the structure/superstructure dialectic, Gramsci emphasized that human intervention, be it organized or chaotic, a social act or one of individual prominence, was fundamental to, and indeed an expression of, the economic base.

To be clear then, Gramsci proposed a radically unique way of incorporating the notion of practical activity – and therewith of power, passion, and transformation – without either hypostatizing its origins or relegating it to the superstructural level as some kind of epiphenomenal appendage of the real. In this context – that is to say, in the context of accounting epistemologically for passionate or wilful change – his was an 'impure' philosophy, in the most profound sense of the word.

> If the Crocean concept of passion as a moment of politics comes up against the difficulty of explaining and justifying the permanent political formations, such as the parties and, still more, the national armies and General Staffs, since it is impossible to conceive of a passion being organised permanently without its becoming rational and deliberate reflection (and hence no longer passion), the solution can only be found in the identification of politics and economics. Politics becomes permanent action and gives birth to permanent organizations precisely in so far as it identifies itself with economics. But it is also distinct from it, which is why one may speak separately of economics and politics, and speak of 'political passion' as of an immediate impulse to action which is borne on the 'permanent and organic' terrain of economic life, but which transcends it.[42]

It is no accident, then, that he chose this kind of 'impure' route, a route that added the 'disturbing element,' to use Gramsci's expression, to the concept of economics.[43] What was this disturbing element? For

Gramsci, it was precisely the human will, which as we saw constituted, expressed, and could maintain both the legitimate force and the
legitimate consent of the people. Its incorporation re-emphasized the
fact that the economic was, for Gramsci, both a repository of 'quantity,'
in the flat, descriptive sense, and a splintered bastion of human 'quality.' In his 'Ponti di mediazione sull'economia,' he thus reflected: 'In
economics the "disturbing" element is the will of man, the collective
will, diversely expressed according to the general conditions in which
men have lived.'[44]

Not only did its incorporation re-emphasize the fact that the economic moment was itself born of political struggle, rooted in the knowl-
edge/power matrix of the human condition; it emphasized the fact that
the rational will was utterly fundamental to and constitutive of the
economic moment, the latter of which could not be 'understood' independent of the superstructure to which it was a part. In that sense, too,
the will could not become ethico-political and, hence, hegemonic over
the whole of the social, without at one and the same time being rooted
in and transcending, as it were, this economic moment.

But having now been brought back to the problem of the will and the
ethico-political hegemony necessary for it to become universal (albeit
this time couched in terms of the dialectic between structure and superstructure), it would be useful to recapitulate the paradox set out in
chapter 4. As was noted, Gramsci had insisted that the concept of the
will be placed at the base of philosophy, and that, perhaps more to the
point, in so placing that will, one could gain some analytic latitude in
highlighting the fundamental connection between the 'intellectuals'
and the 'people-nation.' Moreover, that connection would be posed in
a way that distanced one from either liberalist or fascist previsions
around intellectual and moral reform necessary for the building of new
political order and, ultimately, a new ethical state. Introducing the will
in the way that he did (i.e., as a power/knowledge terrain) meant that
Gramsci was able to resituate the notion of creative development, and
intellectual-moral reform as the *sine qua non* for an 'open,' 'immanent'
ethicality. As we also noted, following this line of reasoning, this immanent ethical-political, which was grounded in history, linked to the will,
and born through a process of hegemony, represented, indeed expressed (precisely because of the specificity of that reasoning), a fundamentally 'open,' consensual democratic society.

But as we also noted, this position had led Gramsci to an epistemological crossroads from which only two possible routes seemed to
emerge: either to accept a radicalization of the concept of hegemony as
opposed to the social whole, which would entail a concomitant disrup-

tion of all totalities, dialectical or otherwise, or to accept a radicalization of totality itself, with the concomitant problem of forwarding a pregiven ethicality (of, in Gramsci's example, the working classes) as the bearers of progress. As we know, the real question for Gramsci was not *which* route to take since, as he saw it, the former choice took him out of dialectics altogether and seemed only to point to an absolute relativism impossible to ground. The real question was rather whether or not one could, in promoting a radicalization of dialectical totality, avoid having to propose a pregiven and fully determined ethicality and still remain faithful in substance and in form to the supposition that no social order ever changed 'outside' the terrain of history, i.e., outside the terrain of human intervention.

The question, simply put, was this: Could one stay within the bounds of dialectical historical materialism, which insisted, in part, that truth is a product of human history, while still maintaining, at the analytic and practico-political level, the obvious political strategy that the working classes were, ipso facto, the bearer of a new, progressive society? For Gramsci, the 'answer' was an unqualified yes; the troublesome task was, of course, how to show it without prioritizing the claim or posing as homogeneous the notion of class itself.

As we have seen thus far, that task required a long foray into the reworking of the base/superstructure dichotomy so as to reflect directly the intensity and complexity of the marxist dialectic. That meant, first and foremost, a clarification and reposing of the dialectic, initially in terms of a structure/superstructure demarcation; then, in terms of a quantity/quality nexus; and, later still, in terms of distinctions within the structure at the more abstract level of the quantity/quality moment. This reposition of the structure as such pointed to a way to incorporate and account for 'change' as part of the economic base. It attempted to do so without posing it as a pre-established or homogeneous entity. And it attempted to do so by placing the will as a constitutive element of economics itself.

But however complex these previous steps had been, the next step was even more so. For choosing the path of radicalizing an historico-dialectical totality required a peculiar 'fine tuning' of the structure/superstructure relation in order to avoid begging the question of grounding notions of progress, social ethicality. It required a positing of 'truth' without accepting a general truth; it required a positing of 'legitimate will' without accepting a general will; it required accepting the notion of the working class as bearers of the ethico-political state, without accepting a general notion of class, organization, or movement.

Despite what would appear to be a logical impasse, Gramsci thus continued fine-tuning, as it were, the distinctions within the structure. From this fine-tuning, he was able to deduce several intimately connected propositions around classes, the political party, and the state in terms of the structural moment itself and the distinctions upon which that moment could be constituted. It is these distinctions and the radical propositions to which they give rise that we now must consider and examine with some care, for there we can map out why Gramsci's strategy of radicalizing the dialectic was so profoundly crucial for producing a set of political strategies and analytic methodologies around the founding of a new social order. But also, we will be able to detect why, in the end, that strategy crippled the project and forced Gramsci into a corner from which there was no escape.

Into the structure and what Gramsci finds there

Gramsci identified as belonging to the structural moment a somewhat odd but seemingly self-evident group of elements, elements carefully divided into two discrete groups and, having been so divided, immediately subdivided once again: on the one hand, those elements that constituted 'relations of force,' subdivided into an economic and military moment, and mediated by the political; on the other hand, those elements that constituted 'crises,' subdivided into the conjunctural and the organic.[45] Not surprisingly, Gramsci situated the entire polemic in the broader context of the (dialectical) relation between structure and superstructure, since to do otherwise would have meant reinventing an instrumental economism, albeit, in this case, one that would have privileged the structure (rather than the superstructure) as the natural reservoir of political and ideological conflict.[46] Indeed, by not casting the whole discussion of structural forces/crises in terms of the historicized/immanent dialectic, one would simply reproduce the same seductive but unfortunate tendencies reminiscent of the 'vulgar sociology' Gramsci had so vigorously condemned. It would spawn, as Gramsci would say, the 'snake biting the snake-charmer – in other words, the demagogue [becoming] the first victim of his own demagoguery.'[47]

But more than a way to attack the various forms of economism, the selection of these discrete elements (forces and crises), and their placement in terms of a dialectic between structure and superstructure, was a way to give substance to the two basic principles set out in the 1859 'Preface' and worth repeating here: '1. that no society sets itself tasks for whose accomplishment the necessary and sufficient conditions do not either already exist or are not at least beginning to emerge and develop; [and] 2. that no society breaks down and can be replaced until it has first developed all the forms of life which are implicit in its internal relations.'[48]

By arguing that the structural moment entailed the distincts of crises and relations of force, Gramsci was attempting to give a specificity to *class formation* that would avoid the trap of posing classes a priori, or external to the socio-economic moment, while simultaneously rejecting a closed or fixed notion of the social whole. Gramsci intended to develop the argument that class was itself the *constructed expression* of a variety of splintered processes of power relations – political, intellectual, moral, economic, and so forth – rather than conceptualize it as an 'element' or 'aspect' of the base. But, to formulate a dialectical expression, Gramsci needed to develop further the argument that class would be understood as something *always in movement* and, more to the point, something that would become both foundational to and yet contained within the structure. And he wanted to make that argument while simultaneously suggesting that the working class, specifically, would become the bearer of the ethical-political.[49]

To put it slightly differently, then, by highlighting the discrete elements of crises and relations of force – rather than class per se – Gramsci hoped to be able to develop the argument that classes were always an expression of 'movement' *within the structure*, but of a kind of movement that was itself never fully determined. In that sense, not only were classes 'always in struggle,' but the 'struggle' itself would become the practical moment or basis of a reality whose 'specificity' or 'error' could never be fully sutured. However, this struggle would remain meaningless or abstract if understood outside the total dialectic to which it was a part.

Given this backdrop, Gramsci turned to the work of Machiavelli and began to outline what he considered were the fundamental aspects of the first of the discrete elements mentioned above, that of the 'relations of force.' For both Gramsci and Machiavelli, force and the relations constituting that force were always premised on the most obvious 'primordial fact,' as Gramsci would put it: that every society, up to and including the present, had always been divided into the 'haves' and the 'have-nots,' the rulers and those they rule, the leaders and the led. Bluntly summarizing the problem of the relations of force in this way, Gramsci wrote:

It cannot be stressed enough that the first things which are forgotten are precisely the first elements, the most elementary things ... The first element is that there *really do exist* rulers and ruled, leaders and led. The entire science and art of politics are based on this primordial and (given certain general conditions) irreducible fact. The origins of this fact are a problem apart, which will have to be studied separately ... but the fact remains that there do exist rulers and ruled, leaders and led.[50]

For Gramsci this most basic and irreducible fact was not without its layers: for force was never wholly force; negation, never a pure nothingness. Likewise then, this most basic division between the 'haves' and the 'have-nots,' the leaders and the led, implied neither a homogeneous notion of a legitimate or absolute right to lead nor, for that matter, a dictatorial or repressive leadership. Rather it stressed the notion of legitimation as itself constituted by, in this case, both force and consent. In other words, posing force as a constitutive unity of both force and consent was to acknowledge that force required some kind of consent (be it passive or active) from the very people who were being 'led.' For unless a society were to be built solely on the grounds of absolute domination – hence requiring, ipso facto, the necessity of founding a nation that would entail the constant (and costly) incarceration or control of every person, save the ruler or ruling groups – then somehow consent had to be elicited from those that were to be ruled.

That force was a constitutive unity, and the negation that constituted it not simply a 'void,' meant, then, not only that power was something other than a pure control over someone or something, but that it involved consent in one form or another. But it also meant that consent could never become a pure or absolute acquiescence. It, too, was a constitutive entity of consent and force; it, too, implied a conception of power as that which was relational or always-in-process.[51] A republic, for example, as Machiavelli instructed, was clearly not a dictatorship; none the less, it remained a composite of both violence and law, a composite entity that had as its overriding feature civil law, but, at the same time, maintained at its disposal the underbelly of official (state) violence. In order for a prince to lead and remain leader of the kind of new social order, i.e., one founded on consent, this prince had to appreciate that consent was itself a power relation involving the complex combination of both force and consent. Given this 'fluidity' of force and consent, Machiavelli thus offered to the Prince the following directive:

You should understand that there are two ways of fighting: by law or by force. The first way is natural to men, and the second to beasts. But as the first way often proves inadequate one must needs have recourse to the second. So a prince must understand how to make a nice use of the beast and the man. The ancient writers taught princes about this allegory, when they described how Achilles and many other princes of the ancient world were sent to be brought up by Chiron, the centaur, so that he might train them this way. All the allegory means, in making the teacher half beast and half man, is that a prince must know how to act according to the nature of both, and that he cannot survive otherwise.[52]

If it could be taken as given, as Gramsci assumed quite straightforwardly it could, that the concept of consent was a constitutive unity of force and consent, Gramsci pushed the logic farther. Arguing that those constitutive elements were themselves never homogeneously circumscribed, he implied that they would remain abstract and meaningless unless or until they were *institutionalized* as such.[53] That institutionalization of, and indeed the actual forging of, the force/consent unity itself (especially in terms of that which would predominate over the other in a given moment of their unity) was, for Gramsci, a product and process of politics. It was precisely the establishment of a hegemonic moment; indeed, it was precisely its expression.[54]

Politics in this sense was present even at – or, rather, exactly at – the very formation of a seemingly homogeneous structure or identity, be that structure a social grouping of the 'leaders' or of the 'led,' or, indeed, the very notion of force/consent itself. To ignore or not be able to account for this more subtle aspect of Machiavelli's original directive was, for Gramsci, an error that led not only to problems at the epistemological level, but to miscalculations at the strategic and tactical levels as well. 'It must be clearly understood,' concluded Gramsci in reference to this particular internal complexity,

> that the division between rulers and ruled – though in the last analysis has its origin in a division between social groups – is in fact, things being as they are, also to be found within the group itself, even where it is a socially homogeneous one ... [Moreover, since] the division between rulers and ruled exists even within the same group, certain principles have to be fixed upon and strictly observed. For it is in this area that the most serious 'errors' take place, and that the most criminal weaknesses, and the hardest to correct, are revealed.[55]

To put it slightly differently, then, for Gramsci, the establishing of what might appear to be a coherent and homogeneous consent or force (or even will) always implied an internality or structure that itself either was simply and expressly a 'finished' product unified through political struggle or was in the process of being established and made permanent, or – for whatever reasons – was not able to be established and maintained (and thus tended to produce a vacuum), and so forth.[56] That is, Gramsci was not only suggesting that the notion of consent or force, or, for that matter, social groupings of leaders and led, etc., be understood merely as an expression of a structured constitutive unity. Nor was he suggesting that that unity be understood as a zero-sum game of positivity and negation. Rather, he was suggesting that the establishing of the internal moments of that constitutive unity must be understood as something other than an automatic, a priori given, and that those moments entailed discrete elements not necessarily in contradiction to each other, but none the less substantively contributing to the meaning and horizon of the political, and, indeed, of 'power' itself.

Given that the internality of the (concrete-universal) concept would be marked by its discrete elements, one would find in Gramsci's structural moment relations of forces and crises whose parameters would themselves always be expressing a power relation, i.e., as one whose consistency remained rooted in, but relative to, the ever-changing terrain of human activity, or, in a word, hegemony.[57] In this context, then, we find that this hegemony, this process of forging the unity or nodal point of consent (constituted as such through the unity of force and consent), was a process rooted in the structure and not, as many of the commentators on Gramsci's work have maintained, in the superstructure.[58]

Posed as such, however, this practico-political concept of hegemony, rich in strategic and tactical implications and crucial for establishing a kind of relative ontology in the structure, was still in need of further refinement. While we will not engage in recapitulating the many lively and controversial debates on the concept of hegemony,[59] it is important to clarify certain aspects of Gramsci's development of the concept.

From hegemony in the structure to the ethico-political state

Initially the concept appeared, if not entirely straightforward, at least somewhat unproblematic, except at the level of translation, where *egemonia* tended to be equated with variations of the word *dirigere* (to lead, rule, direct, etc).[60] In this context, the meaning of the concept of hegemony was identical with that usage Lenin originally gave it in his *Two Tactics of Social Democracy in the Democratic Revolution*.[61] That is, it was a methodological and descriptive criterion synonymous with the supremacy a given social group obtained by virtue of its ability to be both 'dominant' and 'leading,' while, at the same time, calling the process by which a group became the leading or dominant one a struggle for hegemony.[62] 'A class is dominant in two ways,' as Gramsci put it,

> ie, [it is] 'leading' and 'dominant'. It leads the classes which are its allies, and dominates those which are its enemies. Therefore, even before attaining power, a class can (and must) 'lead'; when it is in power it becomes dominant, but continues to 'lead' as well ... [In fact] there can and must be a 'political hegemony' even before the attainment of governmental power, and one should not count solely on the power and material force which such a position gives in order to exercise political leadership or hegemony.[63]

In this context, hegemony tended to take as a direct point of reference an already formed, cohesively inscribed group that was either dominant or sought to be so. It tended to mean, moreover, the ability of that group to create coalitions or allies of perhaps different but like-minded groups (also cohesively inscribed), the latter of which, in consenting to be a part of that coalition or power bloc, would agree either tacitly or explicitly to being 'led' by the leading force within it.[64] The power bloc or ruling group would, in turn, be dominant over those groups excluded from that bloc in power; and, if one were not to be witnessing a dictatorship, then there would also exist some kind of consent elicited from those groups 'not in the know.' This example of hegemony underscored the notion of consent as a constitutive aspect to the creating of a power bloc, which was also maintained by an undercurrent of force, both within that coalition and between the coalition itself and those who were excluded.[65] But it did so by having to take as a given the notion that each 'ally' joining the coalition or power bloc would always already be established. As such, its interests could be deduced accordingly.[66]

Gramsci contended, as he suggested Lenin had so done,[67] that since consent was never pure positivity nor force pure negativity, nor their unity a pure balance between the two (but rather, was something whose internality and constitutive unity was itself rooted in the terrain of history and, therewith, in political practice), that meant that a coalition and, indeed, the groups that made up that coalition were *subjectively* constituted. That is, the identity of the group was itself forged from struggle and, indeed, that identity was 'ideological,' in the most profoundly political sense of the word.[68]

For Gramsci, then, the terrain upon which people would become conscious of their struggle and fight it out was precisely the terrain of the ideological moment. But, as this was a moment imbued with a politics/history, it was a constitutive moment that was both a process of and an expression of hegemony. It was, more precisely still, a 'foundational' or 'structural' moment, setting up the non-fixity of the social whole within the context of totality itself. This particular rendering of the notion of hegemony was one, as noted earlier, to which Gramsci attributed great theoretical and political significance:

> The proposition contained in the 'Preface' to the effect that men acquire consciousness of structural conflicts on the level of ideologies should be considered as an affirmation which provides epistemological and not simply psychological [or] moral value. From this, it follows that the theoretical-practical principle of hegemony has also gnoselogical significance, and it is here that Ilich [Lenin]'s greatest theoretical contribution to the philosophy of praxis should be sought. ... [For] the realization of a hegemonic apparatus, in so far as it creates a new ideological terrain, determines a reform of consciousness and of methods of knowledge: it is a fact of knowledge, a philosophical fact.[69]

The ideological moment – when posed in the context of hegemony, i.e., as a subjective moment, as a process in creating the terrain of the 'is' – meant something radically different from a 'true' or 'false' consciousness. It was never arbitrary or psychological, irrational (meaning without any logic to it) or metaphysical. In fact, posed as a constitutive/synthetic unity (one that was both an expression and a process of hegemony), the ideological moment had 'the same energy,' to use Gramsci's paraphrase of Marx, 'as a material force or something of the kind.'[70] Indeed, it was the 'glue' or 'cement' that held together the social formation; its dissolution or shattering would provoke social crisis.[71] Set in this context, it was precisely a discursive terrain, a terrain that entailed a variety of effective power relations, limits, and possibilities, each nuanced by social crisis and, as well, by force or consent.

If the divisions were 'deep' enough, that is to say, if in some way they compromised a fundamental identity and caused a systemic shift in the power bloc, the resulting difficulties would be considered an 'organic' crisis. If the power bloc were forced to change the composition of its bloc, but still maintained a fundamental control/consent, then the crisis would be said to be 'conjunctural.'[72] In either case, the point would be this: if ideology were to be considered at its very core 'political struggle' and, more specifically, if its coherent unity was an emergent hegemonic unity rather than a predetermined or homogeneously inscribed 'true' or 'false' doctrine, *then ideology (or ideologies) could never stand 'outside' or 'unattached' to the structure*; a crisis could never be singled out merely as superstructural or epiphenomenal reflections of the base.[73] Indeed, and, in this context, ideology for Gramsci would be precisely its (structural) expression; crisis, one of its discrete elements. 'It is surprising,' Gramsci mused, 'that there has been no proper affirmation and development of the connection between the idealist assertion of the reality of the world as a creation of the human spirit and the affirmation made by the philosophy of praxis of the historicity and transience of ideologies on the grounds that ideologies are expressions of the structure and are modified by modifications of the structure.'[74]

To think otherwise, argued Gramsci, would be to perpetuate the 'bad sense' of ideology, that is, to equate it with a 'science of ideas' or a set of 'symbols,' or, worse, simply as 'pure appearance.' Ideology, equated as such, would then, ipso facto, have required a concept of superstructure as simply an (abstract) repository of this (now instrumentalist) ideology. Politics, too, would thus be 'reduced' to its superstructural level, becoming merely a strategic 'game of chess,' or, worse, the lobbying for, or manipulation of, a particular set of issues. As Gramsci saw it, these were common errors that emerged from having incorrectly posed, or neglected altogether, the complex and dialectical expression of ideology, which, as the 'cement' of the structure/superstructure moment, was nuanced by – indeed, constituted by – a politics/history/economics 'hegemony,' itself rooted in the structure. Thus, Gramsci wrote:

> It seems to me that there is a potential element of error in assessing the value of ideologies, due to the fact (by no means casual) that the name ideology is given both to the necessary super-structure of a particular structure and to the arbitrary elucubrations of particular individuals. The bad sense of the word ... [occurs when] ideology is identified as distinct from the structure, and it is [then] asserted that it is not ideology that changes the structures but vice versa.[75]

Posing ideology(ies) as 'organic' to the structure, and at the same time, as its conscious expression, was important for yet another reason. It gave Gramsci the capacity, at the analytic level, to incorporate 'change,' 'movement,' or 'fluidity' as directly connected to both political practice and, therewith, the institutionalizing of that practice. For the degree to which ideology(ies) could coherently be unified as such – that is, the degree to which they could be made 'historically necessary,' i.e., attached to the structural moment (which was itself, a political struggle, a struggle of hegemony) – was the degree to which ideologies could have the capacity to '"organise" human masses, and create the terrain upon which men move, acquire consciousness of their position, struggle, etc.'[76] In contrast, the degree to which ideologies were 'detached' from the structure was the degree to which they would simply express, as Gramsci argued further, 'individual "movements", polemics and so on (though even these are not completely useless, since they function like an error which by contrasting with truth, demonstrates it).'[77]

On an ideological level, then, the struggle of hegemony would become, in part, one of identifying and consciously attempting to make more unified and coherent the disparate and arbitrary wills referred to in chapter 4. These inchoate and fragmented wills expressed the 'common sense' of a community, a common perception of the world that, as Gramsci argued, needed to become more refined and directed in order to form, in its stead, a nucleus of 'good' sense.[78] Given this scenario, the task necessary to bring forth change, and to do so in a way that could become permanent, would be to base one's strategy on the common sense of the people, no matter how disparate or seemingly unsophisticated the vantage, and, from that folklore, shape it to a more refined, more 'thought-through,' and, in a sense, principled, world-view. 'Its most fundamental characteristic,' Gramsci wrote of common sense, 'is that it is a conception which, even in the brain of one individual, is fragmentary, incoherent and inconsequential, in conformity with the social and cultural position of those masses whose philosophy it is ... Nonetheless, the starting point must always be that of common sense, which is the spontaneous philosophy of the multitude ... [and which] has to be made ideologically "coherent".'[79]

The task would become, in other words, *to build from the basis of an already existing power/knowledge terrain* a more cohesive world-view, but one that, if it were to survive, would have to be 'historically necessary,' i.e., rooted in the structure, in a way that would both become its expression and, at the same time, maintain an organic relation to that structure. This task was precisely the process of, and establishment of, 'hegemony'; indeed, it was the task we spoke about earlier: that of 'seeing whether what "ought to be" is arbitrary or necessary; whether it is concrete will on the one hand or idle fancy, yearning, daydream on the other.'[80] To put it in strategic terms directly, this task, this hegemonic struggle, was precisely the task of creating a collective will, a will that would become an organized, unified – above all, organic – expression or constitutive unity of the people. Moreover, it was a task, as we shall discuss in greater detail below, that fell primarily to the political party acting as an 'organic' intellectual.

From this position Gramsci deduced that if a collective will could be created and sustained, one born of and rooted in the structure (a structure that was itself a hegemonic unity of multiplicitous and fractured power relations contextualized in terms of the structure/superstructure dialectic), then the possibility would exist for a passage from one kind of society to another, and, in that sense, from the realm of necessity to the realm of freedom. In other words, the task would become precisely one of organizing an 'integral state,' a state-within-a-society, one that was capable of moving from the economic corporate phase to the ethical-political, where the coercive aspects of the state would eventually 'wither away.'[81] Gramsci clarified this point directly in three separate fragments:

> Between the economic structure and the state, with its legislation and its coercion stands civil society, and the latter must be radically transformed, in a concrete sense and not simply on the statute-books or in scientific books. The state is the instrument for conforming civil society to the economic structure, but it is necessary for the state to 'be willing' to do this; ie, for the representatives of the change that has taken place in the economic structure to be in control of the state.[82]

> It is [thus] possible to imagine the coercive element of the state withering away by degrees, as ever-more conspicuous elements of regulated society (or ethical state or civil society) make their appearance.[83]

> This reduction to economics and to politics means precisely a reduction of the highest superstructures to the level of those which adhere more closely to the structure itself – in other words, the possibility and necessity of creating a new culture.[84]

For Gramsci, the specific vehicle whose necessary task would be to ensure that those conditions might come into existence (or, if existing, then be shaped and directed in a way that would maintain its organic link to the fundamental social groups) was precisely the political party, as noted earlier. But the notion of 'party' for Gramsci was not the usual vanguardist concept. It was to be understood, first and foremost, as an 'organic' intellectual, i.e., as precisely that organism that was able to present or bring into existence, to codify or make more 'coherent,' a world-view in a way that would be 'directive and organizational, i.e., educative, i.e., intellectual.'[85]

In this sense, a political party could be any number of social groupings; it could be the name for something as broad as a popular movement or as seemingly narrow as a newspaper, a theatre company, or even a review. 'Think of the role *The Times* in England or that which the *Corriere della Sera* used to have in Italy,' Gramsci remarked, 'or again of the role of the so-called "informational press" with its claim to being "apolitical"; or even the sporting and technical press';[86] they constitute a party insofar as they could express or articulate the real needs of fundamental social groupings – 'fundamental' and 'real' inasmuch as the groups themselves are the constitutive elements of the structure.[87] In clarifying his position, Gramsci put it this way:

> 1. The political party for some social groups is nothing other than their specific way of elaborating their own category of organic intellectuals directly in the political and philosophical field and not just in the field of productive technique. These intellectuals are formed in this way and cannot indeed be formed in any other way ... [But, in contrast,] 2. The political party, for all groups, is precisely the mechanism which carries out in civil society the same function as the state carries out, more synthetically and over a larger scale, in political society. In other words it is responsible for welding together the organic intellectuals of a given group – the dominant one – and the traditional intellectuals.[88]

The party understood as such, that is, as a vehicle for both providing social awareness and creating a social homogeneity, was precisely the organic intellectual or 'permanent persuader.'[89] Its effectiveness was in part attributable to the degree to which it would be directly linked to the structural moment, that is, to the 'fundamental social groups' of history. In that context, the political party/organic intellectual was an educator in the most profound sense of the word; as a representative of primary social groups, its task was to teach, respond to, and create the terrain for a better exchange of power relations.

This understanding of power was, as earlier mentioned, an elementary and primordial lesson, the profound implications of which were quite well known to the rulers of any society but needed to be explained fully to those being led, i.e., to those who were, as Gramsci put it, 'not in the know.' They were those who, despite their ignorance, would none the less become the bearers of the new and emergent power bloc, against which the status quo would be routed and a better society would take its place. For Gramsci, it was quite obvious whom Machiavelli, in *The Prince*, had thought to be 'not in the know' but, despite this (or perhaps because of it), were to be the bearers of modern republicanism: these were the rising merchant classes, i.e., the rising bourgeoisie. In Gramsci's 'modern prince,'[90] those 'not in the know' were precisely the working classes:

One may therefore suppose that Machiavelli had in mind 'those who are not in the know', and that it was they whom he intended to educate politically. This was no negative political education – of tyrant haters – as Foscolo seems to have understood it; but a positive education – of those who have to recognise certain means as necessary, even if they are the means of tyrants, because they desire certain ends. Anyone born into the traditional governing stratum acquires almost automatically the characteristics of the political realist, as a result of the entire educational complex which he absorbs from his family milieu, in which dynastic or patrimonial interests predominate. Who therefore is 'not in the know' [for us]? The revolutionary class of the time, the Italian 'people' or 'nation', the citizen democracy which gave birth to men like Savonarola and Pier Soderini, rather than to Castruccio or a Valentino. It seems clear that Machiavelli wished to persuade these forces of the necessity of having a leader who knew what he wanted and how to obtain it, and of accepting him with enthusiasm even if his actions might conflict or appear to conflict with the generalised ideology of the time – religion.[91]

For Machiavelli, then, the prince was the vehicle necessary to negotiate the political terrain and, in so doing, create, maintain, and indeed become the expression of a specific set of interests for the founding of a new state.[92] For Gramsci, it was precisely the organized and directed organic intellectual, i.e., the political-party-as-modern-prince, who would become the embodiment, the shaper, and the expression of a collective will of those not in the know, i.e., of the emerging and newly formed 'the people.' Indeed, it was the vehicle necessary to found a new state bearing those interests.[93] That the political party was thus the concrete embodiment and elaboration of a specific world-view, organically linked to fundamental social groupings, meant not only that Machiavelli's prince would be precisely a 'party,' too, in the most profound sense of the word,[94] but that, conversely, 'real' or 'organic' political parties could never be understood as 'static' or vanguardist, since, in order to be 'real,' they had to be always the expression of specific interests and fundamental power relations, which were, themselves, *immanently* constituted in the structure.

On the one hand, then, and similar to Machiavelli's prince, the modern prince would be as much an attempt to make concrete what would otherwise exist *en potentia* of the new social forces as it would become the vehicle necessary to bring that power to fruition. In that sense, then, it was both representative and 'educator,' itself 'educated' by the sociopolitical terrain of which it was intimately a part.[95] Integral to the structure, the organic intellectual as organized political party, i.e., as the 'modern prince,' would encapsulate the possibility (and terrain) for the founding of a new state. And because it was linked to the structure as an immanent and not fully sutured expression, it would, ipso facto, be a movement/party that would always and of necessity 'express' change.

But, more than that, the political party would be as much the embodiment of a particular social class, immanent in its expression, as it would be the embodiment of a myth, that is, of an 'ought to be.' In that sense, too, it would embody a directive awareness of something 'as if already true,' posing, in so doing, the possibility of a future reality as that which could be obtainable. Sorel, from whom Gramsci borrowed extensively on this point, put it this way: 'myth' remains a necessary feature of establishing the meaning – indeed, the 'vision' of socialism itself; and in that sense, it is the role of a party to keep that myth alive, i.e., 'real.' 'The myth in which Socialism is wholly comprised ie, a body of images capable of evoking instinctively all the sentiments which correspond to the different manifestations of the war undertaken by Socialism against modern society ... enclose within them all the strongest inclinations of a people, of a party or of a class.'[96] In that sense, too, 'organic' myths and memories were crucial to the degree to which they could set ideological parameters and thus help forge a collective will of the people, a will that could eventually become sovereign and, hence, become state.[97]

Gramsci proposed for those social groups 'not in the know' a modern prince that would be able to make coherent the collective will of a new 'the people,' new in the sense of becoming consolidated and emergent. He proposed, further, that this consolidation would arise both by posing that emerging power 'as if true,' as if already existing as such, and, at the same time, by attempting to articulate the 'real possibilities,' the 'what ought to be,' of a future better society. The political party would thus embody a state-in-formation of this new emergent social class, an integral state – forging the will of the people into an ethical reality, an ethico-political hegemony, and hence, an ethico-political state.[98] For Gramsci, then, the 'real' or 'true' ethical state could not be created out of the personality or cult leadership of a single individual, but only through the construction of the new social subject, representative of a 'concrete phantasy which acts on a dispersed and shattered people to arouse and organise its collective will.'[99] As we have seen in this case, the new representative was precisely the 'party,' in the most complex sense of that word.

Indeed, according to Gramsci, it could not be otherwise. That is, the ethico-political state could not, for example, emerge from issue-oriented strategies per se, for which trade unionism was, for Gramsci, the strongest exemplar. Practically, trade unions, among other groups, could be incorporated on a tactical level in terms of forging the necessary homogeneity of a collective will (in the context of a generalized vision of 'what ought to be' rooted in the structure). But, unless trade unionism could transcend its own economic/corporate level, it could be not become an 'organic intellectual' in the sense mentioned earlier.[100] Without this transcendence, it lacked the necessary political element, i.e., the socio-subjective moment, to be able, according to Gramsci, to consolidate the various disparate wills into a collective will, and, therewith, into a state.[101]

This was a crucial point which, according to Gramsci, Sorel had missed entirely: he had 'stopped short' of realizing the radical (and practical) implications of extending the notion of ideology-as-myth to include the concept of the social-subjective will. In having thus 'stopped short,' Sorel confused tactics with strategy, properly speaking; indeed, he confused 'change' with 'chance' (or 'spontaneity'). 'For Sorel "myth" found its fullest expression not in the trade union as organization of a collective will,' criticized Gramsci,

> but in its practical action – the sign of a collective will already operative. [In this context, then] the highest achievement of this practical action was to have been the general strike – ie, a 'passive activity,' so to speak, of a negative and preliminary kind (it could only be given a positive character by the realization of a common accord between the various wills involved) an activity which does not envisage an 'active and constructive' phase of its own. Hence in Sorel there was a conflict of two necessities: that of the myth, and that of the critique of myth – in that 'every pre-established plan is utopian and reactionary'. *Hence the outcome was left to the intervention of the irrational, to chance (in the Bergsonian sense, of 'elan vital')
or to 'spontaneity'.*[102]

The emphasis on the trade union over the party as a fundamental vehicle for change was deeply troublesome for Gramsci. For, although it acknowledged the problem of transformation (with the logical addendum of winning state power), it posed it as if self-contained and connected more to chance or 'fortuna' than to conscious practico-political will or 'virtu.'[103] That is, for Gramsci, the former emphasis on trade unionism precluded the moment of political struggle, when a group could move out of its strictly economic/corporate phase and into its most purely political phase.[104] Gramsci's difficulty with Sorel on this point was precisely that, by having posed the trade union as the vehicle for fundamental change (rather than the party), Sorel was forced, implicitly, to forward a flattened notion of political practice – one that had more to do with manipulation and tactics *within* proscribed parameters, i.e., within the arena of the superstructure, detached, as it were, from its structural base. In this sense, political organization and, indeed, power itself could remain only taxonomic and descriptive.

To preclude the political moment, the moment of hegemony, was thus to ignore the importance of 'the passage from the structure to the superstructure' when, as Gramsci outlined, the subaltern social groups could

> transcend the corporate limits of the purely economic class, and ... become 'party', come into confrontation and conflict, until only one of them or at least a single combination of them, tends to prevail, to gain the upper hand, to propagate itself throughout society – bringing about not only a unison of economic and political aims, but also an intellectual and moral unity ... and thus creating the hegemony of a fundamental social group over a series of subordinate groups.[105]

To preclude the political moment of the relations of force was, in other words, to ignore what for Gramsci had been the central feature of the real dialectic: the notion of immanence/becoming, the continual making into a reality of a new (social) truth, i.e., the continual process of creating what had, up to that point, been recognizable only as possibility. To preclude the dialectical nature of politics was to ignore the premiss that the making of 'what ought to be' into the 'what is' was precisely an ethico-political struggle, that is, a struggle of hegemony, the ushering in of a new world-view, a new philosophy, and, therewith, a new social terrain appropriate to it.

In short, relying on trade unionism as the bearer of the (new) ethico-political state was to miss the point that, in the transformation from the 'old' to the 'new,' a synthesis of the one social organization with the next must take place in order for change to remain permanent and be institutionalized as such. Indeed, it was to ignore what Gramsci had found crucial in Sorel's own work: the concept of the 'historic bloc.'[106] Here, the historic bloc would not mean or imply a homogenization of the social whole; but neither would it simply mean a unity formed through the direction of the party of leaders and led. Instead it would point to (and embody) the coherence, and yet 'open fluidity,' of the structural moment whose (dialectical) synthesis with the superstructure would be nothing less than the total realization/expression of a new society. Thus, for Gramsci:

Structures and superstructures form an 'historic bloc'. That is to say the complex, contradictory and discordant *ensemble* of the social relations of production. From this, one can conclude: that only a totalitarian [e.g., 'totalizing'] system of ideologies can give a rational reflection of the contradiction of the structure and represents the existence of the objective conditions for the revolutionising of praxis. If a social group is formed which is one hundred per cent homogeneous on the level of ideology, this means that the premises exist one hundred per cent for this revolutionising: that is, that the 'rational' is actively and actually real. This reasoning is based on the necessary reciprocity between structure and superstructure, a reciprocity which is nothing other than the real dialectical process.[107]

For Gramsci, then, that synthesis would be orchestrated by the organic intellectuals whose practico-political expression would be precisely the political party, albeit in the widest sense of the term.[108] And it would remain as 'party' until the new social vision had become 'universal and totalizing,'[109] that is, until party-as-integral-state could become the 'synthetic' and 'totalizing' expression of the structure/superstructural elements, and therewith not only embody an ethico-political 'moment' of hegemony, but usher in a new and specific society, one that would be directly expressing the needs and desires of a new and specific 'the people.' Gramsci summarized the position as follows:

> In the modern world, a party is such – integrally and not, as happens, a fraction of a larger party – when it is conceived, organised and led in ways and in forms such that it will develop integrally into a State (an 'integral' State, and not into a government technically understood) and into a conception of the world. The development of the party into a State reacts upon the party and requires of it a continuous reorganization and development, just as the development of the party and State into a conception of the world, i.e., into a total and molecular (individual) transformation of ways of thinking and acting, reacts upon the State and the party, compelling them to reorganise continually and confronting them with new and original problems to solve.[110]

In the ensuing battle to go beyond an 'integral state' and establish the ethico-political society-state, there would come into existence, eventually and by necessity, the possibility of establishing a 'concrete' universal. Further, in the passage from integral to ethical state, the party would, ipso facto, establish a 'universality' that always maintained its specificity, and hence always remained 'open,' not fully sutured, immanent in its expression. But, in becoming universal, the party would of necessity 'disappear.' For, precisely when the will of a specific 'the people,' embodied as such in the party, became the ethico-political state, the party would represent the full and total expression of its social subjectivity, however diverse and multiplicitous (i.e., sutured and not fully recuperable) that subjectivity might be.[111] Hence, on the one hand, the party would cease to exist as an 'individual' per se; and yet, on the other, it would become instead a collective, immanent, and universal expression. Thus, Gramsci writes in commenting on the aim of the modern prince, since 'every party is only the nomenclature for a class, it is obvious that the party which proposes to put an end to class divisions will only achieve complete self fulfillment when it ceases to exist – because classes, and therefore their expressions no longer exist.'[112]

In one sense, then, the political party would be understood as the symbolic bearer of an immanent, rather than essential, possibility; in another sense, it would be the concrete vehicle necessary to ensure that that possibility would become 'reality.' As a specific, determinate representative of 'the people,' its task would be that of 'founding a new type of State (one rationally and historically created for that end),' linked to, and born out of, the terrain of the old.[113]

Given this reciprocity between the structure and the superstructure, and given the nature of the party, now cast against (and in terms of) an historic-bloc synthesis, i.e., an ethico-political hegemony – indeed, embedded in the layered notion of 'structure' itself – Gramsci was able to rework the conceptual relation of the state and civil society and, therewith, rework the very concept of a (future) democratic society. In the best possible world, *civil society* (and not the state) would become the totalized expression of the social at every level: political, economic, militaristic, and so forth. Civil society, the immanent repository of the collective will, would thus 'become' and embody the state. In that sense, as Gramsci succinctly put it, 'civil society and the State are one and the same.'[114]

This totalized conception of a civil society immanent in its expression was precisely the reversal of fascistic 'totalitarianism,' which had highlighted the homogeneity of the state at the expense of the diversity of the social. For Gramsci, only the former – the radicalization of social totality itself – could represent the collective will of the people, and thus lay the groundwork for establishing a truly participatory democracy.[115] Conceptualizing a civil society immanent in its social construction, that is to say, as an the expression of hegemony, represented the moment, to paraphrase Gramsci, when the 'structure and the superstructure would become one,' that is, 'when structure ceases to annihilate man,' as

Gramsci would say, and would become instead the terrain upon which the new social order could be realized.[116]

This hegemonic social whole now embodied as the ethico-political society would be precisely the 'organic' realization and expression of the collective will of (a specific) 'the people' and hence the expression of a democratic state par excellence. 'It seems to me that of *all the many meanings of democracy, the most concrete and realistic is connected with the concept of hegemony,*' Gramsci emphasized over and again. 'In the hegemonic system, democracy exists between the leading group and those who are led, to the degree to which (the economy is developed and when) the legislation (that expresses that development) favours the passage (which is molecular) from those who are led to the group which is the ruling group.'[117]

Now, this radical new order, this 'radical democracy/ethico-political society,' could have no predetermined meaning or essence, except inasmuch as 'meaning' had been historically constructed in the struggle of hegemony. Neither did Gramsci argue, following from this, that a radical democracy could be ordered into existence from pre-established notions of what was 'good' or 'better,' nor, for that matter, did he think that the old norms and values would be at all predisposed towards the establishing of the new. Indeed, so passionately was he pitted against forced conformism, on the one hand, or romantic liberalism, on the other, that Gramsci urgently underscored what, for him, was the obvious: 'It is not from the social groups "condemned" by the new order that reconstruction is to be expected, but from those on whom is imposed the burden of creating with their own suffering the material bases of the new order. It is they who "must" find for themselves an "original" and not Americanised system of living, to turn into "freedom" what today is "necessity."'[118]

But, here we must take pause. For the fact of the matter was that Gramsci was not speaking about just 'any' oppressed group of people who would become articulated as such through the process and struggle of hegemony; nor was he proposing just 'any' historically constructed plan for freedom. Gramsci clearly had in mind an already established (albeit not fully constituted) social agency, namely, the working class. As such, that class would be the bearer of the new ethical possibility. Indeed, in Gramsci's estimation, it was never a question as to 'who' these people might be or what kind of ethico-political hegemony they would express. The real problem for Gramsci was that the 'old' was dying and the 'new' could not be born, that is, in the midst of the social upheavals rocking Italy and elsewhere, fascism – and not the democratic modern prince of the workers' movement – had become the organizing principle of the day. Fascism had become the 'new social order' and instead of an immanent, ethico-political democracy, the workers' movement lay shattered and in chaos.

In this context, then, Gramsci not only intended to argue against fascism and all that it represented, he wanted to show *why* the fascist movement – which had pitted itself against 'the old' and presented itself as if 'the new' – was inherently and fully reactionary, not at all progressive, not the least bit democratic, and could only create (as we earlier noted) the bureaucratic state. But, more than that, Gramsci clearly wanted to argue that the workers' movement was precisely the reverse of the fascist predicament; indeed, it was the embodiment of a (progressive) *Sittlichkeit*, immanent in its expression and totalizing in its ethicality.

But given his own arguments around the making of an ethico-political reality within the context of historical totality, he knew he could not pose an already given ethicality as such, that is, as a thing-in-itself. As he saw it, the only other option was to ground that communal ethicality on the terrain of necessity, itself understood to be immanent in its expression. Thus he proposed, as we have now detailed, *to radicalize the notion of totality itself* and, in so doing, pose the working classes as constitutive entities, always 'in struggle,' that is, always immanent in their unfolding and bound by what must become their historic mission. And yet, in radicalizing the social totality and the dialectic it implied, Gramsci was still faced with the problem of having to posit an ontological 'given,' an ethical logos of the centre from which all things would flow.

To resolve this ontological conundrum, he thus premised the whole argument on *the privileging of a radical teleology of civil society*, itself propelled by the 'historic mission' of the oppressed and subaltern classes. 'We are then making an historical prediction,' a sombre Gramsci reflected, 'which consists simply in an act of thought that projects into the future a process of development similar to that which has taken place from the past until today ...[119] [Thus the philosophy of praxis] bases itself entirely on the concrete action of man, who *impelled by historical necessity*, works and transforms reality.'[120]

Gramsci, although realizing the limits to a radical posing of totality as itself a 'non-fixed' sociality (i.e., immanently 'open' and 'fluid'), in the final analysis simply translated the hoped-for resolution into that of a radical teleology. But not only did this conceptual move not solve the previous set of difficulties, it set its own trap: for the insistence on a radical immanence teleologically unfolding in history merely begged the question of grounding universal ethicality as an expression of the working classes. Worse, the posing of class as itself teleological in its expression went directly against Gramsci's own laboriously worked out analyses of the rational/real dialectic, and, in that context, against the crucial notion of class as that which is constituted 'in struggle.' Indeed, it dismissed the depth of Gramsci's own claim that meaning was itself an historical product, a fractured and multiplicitous synthesis made possible by the science and art of politics. In short, it made him beg the question as to how an ethical grounding could be established.

And so, despite what might appear as a circuitous route to incorporate 'life' in all its impure and profane ways, despite his brilliant engagement with the concept of the will as a non-essentialist foundation to an open and immanent social whole, despite his profound rethinking of the ethico-political and the hegemony it implied, and despite his careful rethinking of the political party as an organic intellectual or the integral state and the civil society that would become its democratic expression, Gramsci had to resort, in the final analysis, to the privileging of an already established and homogeneous ethical subject linked to the teleological unfolding of the ethico-political society-state. 'When one bangs their head against the wall enough times,' Gramsci lamented to his sister-in-law, 'one finds out one thing: their head breaks, not the wall.'

He thus consciously took up the position that the class struggle, indeed class itself, which he had so carefully and methodically explored in terms of its instability, its 'error,' its 'always-in-the-process-of-becoming' and of constituting its subjectivity as such, was, in the final analysis, a synthetic unity that had to rely on the teleology of a pregiven ethicality, i.e., the posing of an already constituted and homogeneous communal ethicality or *Sittlichkeit* that, in the case of the 'good' or 'better' community, was, ipso facto, born from its unfolding. True, it was an ethicality forged from the subject positionalities of those subaltern groups, those people materially exploited and systematically dehumanized precisely as a result of their fundamental link in the capitalist system. Indeed, it seemed the necessary premiss required not only to defeat the attacks of 'nihilistic relativism' launched against his absolute historicism, but allowed him in the end to argue, ironically enough, for the building of an ethico-political state devoid of those essentialist trappings. But despite this – or perhaps because of it – it forced him into the weak theoretical proposition of having to accept the notion of an 'historic mission' of the working classes, which, even to paraphrase Gramsci, implied a certain level of mysticism or even a systematic rethinking of Kant's transcendentalism. And it certainly seemed to beg the question around the emergence of fascism itself, particularly within the ranks of the working classes. Painted into a corner, he thus was forced to conclude that teleology and the radical totalizing upon which it is premised must, in the end, 'be sustained and justified in the philosophy of praxis.'[121]

On the one hand, then, it is accurate to say that a thorough investigation of Gramsci's analytic positions reveals that he could not square the circle. He was not able to give us a fully articulate, completely detailed comprehensive theory for building and maintaining a radical democracy. But, on the other hand, what actually mattered for Gramsci was this simple truth: 'That objective possibilities exist for people not to die of hunger and that people *do* die of hunger has its importance, or so one would have thought.[122] ... [For] What counts [in changing that sorry scenario] is not the opinions of Tom, Dick, and Harry, but that ensemble of opinions which become collective, [become] a social element and [thus] a social force.'[123]

It was a plea – a strategic, tactical, methodological, political, and, above all, practical plea – to all those oppressed and exploited, all those 'not in the know,' to become aware of the stakes in refusing to organize and actively fight for the overthrow of a reactionary and oppressive state. More than that, it was a sytematic attempt to strategize against accepting this brutal social 'fate,' and, instead, show that 'the people' could, despite the odds, organize their collective will-power and move onto the progressive terrain of a truly ethico-political democracy.[124]

The obvious question remaining is simply this: Is there a way to accept the profound contributions Gramsci offered around a post-liberal-democratic theory, without having to accept the concomitant position of an ethical grounding teleologically unfolding towards some historic 'mission' or, conversely, having to establish as transcendental the *Sittlichkeit* of an already given social agent? In the concluding remarks, the possible theoretical trajectory opened to us by Laclau and Mouffe, Foucault, Derrida, and others is put forward for possible consideration.

SIX

Gramsci's Contribution to a Post-Liberal-Democratic Theory:

Concluding Remarks

At the outset of this work, the question was posed as to whether Gramsci's philosophy of praxis might enable one not only to go 'beyond' the dilemmas found in a liberal or idealist tradition but, in so doing, to be able to establish an analytic framework for a 'post'-liberal-democratic theory. That is, could one begin to articulate such a theory without having to accept as 'always already' given a homogeneous conception of human interest and need – in fact, of human nature itself – and yet, at the same time, not have to 'ground' that heterogeneity in terms of an external transcendental or teleological universalism. What was at stake in this study, in other words, was precisely the problem of taking Gramsci's claim seriously: that a 'history/politics' constituted the absolute universalism of truth itself and, therewith, the very core of the ethical 'what ought to be.'

Gramsci's contribution

If this claim could be sustained and the logic pushed beyond its Enlightenment roots, the elements constituting a progressive post-liberal-democratic theory would become clearer. As we saw, this democratic theory must also, and of necessity, be founded upon a radical notion of social diversity or pluralism, one that simultaneously held forth a radical autonomy of human subjectivity, while grounding its social ethicality (and cohesiveness) in the profound heterogeneity of a collective will. Moreover, and as we also noted, this will was itself historically 'immanent,' vital, necessary, or, to emphasize Gramsci's word, political. It was thus, and of necessity, a fractured and multiplicitous collective will – one that, as such, provided both the ground and the horizon, the 'is' and the 'ought,' of an ethico-political hegemony. Indeed, it became the expression for that peculiar spatiality existing somewhere between the possible and the impossible or, as Gramsci would say, 'between the realm of necessity and that of freedom, in order to concretize the latter into the former.' In so doing, it became not only the 'concrete universal,' i.e., the historically specific 'totalizing' expression for a 'real' citizen democracy, but the permanent and yet dynamic link, the very fluid knowledge/power terrain between those who were 'the people' and the groups who were to lead.

It could be said, then, that in approaching Gramsci's prison notes with the open-ended question 'What might he be fighting *for*?' it became quite clear that, despite the actual topic of democracy being mentioned in only a handful of fragments, Gramsci's complete reassessment of science, knowledge, and, later, the dialectic and its relation to the will provided a precise rethinking of what, analytically, ought to constitute a 'better' society and why. At the very minimum such a society would be based on the rejection of a pure essence or pure positivity to any given identity or truth game and, hence also, to any given moral or ethical proposition. Instead, the truth as both 'is' and 'ought' was posed in terms of its historically specific 'universality,' ipso facto, constituted by the political moment 'in the most profane and impure sense of the term.' There was no hidden god, no noumenon or archimedean point existing above or beyond reality; there was only the dialectical wholeness of reality itself, an immanent dialectical materialism that bore no concrete otherness existing in relation to, apart from, different from, or even outside of, the so-called real world. It expressed only the dynamic presence of a history/politics, that is, the dynamic presence of a reality that entailed both a fluidity and a discontinuity, both a possibility and an impossibility, both a suturing and an erasing, inextricably linked together to form the whole of truth. It was a society, in other words, that was neither static nor pregiven but, rather, in perpetual movement; one that, at the same time, entailed 'error,' 'specificity,' 'negation,' and that disturbing element called the will.

In fact, as we also noted, this flexible posing of the will was, in turn, premised on a well-thought-out (but often ignored) argument around its discursive nature: i.e., it was the collective expression of a practico-political terrain and, as such, formed the given parameter or boundary for social struggle (or, to put it in philosophical terms directly, provided the 'first' moment, as it were, rife with all that we have mentioned concerning opposite and distinct abstractions). But, it also expressed that 'unquantifiable something,' as Gramsci would put it, which contoured the very processes of political strategy and change. In this sense, the will was the conceptual name given for the 'in-between,' the not-quite-negative/not-quite-positive 'neither/nor'; that is, the rational but creative element that often, and despite all odds, could produce circumstances completely different from what might have otherwise been deduced and yet do so in terms quite apart from accidental or arbitrary happenstance. 'Real' change, that is, permanent or institutionalized change, was thus, for Gramsci, not an epiphenomenal reflection of the structure pitted against or in terms of a superstructure; nor was it something 'determined in the last instance' by an abstract quantitative economic moment. It was, rather, understood to be both a product and an expression of the struggle for hegemony.

In this sense, too, then, it could be said that where the dialectic of historicized immanence was precisely the 'science' of politics, the will was, for Gramsci, its 'art.' Its power lay not in 'discovering' or 'uncovering' – for there was no 'essence' or metaphysical 'law' underwriting the will. Rather, its power lay precisely in its propensity to create, invent, and inscribe. And as this was a political 'art' never external to the structural terrain per se, nor never fully realized or made 'concrete' if posed only in and of itself (and thus outside the structural/superstructural dialectic to which it was a part), this wilful creating and inscribing could never represent 'idle daydream' or irrational 'fancies.'

Indeed, it could never be static or devoid of specificity. Like the terrain from which it emerged, this historically particular (however much 'utopian') imaginary – utopian to the degree that it remained in the realm of possibility and was not as of yet 'reality' – was also (and always) in a process of an historico-political movement or becoming. But as we also saw, it was a becoming rooted in the 'realm of necessity,' that is, in the structural terrain itself, which was also and precisely the 'expression' of the practical political struggle for hegemony (and the fluidity and discontinuities this struggle implied). In this sense, the will as the 'art' of a social imaginary remained 'open,' creative, non-rigid and non-definitive, and, yet, entailed a subjectivity at once both very 'real' and not quite existing as such.

Thus the will became for Gramsci both a will-power terrain and the vehicle providing the necessary intellectual and moral reform from which a radically pluralistic democracy would become its concrete (but universal) expression. This qualitatively immanent/quantitatively historicized collective will would thus also become, for Gramsci, both the arbitrator and the expression of a legitimation process capable of establishing, in an integral sense, the ethico-political state. Moreover, this integral and ethico-political state would, ipso facto, be based on the specific will of a specific people, whose social identity as a people would also (and of necessity) be both immanent and real, universal and, yet, concrete.

In fact, posing the will as such meant that not only would the subjectivity of 'the people' be a direct expression of the 'impure' hegemonic moment – i.e., the political struggle itself – but so, too, would the constituting of a class. Indeed, the whole concept of class, particularly as an abstract economic category, was now reassessed to take on a whole host of 'qualitative' aspects alongside its 'quantitative' ones. Hence, class formation was also (and always) inherently 'political' in the most profound sense of the word: it, too, was predicated on – and an expression of – the open foundational unities forged by specific political struggles. The same could be said about class interests, strategies, needs, and wants; in fact, the whole socio-economic moment was now recast in terms of an absolute historicism that placed at its centre ruptures, struggles, and crises, the resolutions of which forged unities only in and against the specificities of the political.

In this case, too, there was no archimedean point 'outside' society or somehow existing underneath (in terms of a base) or above (in terms of a superstructure) from which social ethicality, strategy, or even the meaning of life itself could be deduced. There was only the historic bloc produced through political struggle; there was only a social totality, immanent in its expression. This was a 'radical' notion of totality in the fullest sense of the word: in terms of getting to the root of the problem in all its diverse ways. That is, Gramsci's was not a radical totality in the sense of creating in its wake a homogeneous world rooted in the notion of an identity, totality, or, for that matter, equality as nothing more than a 'sameness,' strictly speaking.[1] Rather, as we have tried to detail, it was radical for precisely the reverse reason: its equality, unity, and totality rested on a *profound heterogeneity* of discrete social elements.

For, as we have examined, the very notion of a unity or totalized sociality was understood to be a constructed synthesis of fractured elements or distincts that also, in themselves, entailed a discontinuity, a rupture, a 'specificity' or 'error.' Why? Because, as we noted in chapter 2, when discussing Croce's complaints against Hegel, in order to establish any form of equivalence or identity there needed always to be some remainder; that is, there needed always to be a something 'not' included in that equivalence, precisely so as to make the identity have any meaning beyond simple 'sameness.' To put it slightly differently, identity could have concrete substance only when understood against and in the context of its negation – or, to use Gramsci's shorthand, its impurity or 'error.'

By taking discontinuity and error as givens, then, what brought these inchoate elements together and funnelled them into 'good sense,' as Gramsci would put it, was the profound struggle for hegemony. It was the synthesis of history and politics, a synthesis that need not be, indeed could never be, '100 per cent conscious,' but required some kind of direction. Truth, science, knowledge, economics, ideology, and so forth were always, then, for Gramsci, a function of the political, now understood as the first, last, and mediating moment of reality.

In casting the political as the first, last, and mediating moment of this radical social totality, Gramsci was able to clarify (or, as some would argue, alter) Marx's posing of the structure itself. It allowed him to suggest that what contoured the limits or boundaries to the social whole must also be cast in terms of an immanent nexus between the 'is' and the 'ought,' between, that is, the real and the not-yet-possible. That contouring was itself named 'structure,' now understood as the expression of the dialectic between the realm of necessity and the realm of freedom. Thus, at one level of analysis, structure was understood to be not only the synthesis of that reality, but its immanent 'ground' or 'terrain,' a ground that covered both the (practical) imaginary and the real.

And yet, in another sense, and given that, for Gramsci, a radical, immanent totality was an historical process, a hegemonic process par excellence, the structure was also to be understood as a distinct and constitutive element to the social whole, meaningless without its dialectical counterpart, superstructure. Structure at a third level of analysis became precisely the terrain from which the better society, the so-called what ought to be, could be forged into reality, into, that is to say, the 'is.' It was the creating of a civil society, an ethico-political society as state, one, by necessity, immanent, open, and fluid.

One of the advantages of posing the structure in these somewhat mutated terms was that it allowed Gramsci a practico-political way to establish why a (heterogeneous) collective will must, of necessity and not merely by definition, remain the essential requisite to the building of a citizen democracy. For as this will was both a vehicle and an arbitrator, an inventor and a director of a people's interests and antagonisms, and as it was forged directly from a structure that itself emerged and expressed the very premiss and the outcome of historico-political struggle, this will could never relapse into some generic or abstract will, as had been the problem in the earlier liberal and idealist formulations. Rather, it always would express a specific 'the people,' whose fractured and distinct humanity would itself be understood in terms of an historicized becoming, and whose communal ethicality could be ground in and bound by this (historically immanent) *Sittlichkeit*.

What constituted the social 'ought' of a democratic society beyond the bounds of liberalism and its liberal-democratic variant was precisely that the social whole must always be founded upon, and be able to maintain and reproduce, an open and immanent historical synthesis, a so-called living unity of the rational and the real, one rooted in the structure and, as such, expressing the collective will of a people. Thus, as Gramsci noted, with 'the word "democracy" ... what matters is that a bond is being sought with the people, the nation, and that one considers necessary not a servile unity, resulting from passive obedience, but an active unity, a living unity, whatever the content of that life might be.'[2]

Gramsci's theoretical framework for understanding *why* a radical non-essentialism and heterogeneity of the social must become the basis for a post-liberal democracy could be touted as one of the most profound contributions any theorist has made to contemporary political philosophy. But being the political strategist he was, Gramsci also explored in analytic terms the *how* and the *what* of constituting a post-liberal democracy.

As we saw, the *how* would be achieved through the function of the organic intellectual who represented, expressed, educated and was educated by the fundamental social groups within a society. In this sense the 'intellectual' could act as a political party, immanently rooted in the structure, constituting and yet buffeted by the ideological hegemony within a given totality. And yet, as we also saw, because the party was understood to be the practical embodiment of an organic, that is, 'necessary,' collective will, it could no longer be posed as a vanguard or purveyor of the truth. As with the 'truth' it was to represent and express, the political party/organic intellectual was always cast in terms of its subjective constitution; it, too, was always in a process of becoming.

Indeed, it was precisely this process of becoming (itself a political-participatory and hegemonic process) that would move the party-as-integral-state out of the 'distinct' structural moment and onto the effective terrain of the structure/superstructure unity, a unity that expressed the collective will of a people-nation. In this sense, civil society would become both the bearer and the expression of the ethico-political hegemony, the 'is' and the 'ought' of an immanent collective will. Unlike the fascist rendition explored in chapter 4, Gramsci's ethico-political state-as-civil-society sought to premise itself on the bond between the leaders and led, where societal legitimation and consensus, indeed truth itself, would rest in the hands of the people. In the final analysis, then, Gramsci concluded that a real democracy, that is, a citizen democracy, would be both the expression of and the terrain upon which a collective will could be obtained, institutionalized, and reproduced. Indeed, it was precisely an historicized *Sittlichkeit*, the embodiment of an ethico-political hegemony realized in *civil society* as distinct from the hegelian ethical state.

And yet, as we saw, this civil society/ethico-political (integral) state rested, in the final analysis, on the unresolved dilemma as to how to ground the universality of this position. It still seemed to beg the practico-political question, in other words, of why one could say, 'This and not *that* is what we must fight for'; indeed, it still seemed to beg the question of who precisely this 'we' might be. In having insisted so thoroughly on the profundity of politics as the first moment of history, and hence as having presented an historicism absolute in its meaning, Gramsci was faced with two seemingly fruitless analytic resolutions: either radicalize the concept of dialectical totality and therewith place the ethical-political (and the hegemony it implies) as a function of a given social whole, which, in the end, must rest upon an unbroken teleology; or radicalize the concept of hegemony itself and therewith place the ethical-political as an absolute function of rupture, error, or impossible spatiality. The former would lead to a 'ground' based on external agency, homogeneity, and the privileging of a synthetic theoreticism, despite attempts to do precisely the reverse; for, in the final analysis, it would deduce a sociality from a fully sutured social whole, albeit in its 'integral' sense. But, the latter would mean giving up the 'ground,' except inasmuch as grounding itself would remain a function of a profound negativity, resulting therefore in what seemed to be an absolute nihilism posted somewhere beyond the limits of dialectical reasoning.

That is to say, then, and as we saw in the preceding chapter, a radicalizing of 'totality,' despite all the twists and turns of the argument, would lead in the end to accepting as pregiven a rational unity, which, in this case, meant returning to a reductionist notion of class and class interests. Hence, in choosing that route, one had necessarily to accept the dubious argument that the *content* of the ethical-political must be constituted prior to the establishment of the community. But the latter seemed to fall victim to the 'friendly fascism' of Croce's history/anti-history dialectic. It seemed as if it were unable to disengage itself from the charge that, while capable of showing the complexity of truth in all its historical specificity and negation, it was completely incapable of distinguishing oppressive situations from progressive ones. Gramsci saw this as a relativistic nihilism, a nietzschean 'charlatanism,' as he called it, an anti-system system still unable to do any better than to say, along with Croce, that everything (including the oppressive situation in which Gramsci was a part) was just one of the many stepping-stones in the immanent unfolding of the 'story of liberty.'

In choosing the first alternative – what, for Gramsci, was the only option – we saw how his radicalization of totality led to a profound reinscription of diversity and heterogeneity at all levels of the argument save one: the insistence that the inherent radical pluralism of a real democracy must, ipso facto, be rooted in, and expressed as, the historical mission of the working class. Like the gordian knot of antiquity, the more Gramsci worked through these basic premisses around the notion of politics as historicized immanence, or that of the will as an operative awareness of historical necessity, or, finally, of the base as a constitutive unity or structure that could be understood only in the context of a dialecticized reality, the more he became entangled in those premisses. For, given the logic of his argument, and despite attempts to add fluidity and error – indeed, life itself – to analytic categories, by casting the whole attempt in terms of a dialectical reasoning, historical or otherwise, ultimately Gramsci was unable to resolve the ethico-political dilemma.

Ultimately, that is to say, he was unable to get out of metaphysics. And, perhaps, neither are we. For, in order to ground the ethico-political society in terms of the working classes, one would still have to resort to taking as an absolute given the priority (and rational unity) of an 'historic mission,' replete with the faith and dogma all missions seem to require. In theoretical terms, one still had to privilege an analytic teleology of, in this case, a working-class *Sittlichkeit*. Why should this necessarily be a problem? After all, given there was no way out of the dilemma, accepting this predicament must have seemed a very small price to pay. For despite the necessity of having to incorporate an a priori essentialism around a working-class-based ethicality, Gramsci was able to begin to argue, ironically enough, for the building of an ethico-political state utterly devoid of those essentialist trappings.

Yet, by paying that price, Gramsci won a shallow victory. His concept of hegemony, for example, so carefully crafted around dynamic and non-essentialist categories, could be taken, in the end, only to articulate, however complex, *coalition* politics, the building of 'alliances' using already given and homogeneously sealed entities such as 'the' worker, 'the' peasant, 'the' Jew (and, even in contemporary times, 'the' woman, 'the' gay, 'the' person of colour, etc.). Thus, these groups could be understood only at a *descriptive* level, and the political processes involved with creating the subject positionalities of 'worker,' or 'woman,' or 'lesbian,' or 'person of colour' and so on could be understood only as *fait accompli*, added up together to create yet another totalized group called 'the' people. Worst of all, by radicalizing a notion of totality that reformulated but could not resolve the entire dilemma except as a teleological necessity, Gramsci merely begged the question of attributing ethicality to his dictum that will-power, indeed truth itself, was created as such.

The obvious question must therefore be addressed: if after all this, Gramsci's analytic contribution to a democratic theory purporting to go beyond liberalism is so fatally flawed, what possible use can we 'salvage' out of it? Should it be concluded that, in the end, we are left with a teleological 'error' so profound that his work must be categorically dismissed as a 'failure' or, at best, highlighted as a unique set of comments that manage to put forward a few astute observations on the game of politics? Should we conclude, as some have done, that Gramsci's *Quaderni del carcere*, despite its passion and intensity (or perhaps because of them), deserves nothing more than 'to be buried with all the honours due' a dedicated militant of the left who was forced to write under some of the most sordid conditions imaginable during his fascist imprisonment?

The short answer is no. For, on the one hand, and irrespective of the teleological 'error' he necessarily had to assume, Gramsci did, indeed, leave us with a *substantive* contribution about the concept of a post-liberal democracy. It is rooted in the interpretation of a marxism as a philosophy of praxis and, in locating it along that philosophical and political trajectory, provides two intertwining and crucial (albeit no less problematic) points. First, that the *concept* of a 'better society' must be one based on an open and yet discontinuous movement established by placing the political – and hence the creative and intellectual moment – at the root of all meaning. It is one that thus poses, among other things, the concept of structure in terms of an historically produced *constitutive but heterogeneous unity*. This is a unity-in-diversity, an active unity, one that is totalizing to the degree to which hegemony could be established.

But, second, Gramsci's philosophy of praxis shows not only the necessity for incorporating participatory, creative, and intellectual capabilities of the people, it shows *why* this must form the basis of a real democracy. Indeed, it shows why a radical civil society, i.e., an ethico-political hegemony, is the most important 'form' that that democracy can take. And it does so in a way that refuses the generic abstractionism of liberalism by linking – indeed, by grounding – the specificity of a collective will of a people-nation in terms of an historicized *Sittlichkeit* immanent in its creation.

On the other hand, perhaps the greatest contribution to a post-liberal-democratic theory Gramsci's intense labour produced is precisely in having shown that there exists an impossible 'error,' a precipice over which one cannot leap should one refuse to abandon historico-dialectical reasoning, or, for that matter, any form of totalizing, historical or otherwise. For if one is going to take seriously the premiss that we are born on the terrain of history, that we are a part of history and indeed the creators of future history – that is to say, if one is going to take seriously the challenge of life itself and become committed to the politics of making it 'better' – Gramsci shows categorically that there is no way to ground an historically immanent ethicality of the social through dialectical reasoning alone.

Gramsci's 'error,' if it is to be called this, leads to the profound clarification that to accept social totality as a premiss, no matter how 'radicalizing' that unity might be, presents no other option to the grounding of the ethical-political except to accept as teleological an abstract analytic category, in this case class. It would seem, then, that we are left with two options. Either we accept this radicalization of totality, as did Gramsci, and be satisfied with the significant strategic tools a philosophy of praxis provides (however limiting it may be on other levels). Or we take as a given the profundity of the political and the radical pluralism this absolute heterogeneity implies, and search for a new logic.

The continuing search

Given Gramsci's propensity towards the 'impure and the profane,' an obvious linking of his work with what has now come to be known as post-modern or 'discursive' theory may provide a possible resolution.[3] Certainly this link has been a major consideration for theorists like Laclau and Mouffe who, in their ground-breaking *Hegemony and Socialist Strategy*, cast the connection in these terms, worth quoting at length:

> The task of the Left ... cannot be to renounce liberal-democratic ideology, but on the contrary, to deepen and expand it in the direction of a radical and plural democracy ... But if we look for the ultimate core of [what up to this point has galvanized the political imaginary of the Left, the 'what ought to be,' we shall find it in the classic concept of 'revolution'] ... But the classic concept of revolution ... implied the *foundational* character of the revolu-

tionary act, the institution of a point of concentration of power from which society could be 'rationally' reorganized. This is the perspective which is incompatible with the plurality and the opening which a radical democracy requires. Once again radicalizing certain of Gramsci's concepts, we find the theoretical instruments which allow us to redimension the revolutionary act itself ...

It is only when the open, unsutured character of the social is fully accepted, when the essentialism of the totality and of the elements is rejected, that this potential becomes clearly visible and 'hegemony' can come to constitute a fundamental tool ... These conditions arise originally in the field of what we have termed the 'democratic revolution' ... or, in other words, in a form of politics which is founded not upon dogmatic postulation of any 'essence of the social', but on the contrary, on affirmation of the contingency and ambiguity of every 'essence', and on the constitutive character of social division and antagonism. [This means, then, affirmation] of a 'ground' which lives only by negating its fundamental character; of an 'order' which exists only as a partial limiting of disorder; of a 'meaning' which is constructed only as excess and paradox in the face of meaninglessness – in other words, the field of the political as the space for a game which is never 'zero-sum,' because the rules and the players are never fully explicit. This game, which eludes the concept, does at least have a name: hegemony.[4]

Let us examine more closely, then, what elements are required so that we might play this kind of non-zero-sum game, that is, so that we might be able to 'radicalize' hegemony without falling into the traps already discussed throughout this book. It would require, at the very least, a kind of logic without the concomitant privileging of a foundational unity or systematizing of that logos. At the very least, it would require rethinking the limits of the political moment wholly disrupting the notion of 'limit' as being in itself a 'fixed' universalism, dialectical or otherwise. Indeed, it would require a rethinking of that 'undefinable something' (to defer to Gramsci once again), i.e., that peculiar mix of the 'not-yet-possible,' contouring and, in fact, (de)limiting the real. It would require, in other words, a series of elastic 'quasi concepts' around otherness and negation.

As we saw, Gramsci made initial inroads; but he was not alone. The early dadaists and surrealists certainly attempted to do so with their insistence on the breaking of the frame, throwing the boundaries between viewer and painting, not to mention 'high art' and the everyday, into a profound ambiguity. Indeed, the meaning of what precisely one might be looking at was always posed as a negotiation, one that, of necessity, refused any kind of foundational originality to organize its 'truth.'[5] In assessing, for example, René Magritte's infamous painting of a pipe poised above its framed replica wherein it was written 'this is not a pipe,' Foucault characterized the ambiguity thus:

> Standing upright against the easel and resting on wooden pegs, the frame indicates that this is an artist's painting: a finished work ... And yet this naive handwriting [which exclaims within the painting: *Ceci n'est pas une pipe*], neither precisely [denotes] the work's title nor one of its pictorial elements; [nor does it represent] the absence of any other trace of the artist's presence ... everything suggests a blackboard in a classroom. Perhaps a swipe of the rag will soon erase the drawing and the text. Perhaps it will erase only one or the other, in order to correct the 'error' (a drawing that will truly not be a pipe, or else writing a sentence affirming that this is indeed a pipe). But this is still only the least of the ambiguities; there are some others ... To what does the sentence written in the painting relate? 'See these lines assembled on the blackboard – vainly do they resemble, without the least digression or infidelity, what is displayed above them. Make no mistake; the pipe is overhead, not in this childish scraw.'[6]

We have here a painting within a painting, overlaid with a statement declaring that what one is seeing is not at all what it says it must be. There is a playful transgression of boundaries, limits reacting one upon another, producing its (fleeting) meaning in an impossible intersection of their rupture. To put it slightly differently, the object or referent is never quite present, though its absence leaves a trace that doubles back to contour and, in some sense, 'create' (or 'invent') an always negotiated – and therefore not ever fully realized – terrain of the present.[7] Foucault referenced this doubling as kind of 'thought from outside,' where the very notion of the outside was itself multiple and fragmented, entailing a kind of specificity and regularity, albeit one dispersed, scattered, 'disappearing in that naked space.'[8]

Contrary to the cartesian 'I think, therefore I am,' which accepted, ipso facto, a self-referential positivity, and thus directed its ratio to thinking 'the truth,' here we find a dislocating of both the 'indubitable certainty of the "I"' as well as its existence.[9] It is a 'neither/nor,' a quasi negativity/quasi positivity pitted against an entire philosophical tradition that, in directing its logic towards thinking 'the truth,' had, therewith, attempted to 'uncover' and reflect its total certitude.[10] But in posing thought from 'outside,' as it were, the entire dichotomy of truth/falsity is erased, and the entire search to uncover a general Truthfulness of truth is rejected. In its place we find a different kind of spatial and temporal referencing, one that puts truth on the same plane as invention, rather than bracing it against, or in terms of, a falsity or a lie. We have instead the reality of a truth-as-fiction, maintaining in its quasi presence a kind of regularity in dispersion, one that is no less 'real' and, yet, on the other hand, one always premised on strategies of *creating* and, indeed therefore, on strategies of power and change.

This fiction is not 'within' subjectivity itself; rather, it is the 'not' of the subject, 'the impossible verisimilitude of what lies between: [it is] ... the proximity of what is most distant, the absolute dissimulation in our very midst.'[11] Here, then, fiction and the truth to which it points consist 'not in showing the invisible, but in showing the extent to which the contour of the visible is invisible.'[12] It is not an 'outside' in the sense of directing one's attention towards the interiority of consciousness (as did a purely reflexive discourse) or, for that matter, towards any synthetic totalizing confirmation (as did dialectical synthesis). Instead, it leads to 'an outer bound where it must continually contest itself.'[13] It leads to the 'that which confines us': a discursive 'undefinable something,' not visible but nevertheless 'out there.'

Its limit falls more on the side of a radical geography, an impossible spatiality or gap or caesura, constructed in the very nexus between the 'not' and its other. It leads neither to an originary truth nor to a beginning; there is no point of departure or arrival, no propensity towards systematizing a series of fractured and discrete elements into a cohesive and totalizing unity. Indeed, there is no propensity towards systems of any kind. In his 'Introduction to the Non-Fascist Life,' Foucault stressed the ethical and political importance of taking this discursive route:

Withdraw allegiance from the old categories of the Negative (law, limit, castration, lack, lacuna), which Western thought has so long held sacred as a form of power and an access to reality. Prefer what is positive and multiple: difference over uniformity, flows over unities, mobile arrangements over systems. Believe that what is productive is not sedentary but nomadic. Do not think that one has to be sad in order to be militant, even though the thing one is fighting is abominable ... Do not use thought to ground a political practice in Truth; nor political action to discredit, as mere speculation, a line of thought. Use political practice as an intensifier of thought, and analysis as a multiplier of the forms and domains for the intervention of political action ... [For] what is needed is to 'de-individualize', by means of multiplication and displacement, diverse combinations. The group must not be the organic bond uniting hierarchized individuals, but a constant generator of de-individualization.[14]

What is needed is not to remain bound by subjectivity and its inherent self-reflexivity – any more than what was 'needed' was to be bound by an 'objective' truth. What is proposed, instead, is an non-logistical logic, a genealogy rife with multiplicities, series, cuts, pauses, commas, all pointing directly and only to the 'that,' the 'what,' the 'how' – but never to the 'why,' never, that is, to any form of reason or questioning that leads, ipso facto, to a first cause or to the Cause of causes. *God is dead.* And in a post-modern world, there is no attempt to replace him with some other absolute truth.

As we have seen, the attempt is much more modest.

Derrida simply names it a 'speleology,' a kind of quasi logic 'which no longer searches behind the lustrous appearance, outside the "beyond", "agent", "motor", "principle part or nothing".'[15] But, for Derrida, this quasi rationality requires a kind of logic quite different from the varying forms of contingency thus far discussed. It takes as a (kind of) given a radical 'undecidability,' the undecidability, as Derrida puts it, of the hymen. 'With all the undecidability of its meaning,' Derrida explains,

> the hymen only takes place when it doesn't take place, when nothing *really* happens, when there is an all-consuming consummation without violence, or a violence without blows, or a blow without marks, a mark without a mark (a margin), etc ... [But] at the edge of being, the medium of the hymen never becomes a mere mediation or work of the negative; it outwits and undoes all ontologies, all philosphemes, all manner of dialectics. It outwits them and – as a cloth, a tissue, a medium again – it envelops them, turns them over and inscribes them.[16]

Inscription, in this case, becomes, it would seem, a kind of addendum or rider to the hymen. To put it differently, it would seem to pose the 'taking of a decision,' that is to say, the political moment (and the radical contingency it implies) as a supplement.[17] In posing inscription in this way, Derrida seems to suggest (though there is an ambiguity in his work around this point) that the specificity of power processes and, indeed, of change itself is somehow ancillary or given over to happenstance. This would imply, at the very least, that the inscription of a political imaginary – indeed, the political imaginary itself – might simply remain in the nether realm of the (not yet) possible.

On the other hand, though the logic of contingency as a radical hegemony represents one of the, if not *the*, most important analytic/practico-political strategies necessary to overcome that very dilemma, many of the difficulties Gramsci outlined remain unresolved, particularly around the political and strategic question of 'what ought to be.' This is not for a moment to suggest that we retreat from the task at hand, the task of constructing a post-liberal-democratic theory precisely on the 'quasi' ground of a radical hegemony. It is merely to underscore a point Gramsci so eloquently made when lamenting the defeat of the socialist movement: 'The whole problem lies in this: the old is dying and the new has not yet been born.'[18]

Notes

Chapter One

1 C.B. Macpherson, 'Post-Liberal-Democracy?' 172; Macpherson's emphasis
2 The classic development of this position can be found in his *Democracy in America*. Also worth noting are the arguments developed by Edmund Burke, especially in his *Reflections on the Revolution in France (1790)*. We shall return to this point later in the discussion when addressing Hegel's interpretation and critique of Rousseau's general will.
3 The claims made by, among others, Robert Dahl in his *A Preface to Democratic Theory*, and Milton Friedman in his *Capitalism and Freedom*, embrace this position quite thoroughly. They argue, in part, that capitalist relations of production are a necessary requirement for the maintenance and reproduction of a pluralist democracy. A general critique of these claims can be found in Macpherson's 'Elegant Tombstones: A Note on Friedman's Freedom,' and a more sustained critique in his *The Life and Times of Liberal Democracy*.
4 The relation between political rights and market assumptions inherent in liberal and liberal-democratic theory is clearly a complex one and has been detailed in the literature from a variety of perspectives, and for quite some time. See, for example, the classic discussions by, among others, Harold Laski, in his Weil Lectures delivered at the University of North Carolina and published as *Democracy in Crisis*, esp. pp. 233–63, where he critically assesses the link between capitalism and liberal

democracy. A more sustained critique can be found, of course, in Max Weber's well-known *The Protestant Ethic and the Spirit of Capitalism*. Also worth noting is J. Schumpeter's *Capitalism, Socialism and Democracy*, to which Macpherson cites a specific debt regarding his own analytic development. Cf. C.B. Macpherson, *Property*, as well as his major statement on the complexities of political rights and the market in his *The Political Theory of Possessive Individualism: Hobbes to Locke*.

5 Of particular importance is Sheldon Wolin's *Politics and Vision: Continuity and Innovation in Western Political Thought*. See also P. Anderson's *Considerations of Western Marxism: A Critical Reader*; S. Timpanaro, *On Materialism*; and Carol Pateman's *The Problem of Political Obligation: A Critical Analysis of Liberal Theory*.

With the consolidation of the 'new left' in the late 1960s and early 1970s, there was the growth of journals as diverse as *Screen*, *Consciousness and Ideology*, and *New Left Review* and the Birmingham School's important work on ideology and political practice; in Italy, *Rinascita* and *Critica marxista*; in France, *Dialectiques*, the Tel quel group, and so forth – all of which raised and extensively discussed the problem of democracy and its relation to leftist politics and philosophy from a variety of theoretical dimensions: linguistic, psychoanalytic, and discursive. These inspiring debates spawned equally provocative discussions along those varied theoretical tracks. See, for example, R. Coward and J. Ellis's *Language and Materialism*; Franco Lo Piparo's *Lingua, intellettuali, ed egemonia in Gramsci*; Raymond Williams's *Problems in Materialism and Culture*; and Ernesto Laclau and Chantal Mouffe's *Hegemony and Socialist Strategy*. One of the best discussions detailing the variety of those debates and the impact they had on democratic theory can be found in Frank Cunningham's *Democratic Theory and Socialism*.

6 See, for example, the introductory remarks by Richard Bellamy in Norberto Bobbio, *The Future of Democracy*, where he critically assesses works as diverse as Harold Laski's *Studies in the Problem of Sovereignty* (London: George Allen and Unwin 1917) and G.D.H. Cole's *Self-Government in Industry* (London: George Bell and Sons 1918), among others.

7 *The Political Theory of Possessive Individualism*, pp. 263–77

8 T. Hobbes, *Leviathan*, Part I: 'Of Man,' esp. ch. 6, pp. 118–30

9 C.B. Macpherson, 'Introduction,' *Leviathan*, pp. 9–63. See also G. Horowitz and A. Horowitz, *Everywhere in Chains*.

10 While the issue is raised through the first *Treatise*, for a specific discussion on property and, by extension, on class in Locke's work, see his *Second Treatise*, 'Of Property,' ch. 5 in J. Locke, *Two Treatises on Govern-*

ment, pp. 303–21. The concept of property as central to an analysis of liberalism and liberal democracy is first raised by Schumpeter in his *Capitalism, Socialism and Democracy*, although Macpherson draws out the implications more fully in his *Possessive Individualism*, pp. 9–106.

11 This point is particularly well established in C. Bay, 'Foundations of the Liberal Make-Believe: Some Implications of Contract Theory versus Freedom Theory.'

12 Of course, this is not to say, conversely, that all forms of obligation result from having to accept an extrinsic agency, as indeed certain authors in the liberal-democratic tradition discuss. See in particular T.H. Green's critique of Locke's (and Hobbes's) suppositions in his *Lectures on the Principles of Political Obligation (and Other Writings)*, esp. pp. 13–193.

One of the more interesting assessments of the problem of obligation in relation to individual rights and freedoms, and the way in which that obligation can be an expression of the legitimacy of the social order itself, can be found in Pateman's *The Problem of Political Obligation*. In pointing out the obvious difficulty with the concept of obligation in liberal theory as being, as she puts it, 'how and why any free and equal individual could legitimately be governed by anyone else at all' (p. 11), she raises the complex issue of self-assumed obligation as the only real resolution to the liberal dilemma, and presents a detailed analysis of the state and civil society in relation to the role and distinction of 'promising' political authority and political obedience. In this way she is able to tease out a more radicalized concept of obligation itself.

13 Hobbes, *Leviathan*, Part I, ch. 13, 14, and 15, pp. 183–8, 189–201, and 201–17; and Part II, ch. 17 and 18, pp. 223–8 and 228–38

14 Locke, *Two Treatises on Government*, 'Second Treatise,' 'Of Political or Civil Society,' ch. 7, pp. 336–48; and 'Of the Dissolution of Government,' ch. 19, pp. 424–46

15 Some have argued that Locke's changed focus regarding the state of nature was more a result of a nicely sharpened vision, produced by the hindsight view of the 1688 civil war, than of any logico-theoretical proposition per se. Whereas Hobbes, writing prior to the event, could foresee only total destruction, after the Glorious Revolution it was clear that a civil uprising could occur that would leave the state more or less intact, notwithstanding the change in the governing power relations. See, for example, D. Held, 'Introduction: Central Perspectives on the Modern State,' and the more substantive work by J. Dunn, *The Political Thought of John Locke: An Historical Account of the Argument in 'Two Treatises of Government.'* Locke's revamped conception of the state of

nature, however it emerged, allowed him to make certain distinctions concerning the state and civil society and the kind of obligation that would thus be required. See in particular Macpherson's 'Locke: The Political Theory of Appropriation.'

16 *Reflections on the Revolution in France,* pp. 64–65; bracketed remarks, mine. But see also Paine's well-known counterargument in his *Rights of Man,* esp. Part I, pp. 7–100. Also worth noting are the debates between T.B. Macaulay and James Mill. Macaulay's well-known critique of the Benthamite utilitarians and the logic of James Mill's *Essay on Government* lent both philosophical and political support to Burke's comments raised above. See, in particular, T.B. Macaulay, 'Mill's *Essay on Government*: Utilitarian Logic and Politics.'

17 Clearly, the crucial contributions of Bentham and James Mill, as well as those of J.S. Mill, are central here, though their work (and the differences among them) will be alluded to only inasmuch as to set the direction for the way in which Gramsci attempted to resolve the problem at hand. But for Mill's argument around the developmental capacities of personhood and the need to create a democracy that would take personhood as a fundamental given, see in particular his 'The Claims of Labour (1845),' discussed further in his 'Considerations on Representative Government,' in *Three Essays: On Liberty (1851), Representative Government (1861) and The Subjection of Women (1869),* pp. 5–141, 145–423, 427–548.

18 A point that runs through the entirety of Macpherson's work, but see in particular his *Life and Times of Liberal Democracy,* pp. 1–22.

19 *Democratic Theory: Essays in Retrieval,* 'Problems of a Non-Market Theory of Democracy,' pp. 51–2

20 This positioning of the ethical as a communal good can be traced throughout Hegel's work, but, in particular, see Hegel's *Philosophy of Right,* esp. the second and third parts, pp. 75–104 and 105–223. See also his *Phenomenology of Spirit,* 'C. [BB.] Spirit, VI. Spirit,' pp. 263–409, esp. 'A. The True Spirit. Ethical Order,' pp. 266–94.

21 Hegel, *Phenomenology,* 'C. [BB.] Spirit: Culture, II. The Enlightenment,' pp. 328–55 and 'III. Absolute Freedom and Terror,' pp. 355–64. This point and the argument that shall be developed with regard to Hegel and the 'grounding' of *Sittlichkeit* have been drawn from several sources: in the main, from the invaluable scholarship by Charles Taylor, *Hegel,* esp. 'Part IV: History and Politics,' pp. 365–461. See also Shlomo Avineri, *Hegel's Theory of the Modern State*; and the volume edited by Z.A. Pelczynski, *The State and Civil Society: Studies in Hegel's Political Philosophy,* particularly the articles by M.J. Inwood, 'Hegel, Plato and

Greek Sittlichkeit,' pp. 40–54, and Z.A. Pelcyznski, 'Political Community and Individual Freedom in Hegel's Philosophy of State,' pp. 55-76.

22 *Phenomenology*, pp. 328ff, esp. 343–4

23 *Hegel*, p. 401

24 *The Philosophy of Right*, pp. 155–60; see also *Phenomenology*, pp. 356–7,
361–3.

25 *Phenomenology*, pp. 358–60. Cf. *Hegel*, pp. 372–4, 402–8.

26 'It is clear,' writes Taylor, 'that the aspirations to absolute freedom
cannot consort with any articulated differentiation of the society. The
only structures which can be accepted as untouchable are those which
underlie the taking of decisions. But those have to be totally taken by
all. Thus these structures have to be based on and ensure the maximum
homogeneity of citizens. For if all are to take the total decision, then, in
this crucial respect, all are to be seen as identical ... no differentiations
can be allowed which entail different relations to the process of
decision, not even those which would have this as indirect result, such
as inequality of property. The society must be a homogeneous one.'
Hegel, p. 406; see also 403–8.

27 *Philosophy of Right*, p. 157, referenced in *Hegel*, p. 403. But, see also
Phenomenology, p. 359, where Hegel writes: '589. Just as the individual
self-consciousness does not find itself in this *universal work* of absolute
freedom *qua* existent Substance, so little does it find itself in the *deeds*
proper and *individual* actions of the will of this freedom. Before the
universal can perform a deed it must concentrate itself into the One of
individuality and put at the head an individual self-consciousness; for
the universal will is only an *actual* will in a self, which is a One. But
thereby all other individuals are excluded from the entirety of this
deed and have only a limited share in it, so that the deed would not be
a deed of the *actual universal* self-consciousness. Universal freedom,
therefore, can produce neither a positive work nor a deed; there is left
for it only *negative* action; it is merely the *fury* of destruction.'

28 As a point of interest, it is worth noting not only the obvious objections
to the coupling of Kant and Rousseau in the way proposed by Hegel
with its subsequent connection of absolute freedom with that of terror,
but also the objection to Hegel having posited Rousseau's notion of the
general will as leading to 'homogenization.' See, for example, Galvano
della Volpe, 'IV. Clarifications,' in his *Rousseau and Marx: And Other
Writings*, pp. 75–105, and, as well but for entirely different reasons, A
Sher Horowitz, *Rousseau, Nature and History*.

29 *Phenomenology*, 'C. [BB.] Spirit: Culture, III. Absolute Freedom and
Terror,' esp. 586–94, pp. 357–63

30 *Philosophy of Right*, pp. 156–7. See also *Hegel*, pp. 366–72. Taylor writes:
   'This view starts, in a sense, with Rousseau ... It wants to found our
   obligation on the will but in a much more radical sense than Hobbes ...
   This [Kant] proposed to do by applying a purely formal criterion to
   prospective actions, which was binding on the will as rational ... A will
   operating on this principle would be free from any ground of determi-
   nation *(Bestimmungsgrund)* in nature and hence truly free. *A moral
   subject is thus autonomous in a radical sense. He obeys only the dictates of his
   own will. Reason, as rational will, is now the criterion, but in a third sense,
   one opposed to nature,'* pp. 368–9; emphasis, mine.
31 *Phenomenology,*' C. [BB.] Spirit, 'A. The True Spirit. The Ethical Order,'
   pp. 266ff; and esp. pp. 277-8
32 See also the second and third parts of his *Philosophy of Right*, particularly 'Morality,' pp. 75-104; 'The Civil Society,' pp. 104-10 and 122–55; and
   'The State,' pp. 155–223. Cf. *Hegel*, 'Ethical Substance,' pp. 365–88, and
   'The Realised State,' pp. 428–61.
33 *Hegel*, p. 430; compare *Philosophy of Right*, 3, 'The Good and Conscience,
   [135], pp. 39–90. See also *Phenomenology*, 'C. [AA.] Reason: b. Reason as
   Lawgiver,' 402, pp. 252–3; and 'C. [BB.] Spirit: a. Culture and Its Realm
   of Actuality,' (507)–(526), pp. 308–21.
34 *Philosophy of Right*, (Second Part), Morality: 'III. Good and Conscience,'
   135, p. 89, as referenced in *Hegel*, p. 430; see also *Hegel*, pp. 377–85.
35 *Hegel*, p. 430
36 *Hegel*, p. 376
37 K. Marx, 'Theses on Feuerbach,' pp. 12–13

Chapter Two

1 Antonio Gramsci, *Quaderni del carcere*, II, 11:33, 'Questioni generali,' pp.
   1447, 1448; cross-reference to the annotated English edition: Antonio
   Gramsci, *Selections from the Prison Notebooks*, p. 431. Hereafter, all
   references to Gramsci's prison notebooks will be to the standard
   edition in Italian and in the form shown above, indicating the volume
   number, followed by the notebook number, section, title (where given),
   and page number. Wherever possible cross-reference will be made to
   the English edition, referred to as *Prison Notebooks*, followed by section,
   title (where given), and page number.
2 For an overall review of the variety and complexity of the debates
   around this problem of locating the politically correct Gramsci of the
   Quaderni, these few articles and books still remain pertinent: Alastair
   Davidson's 'Gramsci and Reading Machiavelli,' as well as his later
   book, *Antonio Gramsci: Towards An Intellectual Biography*; Joseph Femia's

'Hegemony and Consciousness in the Thought of Antonio Gramsci';
Chantal Mouffe and A. Showstack-Sassoon, 'Gramsci in France and
Italy: A Review of the Literature'; and Phil Cozens's *Twenty Years of
Antonio Gramsci: A Bibliography of Gramsci and Gramsci Studies Published
in English, 1957–1977.*

3. This is not to imply that censorship or, indeed, prison life itself did not
take an exacting toll on Gramsci's physical and mental well-being.
Rather, it is to suggest that some scholars have become so struck by the
repressive brutality of his imprisonment that it becomes an explanatory
feature not only of why Gramsci relied on using code names for Lenin
(Ilich) or Trotsky (Bronstein), for example, but for his having used
unfamiliar concepts or those originating in philosophical systems
unrelated to marxism, as if they, too, are part of a code. It must be
stated that sometimes he did, indeed, use code names and phrases to
camouflage his work, making the assessment of that work all the more
difficult. But it must be stressed that he also used these phrases to
specify – and not camouflage – certain concepts often seen as contradictory or, in any case, not specifically related to marxism. For commentary on his use of code, see Lynn Lawner's 'General Introduction'
to *Prison Notebooks*, pp. xxi–xxv. For a sympathetic but critical approach
to the related problems of romanticizing Gramsci's prison writing, see,
for example, the excellent article by F. Rosengarten, 'Three Essays on
Antonio Gramsci's *Letters from Prison.*'

4 Various attempts to uncover the 'real' Gramsci are scattered throughout the literature. Well-known discussions placing the *Quaderni* as
fragmented leninism can be traced back to literature dealing with the
debates within the Italian Communist Party (PCI). See for example R.
Alcara, *La formazione e i primi anni del Partito communista italiano nella
storiografia marxista*, as well as A. Pozzolini, *Antonio Gramsci: An
Introduction to His Thought*. In that regard, see also Palmiro Togliatti,
Gramsci, and the later English edition, *On Gramsci and Other Writings*.
Also of importance here is the earlier work of Carl Boggs, *Gramsci's
Marxism*, where he characterizes Gramsci as an 'Italian Lenin.' Later, in
his *The Two Revolutions: Gramsci and the Dilemmas of Western Marxism*,
Boggs retracts the singularity of this vision.

For a characterization of Gramsci as falling somewhere 'between'
Croce and Lenin, see the earlier work of Ruggero Orfei, *Antonio
Gramsci: Coscienza critica del marxismo*. For a rigorous attempt at moving
the interpretation of Gramsci's work beyond PCI leninism, see for
example Christine Buci-Glucksmann, *Gramsci and the State*, where her
interpretation is framed in terms of an althusserian/structuralist slant.
For an account of Gramsci's work that tries to contextualize the various

debates on all sides of the political spectrum, see the important and extremely accessible volume edited by Chantal Mouffe, *Gramsci and Marxist Theory*. See also G.C. Jocteau, *Leggere Gramsci: Una guida alle interpretazioni*.

In what some have characterized as a backlash against official translations of both the PCI and those who sought to read Gramsci as a leninist, several articles and books have appeared, which, in trying to recuperate the complex nuances of Gramsci's thought lost in the earlier interpretations, replaced the various characterizations of leninism with that of idealism. See, for example, the early discussion by E. Genovese, 'Review of John Cammett's *Antonio Gramsci and the Origins of the Italian Communist Party*.' Also see the well-known article by Paul Piccone, 'Gramsci's Hegelian-Marxism,' whose arguments presenting a hegelian Gramsci are forwarded in a book Piccone co-edited with Pedro Cavalcanti, *History, Philosophy, and Culture in the Young Gramsci*. Of interest here, too, is Maurice Finocchiaro, 'Gramsci's Crocean Marxism,' whose argument is reflected at greater length in Piccone's more recent book, *Italian Marxism*.

5 These terms will be explored in more detail later in this chapter, but for a general indication of the way in which they will be used, particularly with regard to the more complex concept of ethico-political hegemony and the society it implies, see his remarks in *Quaderni* III, 13: 1 pp. 1556–61; *Prison Notebooks*, 'The Modern Prince: Brief Notes on Machiavelli's Politics,' pp. 126–33.

6 *Quaderni* II, 10: 54, pp. 1343–6; *Prison Notebooks*, pp. 351–7

7 *Quaderni* II, 11: 17, p. 1411; *Prison Notebooks*, pp. 440–1

8 *Quaderni* II, 13: 10, p. 1486; *Prison Notebooks*, p. 346

9 See also *Quaderni* II, 10: 40, pp. 1290–1; *Prison Notebooks*, pp. 367–8. It is also worth noting that Gramsci's insistence on the concept of a 'fluxed' terrain of history, as well as that of truth as being a part of (rather than 'external' to) the political is quite similar to the foucauldian notion of discursive subjectivity, indeed, to the notion of discourse itself. This point will be explored in chapter 6, but, for a preliminary indication of Foucault's use of inside/outside and his notion of discontinuity, see Michel Foucault, *Maurice Blanchot: The Thought from Outside*, pp. 9–58.

10 'Theses on Feuerbach,' particularly nos 1, 3, 5, 6, and 11

11 'Cleanse' is precisely the word Gramsci uses when referring to a resystematizing of idealist, transcendental, or positivist philosophy for use in a philosophy of praxis. Cf. *Quaderni* II, 11: 30, p. 1443; *Prison Notebooks*, p. 466

12 *Quaderni* II, 7: 33, 'Posizione del problema'; 11: 7, 'Antonio Labriola'; and *Quaderni* III, 16: 2, 'Questioni di metodo,' pp. 881, 1507–9, and

1840–4, respectively; *Prison Notebooks*, pp. 361, 386–8, 382–6, respectively. It should be noted here that this reliance on Vico is not an original position of Gramsci but can be found in the work of Marx as well as Labriola. See for example J. O'Neill, 'On the History of the Human Senses in Vico and Marx.'

13 Vico's most well-known work, *The New Science*, went through several editions where various changes occurred in the logic. But the most profound break occurred in the 1730 version (revised slightly in 1744 and republished as the third edition). Unless otherwise noted, all references to Vico's argumentation have been taken from this later edition: *The New Science of Giambattista Vico: Translated from the Third Edition [1744]*, hereafter cited as *The New Science (III)*.

14 Benedetto Croce, *The Philosophy of Giambattista Vico*, pp. 2, 5. Cf. *Quaderni* II, 11: 54, p. 1482; earlier version: 8: 199, 'Unita della teoria e della practica,' p. 1060; *Prison Notebooks*, p. 364

15 Giambattista Vico, *The Selected Writings of Giambattista Vico*, pp. 104–28. See also Henry Packwood Adams, *The Life and Writings of Giambattista Vico*, esp. ch. 13 and 14, pp. 147–71 and pp. 183–93, respectively.

16 Vico, *The New Science (1725)*, para. 321 and 137 as cited in *Prison Notebooks*, p. 35 n11

17 Vico, *Selected Writings*, pp. 84–91

18 Ibid, pp. 91–101

19 Vico, *The New Science (III)*, esp. Book 4, Section IX: 'Three Kinds of Reason,' pp. 313–16, and Section X: 'Three Kinds of Judgments,' pp. 317–18, 321–4. See also Croce, *Vico*, pp. 24–35, as well as Isaiah Berlin, *Vico and Herder: Two Studies in the History of Ideas*, both of whom address this point directly.

20 Croce, *Vico*, pp. 32, 33–5. On this point, see also Alfonsina Grimaldi, *The Universal Humanity of Giambattista Vico*, pp. 247–53.

21 For an extended discussion of this point, see in particular Berlin, *Vico and Herder*, pp. 99–142.

22 Vico, *The New Science (III)*, 40–42, pp. 21–3, and the concluding sections of the work, 1097–1112, pp. 377–83, respectively. See also Berlin, *Vico and Herder*, pp. 21–41.

23 Vico's connection between science and human activity was read by Croce as a way to establish the argument that, as with history, morality and ethics were also products of knowledge, and as such could never be 'arbitrary' or 'irrational.' Indeed, ethics and morality were, instead, the epitome of rational thought. The ramifications of this position, and Gramsci's response to it, will be considered below.

24 Croce, *Vico*, esp. ch. 9 and 13, pp. 103–4, respectively. It is interesting to note that Gramsci will embellish Vico's notion of accessibility and

creativity with Bergson's theory of relativity, much of which is outlined
in Bergson's *The Creative Mind*, esp. pp. 33–106. We will return to
Bergson's influence in chapter 4.

25 As Gramsci will put it, 'task becomes duty; will becomes free': human
emancipation begins with recognizing the extent to which one is part
of – and not simply 'subjected' to – history. In so recognizing this, it
becomes clearer how (and why) individuals themselves can be empowered and can begin to articulate strategies for change. We will come
back to this point in the next chapter, but see in particular *Quaderni* II,
7: 4, p. 855; *Prison Notebooks*, pp. 409–10. For a related point from a
different vantage, see for example Thomas Nemeth, *Gramsci's Philosophy: A Critical Study*. Nemeth, albeit interpreting Gramsci, in part,
through the work of Husserl, underscores a similar connection to Vico,
but goes farther and connects Gramsci to Dilthey. 'Thus, we find
Gramsci close indeed to the Vico-Dilthey contention that man under-
stands best what he himself has created' (p. 104).

26 While this point, and the consequences that follow, will be examined in
detail below, it should be mentioned at the outset that it forms one of
the fundamental arguments in Croce's four-volume *The Philosophy of
Spirit*, in particular, Vol. 2, *Logic as the Science of the Pure Concept*.

27 This point is brought to bear more fully in Croce's *Vico*, pp. 5–6. But see
also Hoare and Smith's comment regarding this point in *Prison
Notebooks*, p. 364 n53.

28 *Quaderni* III, 13: 10 and 13: 13, and *Quaderni* II, 11: 52, pp. 1568–70, 1572–
6, and 1477–81, respectively; *Prison Notebooks*, pp. 136–8, 140–3, and
410–14, respectively.

29 This explication of Croce's 'peculiar' rendering of Hegel has been
developed, in the main, from two of his works: Croce's *What Is Living
and What Is Dead in the Philosophy of Hegel*, and his *Logic as the Science of
Pure Concept*. As mentioned earlier, the *Logic* was the second in a series
of his four-volume *The Philosophy of Spirit*. Volume 1, *Aesthetic as Science
of Expression and General Linguistic*, and Volume 3, *The Philosophy of the
Practical (Economic and Ethic)*, are drawn upon as well in this chapter,
but to a much lesser extent.

30 Croce, *Logic*, p. 305

31 Ibid, pp. 303–9

32 Ibid, pp. 310–26, 579–80, 582

33 Indeed, the whole of Croce's *Logic*, and to a lesser extent his *Philosophy
of the Practical* and the *Aesthetic*, are devoted to explicating this point at
length. See, in particular, *Logic*, pp. 493–509. An interesting discussion
of this point can be found in Wilden H. Carr, *The Philosophy of Benedetto
Croce: The Problem of Art and History*, pp. 19–20, 24, 80–1, 89.

34 *Aesthetic*, pp. 230–1, 232. See also Croce, 'Pure Intuition and the Lyrical

Character of Art,' a lecturer delivered at Heidelberg at the second
general session of the Third International Congress of Philosophy,
reprinted as an appendix to his *Aesthetic*, pp. 371–403.

35 *What Is Living and What Is Dead*, pp. 175–91, 203–17
36 Ibid
37 *Quaderni* II, 11: 17 and 11: 64, pp. 1411–16 and 1491–2; *Prison Notebooks*,
   pp. 440–6 and 371–2, respectively. See also A. Lepre, *Gramsci secondo
   Gramsci*, esp. pp. 65–135.
38 *Logic*, pp. 603–6. For Croce's detailed development of Kant's a priori
   synthetic judgment as related to the hegelian dialectic, see *Logic*, pp.
   532–41, 571, 572–82.
39 For this point I have relied on the contributions of Merle E. Brown in
   his *Neo-Idealistic Aesthetics: Croce-Gentile-Collingwood*, esp. pp. 29–33.
40 *What Is Living and What Is Dead*, pp. 88–99; *Logic*, pp. 91–107, 204–6,
   213–17, 224–31, 463–5, 528–9. The question of 'distincts' in Gramsci's
   work will be raised in chapter 3 and discussed in more detail in chapter
   5, but see *Quaderni* II, 10: 41, pp. 1315–17, as well J. Nemeth's comments
   in his *Gramsci's Philosophy*, pp. 165–9.
41 *Logic*, p. 95; see also *What Is Living and What Is Dead*, p. 25. It must be
   stated here that Croce saw no problem with understanding the
   complexity of the hegelian dialectic as a simple triad, a point many
   Hegel scholars would be hard-pressed to accept In fact, almost the
   whole of *What Is Living and What Is Dead* is based on this interpretation,
   a reading that allows Croce to conclude, in his typically sardonic tone:
   'it sometimes seemed as if Hegel was not in full possession of his
   thoughts' (p. 191).
42 *What Is Living and What Is Dead*, pp. 90–9, 100–19
43 Ibid, pp. 25–6
44 *Logic*, pp. 535–9. See also his 'Fake Application of the Dialectic (a, a–),
   in *Logic*, pp. 101ff; and, as well, his 'Dualism Not Overcome,' in *What Is
   Living and What Is Dead*, pp. 193ff.
45 *Logic*, pp. 43–53, 66–7, 72–9. See also Carr, *The Philosophy of B. Croce*, pp.
   84–91.
46 *Logic*, pp. 76, 77–9, 83, 91–9
47 Ibid, pp. 204–31, 330–55, and 391–405. Since this discussion is only
   meant to highlight the implications Croce draws from his conception of
   distincts, suffice it to say that the distincts and the relation they have to
   concrete universals ('being,' as mentioned above, or even as in 'truth,'
   or in terms of the abstract relation they underscore in notions such as
   the 'useful' and 'good') help Croce to resituate the notion of subject/
   predicate in both Hegel and Kant, and allow him, as a consequence, to
   incorporate a more nuanced concept of negation.
48 *Logic*, pp. 108–20. According to Croce, this reading of Kant meant that

Kant was attempting to argue that when making a 'true' rather than a 'pseudo' judgment, the subject of that judgment would always already be predicated on something. So, if one were to say that 'A is pleasant,' one would imply that the existence of A itself is expressed, 'at least and always,' to use Croce's summation, as an act of thought. Thus Croce writes: 'The *a priori* synthesis is a unity of necessary and contingent, of concept and intuition, of thought and presentation, it is thus the pure concept; the concrete-universal': Croce, *Logica*, p. 374, as cited in Carr, *The Philosophy of B. Croce*, p. 93.

49 *Logic*, p. 173. We will bracket for the moment the problem of totality inherent in Kant's positing of an a priori synthetic unity, which Croce quite obviously accepts.

50 *Logic*, p. 173

51 Ibid, pp. 17–8. See also the third part of his *Logic*, 'The Forms of Error and the Search for Truth,' pp. 391ff.

52 See, in particular, the *Logic* once again, where Croce, lapsing into some kind of metaphoric dilettantism, launches into an explanation of truth and error in terms of the almighty devil himself: to wit, that the spirit that 'errs' cannot (like 'the devil') stand 'the light of truth' and, therefore, attempts to 'flee' from it. That spirit, however can and 'must be converted into the spirit of search ... [For] Truth, to one who searches, is at the top of the staircase of errors' (pp. 467–8); compare pp. 466–78. For a sustained critique of Croce's entire concept of distincts, see, for example, Brown's *Neo-Idealist Aesthetics*, pp. 44–77.

53 *Logic*, pp. 463–5, 79

54 Ibid, pp. 605–6

55 For an expanded discussion and supportive critique of this 'gradation,' see, for example, Carr, *The Philosophy of B. Croce*, pp. 57ff.

56 Ibid, pp. 136–7

57 The whole of Croce's *Aesthetic* is written to underscore this point, but see, in particular, *Aesthetic*, pp. 77–89; cf. Carr, *The Philosophy of B. Croce*, pp. 99–135.

58 Although almost the entirety of the *Philosophy of the Practical* argues this point, see, in particular, pp. 33–52. It should also be stated here – though it will become quite obvious when we reach Gramsci's usage of it – that Croce's notion of the will is markedly different from Gramsci's development of it.

59 *Practical*, pp. 309–22, 348–63. This is a somewhat layered point with regard to Gramsci's work and as such we will take it up again later in this chapter and in more detail still in chapter 3. But it is worth mentioning at this point that Gramsci's directive to 'make more

coherent a collective will' so as to produce an 'ethico-political' society, might appear substantively similar to Croce's rendition of the ethical-political, and, of course, in certain ways it is quite similar. For some, this seemingly direct parallelism is precisely the 'proof' needed to raise suspicions that eventually cast the 'real' Gramsci as a speculative idealist cleverly camouflaged as a marxist-leninist or, at the very minimum, as a marxist with speculative 'tendencies.' As we shall see, this is another example of mistaken identity, but not for the reasons usually cited. See for example, the very well-argued discussion in R. Kilminster, *Praxis and Method: A Sociological Dialogue with Lukacs, Gramsci and the Early Frankfurt School*, pp. 119–22.

60 In particular see 'Philosophy, History, and the Natural and Mathematical Sciences,' in Croce's *Logic*, Part 2, pp. 247ff; see also *Practical*, pp. xvii–xix.

61 *Logic*, pp. 247–390 and 603–6; and *Practical*, pp. 33–72

62 *Practical*, pp. 33 and 33–4. See also pp. 183–91; compare *Logic*, pp. 342–61. While this point will be drawn out in full in terms of Gramsci's usage of it, see also Gramsci's discussions in both 'The Modern Prince' and 'Problems in Marxism: Passage from Knowing to Understanding and to Feeling and vice versa from Feeling to Understanding to Knowing,' *Quaderni* III, 13: 1, pp. 1555–61; and *Quaderni* II, 11: 67, pp. 1505–6, respectively; *Prison Notebooks*, pp. 125–33 and 418–19.

63 *Logic*, pp. 395, 466–78; cf. Carr, *The Philosophy of B. Croce* pp. 7–22. For a fuller discussion on this point, see also Croce's *History as the Story of Liberty*.

64 In the context of his naming of the practical and theoretic moments of Spirit and the twofold degree, see Croce's *Aesthetic*, pp. 36–52.

65 See also the essay by G.R.G. Mure, 'The Economic and the Moral in the Philosophy of Benedetto Croce.'

66 *Logic*, pp. 256–8, 310–26. The subsequent comments in the text are, in part, also drawn from Carr, *The Philosophy of B. Croce*, pp. 151–2.

67 To be clear and to the point, this meant an *idealized* history, rather than a *historicized* idealism, a point that Gramsci will try to 'correct' when discussing the marxist dialectic and, concomitantly, the base-superstructure relation.

68 *Logic*, pp. 579, 581–2

69 Ibid, pp. 605, 606

70 For a useful assessment from a historical materialist standpoint that neatly counteracts this argument, see, for example, Dick Howard, *From Marx to Kant*.

71 *History as the Story of Liberty*, pp. 59–62

72 For a typical example of Croce's attack on the communist left, see, in particular, his 'The Bourgeoisie: An Ill-Defined Historical Concept,' in his *Politics and Morals*, pp. 155–82.

73 For Croce's half-hearted attack on Locke and Hobbes, as well as on J.S. Mill (half-hearted because he disagreed so profoundly with them), see, in particular, his *Logic*, pp. 530–48. Indeed, by the time Croce reflects on the work of Mill, his half-hearted attack turns into a high-pitched frenzy; to wit: 'With this Empiricism is associated the deplorable *Logic* of John Stuart Mill, one of those books which do the least honour to the human spirit. That less than mediocre reasoner does not even succeed in producing a logic of the natural science ... [And nothing] is more puerile than his nominalism': *Logic*, pp. 547–8.

74 G. P Calabro, *Antoni Gramsci: La 'transizione' politica*, especially the introductory chapter and ch. 3.

75 The political assumptions implicit in the way Croce develops the concept of liberty (not to mention that of 'necessity,' the 'will,' and the 'ethico-political morality') are highly problematic, being labelled by some as a 'friendly' form of fascism. Though Croce never explicitly writes directly in support of the fascists it is true that Croce's adulation of Mussolini becomes less closeted after the publication of his *Philosophy of Spirit*, and in particular in Part 1 of his *History as the Story of Liberty*, pp. 15–64. For a jubilant account of his theoretical positions giving specific credence, if not outright support, to the fascist rule in Italy, see also Croce's 'Liberalism as a Concept of Life' and 'Free Enterprise and Liberalism,' in his *Politics and Morals*, pp. 111–25 and 147–54, respectively.

76 *Practical*, pp. 364–90

77 Croce did not always have such a dim view of historical materialism, at least early in his career. See for example his *Historical Materialism and the Economics of Karl Marx*. This small collection of essays, written between 1896 and 1900, is an attempt by Croce to find the 'living' part of marxist theory and carefully remove it from what the good doctor called the 'false' tissue surrounding it. As noted earlier, a similar surgical procedure was happily performed on Hegel. Gramsci's wry comment on Croce's change of heart sums it up: 'It also appears from this letter that the position of Croce, held a few years ago on the subject of historical materialism, has completely changed. Now Croce dares to maintain that historical materialism marks a return to a kind of medieval theology and to pre-Kantian and pre-Cartesian philosophy. This is really astonishing and makes one wonder whether he is not perhaps, in spite of his Olympian serenity, dozing off a little too often, more often than Homer did ... Croce's position in relation to historical materialism is similar to that of men of the Renaissance toward the

Lutheran Reformation. "When Luther enters, civilization disappears", said Erasmus; and yet, today, historians, even Croce himself, recognised that Luther and the Reformation were the beginning of all modern philosophy and civilization, including Croce's own philosophy': In a letter to Tatiana Schucht, 1 December 1930, in Gramsci, *Letters from Prison*, no. 51, pp. 189–90.

78 *Quaderni* III, 13: 1, p. 1557; *Prison Notebooks*, pp. 127–8

79 Gramsci, *Letters from Prison*, no. 68, 9 May 1932, Turi, pp. 236–8

80 See, for example, the remarks by Lynne Lawner in her 'Introduction' to Gramsci's *Letters from Prison*, p. 47.

81 *Letters from Prison*, pp. 237–8

82 Ibid

83 Ibid, p. 238

84 *Quaderni* II, 10: 9, pp. 1227–8; *Prison Notebooks*, pp. 118–19, where he writes: 'is it fortuitous or is it a tendentious motive, that Croce begins his narrative from 1815 and 1871; i.e., that he excludes the moment of struggle; the moment in which the conflicting forces are formed, are assembled and take up their positions; the moment in which one ethical-political system dissolves and another is formed by fire and steel? ... The problem arises of whether this Crocean construction, in its tendentious nature, does not have a contemporary and immediate reference ... But, in the present conditions is it not precisely the fascist movement of moderate and conservative liberalism in the last century?'

85 Croce, 'Protest against the Fascist Intellectuals,' *La Critica* 23 (1925), 310–12, as referenced in Giovanni Gentile's *The Philosophy of Art*, pp. xvi–xvii. It is interesting to note that Croce's 'protest' was directed against Gentile's having insisted on 'mixing party politics with philosophical speculation,' and not against fascism per se.

86 *Letters from Prison*, p. 236

87 As we will see, Gramsci completely alters Croce's meaning of 'immanence,' of the 'will,' and of the ethical-political, all of which we will explore in greater detail in later chapters. But, for a general indication of the argument, see also *Quaderni* II, 10: 6, 'La filosofia di B. Croce: Introduzione allo studio della filosofia,' pp. 1244–5; *Prison Notebooks*, pp. 366–7.

88 *Quaderni* II, 7: 33, p. 881; *Prison Notebooks*, p. 381

Chapter Three

1 *Quaderni* II, 11 (II): 14, 'Sulla metafisica,' pp. 1401–2; *Prison Notebooks*, 'On Metaphysics,' p. 436

2 Bukharin, *Historical Materialism: A System of Sociology*, referred to by

Gramsci in the *Quaderni* as the *Popular Manual*. All subsequent references to it will use Gramsci's title.

3 *Quaderni* II, 6: 79, p. 750

4 For two of his earliest statements on the problem, couched in an attack against a dogmatic reading of marxism, see Gramsci, 'La Citta Futura,' in P. Spriano, ed., *Scritti Politici* (Roma: Emuadi 1967), pp. 42–6, and 'La Rivoluzioni contro il "Capitale," ' in *Avanti!*, 24 December 1917, in ibid, pp. 80–3, reprinted in A. Gramsci, *Selections from Political Writings, 1910–1920*, pp. 34–7.

5 The whole of notebook 13, 'Notrelle sul Machiavelli,' tackles this problem, but, in particular, 13: 10, pp. 1568–70; *Prison Notebooks*, pp. 136–8. For an account of Gramsci's pre-prison comments on this point, see, in particular, Giuseppe Fiori, *Antonio Gramsci: Life of a Revolutionary*.

6 *Quaderni* III 13: 10, pp. 1568–9; *Prison Notebooks*, p. 137

7 This emphasis by Gramsci contrasts to the well-known problem of taking as a starting-point the question of concept *as if* unitary, homogeneous, or pre-established. This view of concept can only lead to an abstractionism that excludes the historical process itself, a point Marx addresses directly in *The Grundrisse*, pp. 100–7.

8 *Quaderni* II, 7: 35, pp. 883–6; *Prison Notebooks*, pp. 354–7

9 Theorists such as Althusser and Balibar take exception to what they perceive to be an analysis of the political that, in proposing an 'absolute historicism,' leads to a kind of relativity devoid of certain fundamental truths. They argue, in part, that accepting an absolute historicism would destroy, ipso facto, the notion of science appropriate to a marxist epistemology. This is a serious complaint and is taken up in detail in the discussion on science later in this chapter. For their position on the matter, see, in particular, L. Althusser and E. Balibar, *Reading Capital*.

10 *Quaderni* II, 11: 28, 'L'immanenza e la filosofia della praxis,' pp. 1438–9; *Prison Notebooks*, 'Immanence and the Philosophy of Praxis,' pp. 449–52. See also *Quaderni* II, 11: 24, 'Il linguaggio e le metafore,' and 11: 22.IV, pp. 1426–8 and 1424–6, respectively; *Prison Notebooks*, 'The Dialectic,' pp. 450–2 and 434–36, respectively. For a brief comment on the 'distincts,' see also *Quaderni* III, 13: 10, pp. 1568–70; *Prison Notebooks*, pp. 137–8. The actual use by Gramsci of equivalence similar to that found in semiotic appropriation of identity (as representation) has been pointed out by Franco Lo Piparo, *Lingua, intelletuali, e egemonia in Gramsci*.

11 On this point, see C. Donzelli, 'Introduzione a Gramsci,' in A Gramsci, *Quaderno 13, 'Notrelle sulla politica del Machiavelli,'* pp. ix–cii.

12 *Quaderni* II, 11: 24, 'Il linguaggio e le metafore,' pp. 1427–8, *Prison Notebooks*, pp. 450–2; and 11: 16, 'Quistioni di nomenclatura e di contenuto,' pp. 1406–11, *Prison Notebooks*, pp. 452–7. Gramsci is not suggesting, given this totalized notion of 'reality,' that that which is unknown to man is consequently 'external' to reality (or, conversely, that all that can be known has already been discovered). That Gramsci insists, on the contrary, that meaning is directly political and historical is precisely a problem raised in the early studies in linguistics, particularly by F. de Saussure, *Course in General Linguistics [1916]*, arguments Gramsci studied at university.

13 *Quaderni* II, 11: 44, 'La tecnica del pensare,' pp. 1462–6

14 *Quaderni* II, 6: 35, 'Pasato e presente: Il fordismo,' pp. 799–800. Gramsci's use of the dialectic as creating a foundation for specificity is discussed in more general terms in an early article written by A. Martinelli, 'In Defense of the Dialectic: Antonio Gramsci's Theory of Revolution.' See also Lucio Colletti, 'Marxism and the Dialectic.'

15 *Quaderni* II, 7: 4, 'Scienza morale e materialismo storico,' p. 855; *Prison Notebooks*, 'Moral Science and Historical Materialism,' p. 410

16 Ibid

17 It should be stressed here that while Gramsci relies throughout the *Quaderni* on the coupling of the 'realm of necessity' with that of 'possibility/freedom,' he is *not* attempting to derive or deduce an ethics out of the concept of necessity per se. After all, it could be argued that the 'final solution' of the Holocaust, indeed the Holocaust itself, could be seen as being 'necessary' from a fascist perspective. Gramsci, utterly opposed to that (functional) conception of necessity, is rather attempting to find a fluid, heterogeneous meaning for truth/ necessity without resorting to an essentialist or idealist framework. See, in particular, *Quaderni* II, 10: 48.1, II, 'Progresso e divenire,' pp. 1335–6; *Prison Notebooks*, 'Progress and Becoming,' pp. 357–60. Also of interest on this point is Gramsci's 'Che cosa e l'uomo?' 10: 54, pp. 1343–6; *Prison Notebooks*, 'What Is Man?' pp. 351–7.

18 See, for example, A. Baldan, *Gramsci come storico: studio sulle fonte del 'Quaderni Del Carcere,'* pp. 4–41. See also Lo Piparo, *Lingua*, especially Part 4, 'La lingua come metafora del sociale e il Quaderno 29,' pp. 237–60.

19 See, for example, Gramsci's comments on Croce's use of *concordia discours*, in his *Letters from Prison*, pp. 242–4, where the question of error, contradiction, and 'openness' is broached. See also *Quaderni* II, 7: 35, 'Materialismo e materialismo storico,' pp. 883–6; *Prison Notebooks*, 'What Is Man?' pp. 354–7.

20 *Quaderni* II, 11: 21, 30, and 36, pp. 1420–2, 1422–5, and 1451–5, respectively; *Prison Notebooks*, pp. 457–8, 465–8, and as 'Science and "Scientific" Ideologies,' translated by M.A. Finocchiaro, *Telos* 39 (Spring 1979), 151–5, respectively. For an elaborated discussion on this point, see also, for example, Joseph Femia, *Gramsci's Political Thought: Hegemony, Consciousness and the Revolutionary Process.*

21 *Quaderni* III, 13: 20 and (earlier formulation) *Quaderni* I, 4: 8, 'Machiavelli e Marx,' pp. 1598–1601 and 430–1; *Prison Notebooks*, 'Machiavelli and Marx,' pp. 133–6

22 *Quaderni* III, 20: 4, 'Cattolici integrali, gesuiti, modernisti,' pp. 2101–3

23 Gramsci's attack on a 'formalistic' reading of marxism-leninism and the problems such a reading generated is raised against a variety of targets, including, for example, Leon Trotsky. Gramsci accuses him of maintaining a kind of formalism that poses class struggle as if always part of a 'permanent revolution,' regardless of the size and type of capitalist development. See for example the *Prison Notebooks*, pp. 165–6, and the comment by Hoare and Smith, p. 165, n64.

24 'Letter to Togliatti,' Moscow, 18 May 1923, in A. Gramsci, *Selections from Political Writing, 1921–26*, p. 140.

25 *Quaderni* II, 8: 195, 'La proposizone che "la societa non si pone problemi per la cui soluzione non esistano gia le premesse materiali,"' pp. 1057–8; *Prison Notebooks*, 'Number and Quality in Representative Systems of Government,' pp. 194–5. Reference also to Antonio Labriola, *Socialism and Philosophy*, esp. ch. 7, 'Science and "Scientific" Marxism,' pp. 115–24. While we will touch on this in greater detail, shortly, it should also be mentioned that this set of equivalences (in this case, history = politics) is pointing to, among other things, the complex mediation between the two, derived, in part, from Marx's 'Theses on Feuerbach,' as well as from the proposition outlined in the 'Preface to The Contribution to a Critique of Political Economy.'

26 *Quaderni* II, 10: 2, 'Identita di storia e filosofia,' pp. 1241–2; *Quaderni* III, 13: 10, p. 1569; *Prison Notebooks*, 'Politics as an Autonomous Science,' p. 137

27 *Quaderni* II, 7: 35, 'Materialismo e materialismo storico,' p. 885; *Prison Notebooks*, 'What Is Man?' p. 355 (bracketed remark as footnote 42 in the translation)

28 While Gramsci clearly sought to theorize the 'specificity' of the political moment, i.e., its historical concreteness, the phrase 'specificity of the political' is not precisely a gramscian term, and it certainly was not popularized by him. Its familiarity and, indeed, profound implications were established and clarified by Laclau in the well-known

Poulantzas and Miliband debates. See Ernesto Laclau, 'The Specificity of the Political,' in *Politics and Ideology in Marxist Theory: Capitalism-Fascism-Populism*, pp. 51–79. See also S. Hall, B. Lumley, and G. McLennan, 'Politics and Ideology: Gramsci,' as well as E. Hobsbawn, 'Gramsci and Marxist Political Theory.' Of particular note as well, see also Chantal Mouffe, 'Hegemony and the Integral State in Gramsci: Towards a New Concept of Politics.'

29 The following discussion on Gramsci's use of 'science' has been drawn primarily from *Quaderni* II, 11: 30, pp. 1442–5; *Prison Notebooks*, pp. 465–8; as well as 11: 15, pp. 1403–5; *Prison Notebooks*, pp. 437–40. In terms of the 'real' dialectic, immanence, and the question of the ethical-political, see, for example, *Quaderni* II, 10: 48. II, 'Progresso e divenire,' p. 1338; *Prison Notebooks*, 'Progress and Becoming,' p. 360. See also *Quaderni* II, 11: 59, p. 1485, *Prison Notebooks*, p. 345; as well as 11: 12, Note II–IV, pp. 1376–80, *Prison Notebooks*, pp. 324–7.

30 *Quaderni* II, 11: 15, 'Il concetto di "scienza",' pp. 1403–6; 10: 48.II, 'Progresso e divenire,' pp. 1335–8; and 11: 59, pp. 1485–6; *Prison Notebooks*, 'The Concept of Science,' 'What Is Man?' ' "Creative" Philosophy,' pp. 437–40, 357–60, and 345–6, respectively.

31 *Quaderni* II, 11: 50, 'Storia della terminologia e della metafore,' pp. 1473–6. See also 10: 27, 'Punti di meditazione per lo studio dell'economia,' p. 1265; *Prison Notebooks*, p. 400 n39.

32 *Quaderni* II, 11: 29, 'Lo "strumento tecnico",' pp. 1439–42; *Prison Notebooks*, 'The "Technical Instrument",' pp. 458–62

33 *Quaderni* II, 11: 66, pp. 1495–6. See also E. Bernstein, *Evolutionary Socialism: A Criticism and an Affirmation*, and, of course, Lenin's well-known attack on this position in V. Lenin, 'State and Revolution: The Marxist Theory of the State and the Tasks of the Proletariat in Revolution,' *Selected Works*, pp. 264–351.

34 *Quaderni* II, 16: 25, pp. 1988–9

35 General critiques of Loria's position run throughout the *Quaderni*, but see, for example, *Quaderni* III, 28 (III), 'Lorianismo,' pp. 2321–37; earlier version: *Quaderni* I, I, pp. 20–2

36 Loria, *Marx*, pp. 87–8

37 *Quaderni* IV, 28, esp. pp. 2321–6. All discussions in this notebook are directed against *lorianismo*. See also *Quaderni* III, 15: 74, pp. 1833–4 and 17: 40, p. 1942. See also *Letters from Prison*, no. 42, p. 163, and its addendum note.

38 We will be returning to this question of 'technical instrument' and Gramsci's conception of class later in the chapter, and in greater detail in chapter 5, but it is worthwhile noting that a statement of the

problem pre-dating the *Quaderni* can be found in the debate between Tasca and Gramsci over the role of 'class' and class struggle in the formation of the factory council movement., See A. Gramsci, *Selections from Political Writings, 1910–1920*, especially Tasca's attack (12 and 19 June and 3 July 1920), pp. 269–90, and Gramsci's response (14 and 28 August 1920), pp. 291–7.

39 *Quaderni* II, 11: 12, pp. 1388, 1389; *Prison Notebooks*, pp. 336–7. See also the entire fragment, 'Alcuni punti preliminari di riferimento,' pp. 1375–98; general selections in *Prison Notebooks*, pp. 323–43.

40 *Quaderni* II, 11: 70, pp. 1507–9; *Prison Notebooks*, pp. 386–8

41 *Quaderni* II, 11: 70, p. 1508; *Prison Notebooks*, p. 387. In the same fragment, Gramsci dismisses those marxists who tried to counter Plekhanov by relying on Kant and other philosophers. Of Otto Bauer and the other 'Austro-marxists,' Gramsci writes: '2. The orthodox tendency has determined the growth of its opposite: the tendency to connect the philosophy of praxis to Kantianism and to other non-positivist and non-materialist philosophical tendencies. This reached its "agnostic" conclusion with Otto Bauer, who writes his book on religion that Marxism can be supported and integrated by any philosophy, even Thomism. This second tendency is not really a tendency in the strict sense, but an *ensemble* of all the tendencies – including the Freudianism of De Man – that do not accept the so-called "orthodoxy" of Germanic pedantry.' As we shall note shortly, Gramsci challenges both tendencies of this kind of 'orthodox' marxism.

42 Gramsci is clearly following Marx (and Engels) on this point. Apart from Marx's 'Theses on Feuerbach,' cited earlier, see, for example, Engels's well-known summation of the problem in his 'Socialism: Utopian and Scientific.' For a useful synopsis of these debates, see also the well-known work by Leszek Kolakowski, 'Socialist Ideas in the First Half of the Nineteenth Century as Compared with Marxian Socialism,' in *Main Currents of Marxism*, Vol. 1, pp. 183–233, esp. pp. 218–24.

43 An analogous point is raised in Alvin Gouldner's early discussion on the need for a 'qualitative' methodology that can get beyond 'technical' positivism. See A. Gouldner, *The Coming Crisis of Western Sociology.* But see also Darko Suvin, 'On Two Notions of "Science" in Marxism.'

44 K. Marx, *The Poverty of Philosophy: Answer to the 'Philosophy of Poverty' by M. Proudhon*, p. 161

45 *Quaderni* II, 11 (II): 14, 'Sulla metafisica,' pp. 1401–2; *Prison Notebooks*, 'On Metaphysics,' p. 436

46 *Quaderni* II, 11: 22.III, 'Questioni generali,' p. 1424; *Prison Notebooks*, 'Science and System,' p. 434, where he writes: '[Bukharin's] vulgar

contention is that science must absolutely mean "system", and consequently, systems of all sorts are built up which have only the mechanical exteriority of a system and not its necessary coherence.' See also *Quaderni* II 9: 59, 'Nozioni enciclopediche. Empirisimo,' p. 1131, as one of his most direct assaults on 'empiricism' as a category of truth.

47 *Quaderni* II, 11: 31, 'La causa ultima'; 11: 14, 'Sulla metafisica,' pp. 1445 and 1401–3, respectively; *Prison Notebooks*, combined in 'On Metaphysics,' pp. 436–7

48 *Quaderni* II, 11: 17, 'La cosí detta "realtà del mondo esterno," ' p. 1412; *Prison Notebooks*, 'The So-Called "Reality" of the External World,' p. 442

49 *Quaderni* II, 11: 14, 'Sulla metafisica,' p. 1403; *Prison Notebooks*, 'On Metaphysics,' p. 437

50 *Quaderni* II, 11: 14, 'Sulla metafisica,' pp. 1402–3; *Prison Notebooks*, 'On Metaphysics,' p. 437; emphasis mine

51 Ibid, 'Sulla metafisica,' pp. 1401–3; *Prison Notebooks*, pp. 436–7

52 As will be discussed shortly, Gramsci attempts to circumvent this problem by resituating the identity of the rational and the real in the context of an objectivity which can never be divorced from historical error and, therewith, from its subjective political moment. To do otherwise, argues Gramsci, is simply to fall into the trap of deducing future possibilities from abstract and empty truths. 'And how could prediction be an act of knowledge,' Gramsci asks rhetorically, 'for one knows only what has been and what is, not what will be, which is something "non-existent" and therefore unknowable by definition': Quaderni II, 11: 15, p. 1404; *Prison Notebooks*, p. 438.

53 *Quaderni* II, 11: 15, pp. 1403–4; *Prison Notebooks*, pp. 437–8

54 Ibid, p. 1404; *Prison Notebooks*, p. 439

55 Ibid, p. 1403; *Prison Notebooks*, p. 438

56 *Quaderni* II, 11: 14, p. 1401; *Prison Notebooks*, p. 436, where he writes: '[Bukharin] does not succeed in elaborating the concept of the philosophy of praxis as "historical methodology", and of that in turn as "philosophy", as the only concrete philosophy. He does not succeed in positing and resolving, from the point of view of the real dialectic, the problem which Croce has posed and has attempted to resolve from the speculative point of view.'

57 *Quaderni* II, 8: 176, 'La "nuova" scienza,' and 11: 36.III, 'La scienza e le ideologie "scientifiche," ' pp. 1047–8 and 1451–5, respectively; Gramsci, 'Science and "Scientific" Ideologies'

58 *Quaderni* II, 7: 35, pp. 883–6; *Prison Notebooks*, pp. 354–7

59 *Quaderni* II, 10: 2, 'Identita di storia e filosofia,' pp. 1241–2. See also 11: 12, 'Alcuni punti preliminari di riferimento,' pp. 1375–95; *Prison Notebooks*, 'Some Preliminary Points of Reference,' pp. 323–43.

60 *Quaderni* II, 10: 2, 'Identita di storia e filosofia,' pp. 1241–2.

61 *Quaderni* II, 7: 35, p. 886; *Prison Notebooks*, pp. 355–6, 357. It is worth pointing out that the passage quoted above not only concerns the question of a unity of equivalences, but also addresses the problem of the unity of opposites. Gramsci, clarifying this, writes in part: 'Social relations are expressed by various groups of men which each presupposes the others and whose unity is dialectical, not formal. Man is aristocratic in so far as man is a serf, etc. One could also say that the nature of man is "history" and in this sense, given history as equal to spirit, that the nature of man is spirit if one gives to history precisely this significance of "becoming", which takes place in a *concordia discours* and which does not start from unity, but contains in itself the reasons for a possible unity': ibid. In his attempt to 'ground' the equivalences on the historical terrain, and, in that sense, in the political moment, we see here that Gramsci brings in the concept of 'becoming.' We shall discuss this last piece to the gramscian puzzle concerning 'science' and 'immanence' shortly.

62 *Quaderni* II, 11: 22.IV, p. 1425; *Prison Notebooks*, pp. 435–6. Here Gramsci is clearly taking as a given Marx's third thesis on Feuerbach, where it is asked, 'Who educates the educator?'; the answer: historical circumstance, past and present.

63 *Quaderni* II, 11: 52, 'Regolarità e necessità,' p. 1479: *Prison Notebooks*, 'Regularity and Necessity,' p. 412

64 Ibid. Likewise, this is not to imply that the 'real' does not also entail the 'theoretic,' but see also Marx, 'Theses on Feuerbach,' p. 13.

65 *Quaderni* II, 11: 18, 'Giudizio sulle filosofie passate,' p. 1417; *Prison Notebooks*, 'Judgment on Past Philosophies,' p. 449. In connecting the rational and real in this way, Gramsci was also (particularly in this fragment) criticizing those positions that cast the development of past history, including its cruel and myopic moments, as 'irrational, – a position Gramsci was strongly attempting to uproot. He writes: 'To judge the whole of past philosophy as delirium and folly is not only an anti-historical error in that it makes the anachronistic claim that people in the past should have thought as we do today; it is also a real hangover from metaphysics in that it presumes a dogmatic form of thought valid at all times and in all countries, in the light of which the past can be judged. Methodological anti-historicism is sheer metaphysics.' This position is particularly provoking in light of claims made today; to wit: that the entire history of civilization has been white, masculinist, sexist, and, therewith, pitted against women and people of colour for all past and present eternity.

66 *Quaderni* II, 10: 48, pp. 1335–8; *Prison Notebooks*, pp. 357–60. 'Man in this

sense,' says Gramsci, 'is concrete will, that is, the effective application of the abstract will or vital impulse to the concrete means which realise such a will' (p. 360). We shall return to this point in greater detail in chapter 4.

67 *Quaderni* II, 10 (II): 28(2), 'Introduzione alla studio della filosofia,' p. 1266; *Prison Notebooks*, 'History and Anti-History,' p. 369

68 Ibid, but, for a similar point, see also *Quaderni* II, 11: 62, pp. 1488–9; *Prison Notebooks*, pp. 406–7.

69 *Quaderni* III, 15: 22, 'Introduzione allo studio della filosofia,' p. 1780; *Prison Notebooks*, 'Theory and Practice,' p. 365

70 *Quaderni* III, 13: 10; *Quaderni* II, 10: 44, 'Introduzione allo studio della filosofia,' pp. 1568–70 and 1330–2; *Prison Notebooks*, 'Politics as Autonous Science' and ' "Language", Language and Common Sense,' pp. 136–8, 350–1, respectively.

71 *Quaderni* II, 11: 20, 'Oggettivita e realita del mondo esterno,' p. 1420; *Prison Notebooks*, 'The So-Called "Reality" of the External World,' p. 448. The question of 'structure' in Gramsci's work is central and we will return to it in great detail in chapter 5.

72 *Quaderni* II, 7: 35, pp. 883–6; 11: 14, pp. 1401–3; 11: 15, pp. 1403–6; *Prison Notebooks*, pp. 354–7, 436–7, and 437–40, respectively

73 *Quaderni* II, 10 (II): 9, p. 1246; *Prison Notebooks*, p. 399

74 Ibid, pp. 1246–7; *Prison Notebooks*, pp. 399–400

75 *Quaderni* I, 4: 41, 'La scienza,' pp. 466–7; also 11: 37, pp. 1455–6.

76 *Quaderni* II, 10 (II): 9, p. 1247; *Prison Notebooks*, pp. 399–400. For his reiteration of the position of marxism as the 'coronation of modern culture,' see also *Quaderni* III, 9, 'alcuni problemi per lo studio dello svolgimento della filosofia della praxis,' p. 1855; *Prison Notebooks*, 'The Philosophy of Praxis and Modern Culture,' p. 388.

77 *Quaderni* II, 11: 27, p. 1434; *Prison Notebooks*, p. 462

78 *Quaderni* II, 11: 64, ' "Obbiettività" della conoscenza,' p. 1492; *Prison Notebooks*, ' "Objectivity" of Knowledge,' p. 372

79 *Quaderni* II, 11: 17, 'La cosí detta "realtà del mondo esterno,"' p. 1415; 11: 20, 'Oggettività e realtà del mondo esterno,' pp. 1419–20; *Prison Notebooks*, combined in 'The So-Called "Reality of the External World,"' pp. 445, 447–8. As Gramsci expressed it, ' "Objective" always means "humanly objective" ... [For] what would North-South or East-West mean without man? ... Obviously East and West are arbitrary and conventional ... since outside history every point on earth is East and West at the same time ... And yet these references are real; they correspond to real facts, they allow one to travel by land and by sea, to arrive where they have decided to arrive, to "foresee" the future, to objectify reality, to understand the objectivity of the external world.

Rational and real become one.' Quaderni II, 11: 17, p. 1415; *Prison Notebooks*, p. 445

80 *Quaderni* II, 11: 17, pp. 1415–16; *Prison Notebooks*, p. 445
81 In this context, too, 'historical error' is also used by Gramsci as an attack on Gentile's attempts to revise the concept of the practical to mean simply a 'pure act' devoid of any intellectual/theoretical 'mistake.' See, for example, Giovanni Gentile, *The Theory of Mind as Pure Act*. See also *Quaderni* III, 13: 10, pp. 1568–70; *Prison Notebooks*, pp. 136–8, 372 n66.
82 *Quaderni* III, 15: 10, 'Machiavelli, Sociologia e scienza politica,' pp. 1765–6; *Prison Notebooks*, 'Sociology and Political Science,' pp. 244–5
83 The initial attempts at resolving the question of ethicality in terms of an historicist immanence will be raised here, but will be discussed in detail in the next chapter. For a discussion that links Gramsci's notion of absolute historicism (and the totality this implies) to the founding of reactionary and nihilistic philosophy incapable of distinguishing 'good' from 'evil,' see, for example, Georg Lichteim, *Marxism: An Historical and Critical Study*. One of the most well-known discussions of this problem (locating meaning in terms of subjectivity) and its possible reactionary implications can be found, of course, in the writings of the Frankfurt School scholars. See, in particular, M. Horkheimer's vehement attack in his *Eclipse of Reason* (New York: Continuum 1985).
84 *Quaderni* II, 10 (II): 9, 'Introduzione allo studio della filosofia. Immanenza speculativa e immanenza storicistica o realistica,' pp. 1246–7; *Prison Notebooks*, 'Speculative Immanence and Historicist or Realist Immanence,' pp. 399–402
85 As he puts it: 'It has been forgotten that in the case of a very common expression [historical materialism], one should put the accent on the first term – "historical" – and not on the second, which is of metaphysical origin. The philosophy of praxis is absolute "historicism", the absolute secularization and earthliness of thought, an absolute humanism of history. It is along this line that one must trace the thread of the new conception of the world': *Quaderni* II, 11: 27, 'Concetto di "ortodossia," ' p. 1437; *Prison Notebooks*, 'Concept of "Orthodoxy," ' p. 465.
86 'Theses on Feuerbach,' p. 13
87 *Quaderni* II, 10: 9, p. 1246–9; *Prison Notebooks*, pp. 399–402. See also *Quaderni* II, 11: 30, 'La "materia," ' pp. 1442–5; *Prison Notebooks*, 'Matter,' pp. 465–8
88 *Quaderni* II, 10 (II): 9, 'Alcuni problemi per lo studio dello svolgimento dela filosofia della praxis,' p. 1361; *Prison Notebooks*. 'The Philosophy of Praxis and Modern Culture,' p. 396. In a similar vein, one finds Labriola's remarks quite instructive: 'So here we have arrived once

more at the philosophy of praxis ... It is the immanent philosophy of things about which people philosophize. The realistic process leads first from life to thought, not from thought to life. It leads from work, from the labour of cognition, to understanding as an abstract theory, not from theory to cognition. It leads from wants, and therefore from various feelings of well-being or illness resulting from the satisfaction or neglect of these wants, to the creation of the poetical myth of supernatural forces, not vice versa. In these statements lies the secret of a phrase used by Marx, which has been the cause of much racking of some brains: He said that he had turned the dialectics of Hegel right side up. This means in plain words that the rhythmic movement of the idea itself was set aside and the rhythmic movements of real things adopted a movement, which ultimately produces thought. Historical materialism, then, or the philosophy of praxis, takes account of man as a social and historical being. It gives the last blow to all forms of idealism which regard actually existing things as mere reflexes, reproductions, limitations, illustrations, results of so-called a priori thought': Antonio Labriola, *Socialism and Philosophy*, 'Letters to Sorel,' pp. 94–5.

89 *Quaderni* II, 10 (II): 9, 'Introduzione allo studio della filosofia. Immanenza speculativa e immanenza storicistica o realistica,' pp. 1246–7; *Prison Notebooks*, 'Speculative Immanence and Historicist or Realist Immanence,' pp. 399–400

90 'Theses on Feuerbach,' p. 13, where Marx states: 'III. The materialist doctrine that states men are products of circumstances and upbringing, and that, therefore, changed men are products of other circumstances and changed upbringing, forgets the fact that it is man that changes circumstances and that the educator himself needs educating. Hence this doctrine necessarily arrives at dividing society into two parts, of which one is superior to society (see for example Robert Owen).'

91 *Quaderni* II, 11: 32, 'Quantità e qualità,' p. 1446; *Prison Notebooks*, 'Quantity and Quality' pp. 468–9

92 *Quaderni* II, 10: 44, pp. 1330–2; *Prison Notebooks*, pp. 348–51

93 Ibid, p. 1332; *Prison Notebooks*, p. 350

94 This point is developed by Gramsci not only from Marx's third thesis, but also from the sixth thesis, where he writes: 'VI. Feuerbach resolves the religious into the *human* essence. But the human essence is no abstraction inherent in each single individual. In its reality, it is the ensemble of social relation': p. 14. Cf *Quaderni* II, 10: 54, 'Introduzione allo studio della filosofia. Che cosa e l'uomo?,' pp. 1343–6; and 7: 35, pp. 883–6; *Prison Notebooks*, 'What Is Man?' pp. 351–4 and 354–7, respectively.

95 *Quaderni* II, 10: 54, p. 1343; *Prison Notebooks*, p. 351. Similarly, he

concludes in a later fragment, 'The problem of what is man is always therefore the so-called problem of "human nature" ... It is thus an attempt to create a science of man (a philosophy) which starts from an initially unitary concept, from an abstraction in which everything that is human can be contained. But is the "human" a starting point or a point of arrival, as both a concept and as a unitary "fact"? Or might the whole attempt, in so far as it posits the human as a starting point, be a "theological" or "metaphysical" residue? Philosophy cannot be reduced to a naturalistic "anthropology": the nature of the human species is not given by the "biological" nature of man': *Quaderni* II, 7: 35, p. 884: *Prison Notebooks*, p. 335.

96 *Quaderni* II, 7: 35, pp. 884–5; *Prison Notebooks*, pp. 356–7
97 *Quaderni* II, 11: 28, 'L'immanenza e le filosofia della praxis,' pp. 1438–9; and 11: 24, 'Il linguaggio e le metafore,' pp. 1426–8; *Prison Notebooks*, combined into 'Immanence and the Philosophy of Praxis,' pp. 449–52
98 *Quaderni* II, 10: 48.II, 'Progresso e divenire,' p. 1338; *Prison Notebooks*, 'Progress and Becoming,' p. 360
99 *Quaderni* II, 11: 16, 'Quistioni di nomenclatura e di contenuto,' p. 1411; *Prison Notebooks*, 'Questions of Nomenclature and Content,' pp. 456–7
100 *Quaderni* II, 11: 22.IV, 'Quistioni generali,' p. 1426; *Prison Notebooks*, 'The Dialectic,' p. 435
101 *Quaderni* II, 10: 6, p. 1244; *Prison Notebooks*, p. 366. We will discuss the concept of the 'ethico-political hegemony' and the will in the next chapter, as well as in chapter 5. But see, for example, Chantal Mouffe, 'Hegemony and New Political Subjects: Toward a New Concept of Democracy.'
102 *Quaderni* II, 10: 6, p. 1244; *Prison Notebooks*, pp. 366–7. But see also *Quaderni* II, 8: 182, 'Struttura e sovrestruttura,' pp. 1051–2; *Prison Notebooks*, 'Structure and Superstructure,' pp. 365–6. This point raises two others, the first having to do with the creating of a 'historic bloc' (attributed to Sorel), the second having to do with the notion the structure and superstructure. Both points form the basis for chapter 5, but see also *Quaderni* II, 10 (II): 'Introduzione allo studio della filosofia;' 10 (II): 17, 'Principi e preliminari,' pp. 1249–50, 1255–6; *Prison Notebooks*, 'Structure and Superstructure' and 'Philosophy and History,' pp. 365–6, 344–5, respectively.

Chapter Four

1 *Quaderni* II, 6: 79, 'Riviste tipo,' p. 750
2 *Quaderni* II, 11: 59, pp. 1485–6; *Prison Notebooks*, ' "Creative" Philosophy,' pp. 345–6

3 Indeed, analytic discussions on the use of the 'will' in Gramsci have been sparse. However, for a discussion linking the 'collective will' with establishing a workers' democracy, see, for example, the importance discussion by Paolo Spriano, *Storia del partito communista italiana*, Vol. 1, (Torino: Einaudi 1967) as excerpted in Federico Romano, *Gramsci e il liberalismo – antiliberale*. One of the earliest discussions in English that raises the problem of 'will' and tries to differentiate it from 'possibility' can be found in Immanuel Wallerstein, 'The State and Social Transformation: Will and Possibility.' Also of particular note is Thomas Nemeth, *Gramsci's Philosophy: A Critical Study*, though the political implications of Gramsci's posing of 'will' tend to be submerged in the philosophical problematizing of the distincts. The direct referencing of the will in terms of its constituting a practico-political act can be found in Lezek Kolakowski, *Main Currents of Marxism, Vol 3: The Breakdown*, pp. 231–6.

4 Some of the most central discussions of Gramsci's work often overlook the problem of the will, particularly, though not exclusively, those written in English. See, for example, the otherwise pioneering works by John M. Cammett, *Antonio Gramsci and the Origins of Italian Communism*; Chantal Mouffe, ed., *Gramsci and Marxist Theory*; and Anne Showstack Sassoon, *Gramsci's Politics*.

5 This phrase is attributed to Romain Rolland in remarks pre-dating his imprisonment. Gramsci writes: 'The socialist conception of the revolutionary process is characterised by two fundamental features which Romain Rolland has summed up in his watchword: "pessimism of the intellect, optimism of the will". To expect masses who are reduced to such conditions of bodily and spiritual slavery to express their own autonomous historical will; to expect them spontaneously to initiate and sustain a revolutionary action – this is purely an illusion on the part of the ideologues': *L'Ordine Nuovo*, 3–10 April 1920, Vol. 1, no. 43, reprinted in *Selections from Political Writings 1910–1920*, 'Address to the Anarchists,' pp. 188–9. See also, for example, *Quaderni* III, 28: 11, 'Graziadei e il paese di Cuccagna,' p. 2332.

6 See the early work of Carlo Marzani, *The Open Marxism of Antonio Gramsci*. For a more recent appropriation of the will as a political rallying point, see W. Graham, 'Re-discovering Gramsci's Optimism of the Will.'

7 *Quaderni* II, 7: 18, 'Unità negli elementi costitutivi del marxismo,' p. 868; *Prison Notebooks*, 'Unity in the Constituent Elements of Marxism,' pp. 402–3; and, as a way to criticize the fascists, *Quaderni* II, 11: 52, 'Regolarità e necessità,' pp. 1477–80; *Prison Notebooks*, 'Regularity and Necessity,' pp. 410–14

8 Giovanni Gentile, *Origini e dottrina del fascismo*

9 Of Bergson's work, see, in particular, his *Creative Evolution* and *The Creative Mind*, written between 1903 and 1926.

10 See, for example, where Mussolini characterizes the importance of the will as follows: 'I speak of movement [of will] and not of party, because my conception always was that Fascism must assume the characteristics of being anti-party ... It was necessary to imagine a wholly new political conception, adequate to the living reality of the twentieth century, overcoming at the same time, the ideological worship of liberalism, the limited horizons of various spent and exhausted democracies, and finally the violently Utopian spirit of Bolshevism ... It was necessary to lay the foundation of a new civilization. To this end I aimed all my strength. I had a perfect and sure consciousness of the end I was driving at. This was my problem: to find the moment, to find the form': B. Mussolini, *My Autobiography*, pp. 68–9. See also Leni Riefenstahl's well-known film *Triumph of the Will* (1934–6), the official film recording of the sixth Nazi Congress held at Nuremberg in 1934, which sets the problem of the 'triumph' in brutal clarity.

11 *Quaderni* II, 11: 59, p. 1485; *Prison Notebooks*, p. 345

12 *Aesthetic*, pp. 77–80

13 Ibid, pp. 90–1 and 386–4

14 *Philosophy of the Practical*, pp. 173–276

15 Ibid, p. xvii

16 This distinction by Croce is clearly based on the hegelian rendering of will, which posits a 'will' prior to knowledge but argues that the theoretic and practical will 'reciprocally integrate themselves precisely because they are distinguished in the manner indicated': G.W.F. Hegel, *Philosophy of Mind, Part III of The Encyclopedia of the Philosophical Sciences, 1830*, esp. Section 443, pp. 184–6. As we will examine shortly, Gramsci rejects any notion of will as existing prior to knowledge.

17 *Aesthetic*, pp. 77–8

18 Ibid

19 *Quaderni* II, 11: 54, 'Unità della teoria e della practica,' p. 1482; *Prison Notebooks*, 'Theory and Practice,' p. 364

20 *Quaderni* II, 11: 59, p. 1485; *Prison Notebooks*, p. 345. It should be emphasized here that the similarity to Croce is precisely in conceptualizing 'the will' as never devoid of content, although Gramsci clearly situates it in terms of a historicized immanence, as discussed in the previous chapter. In Croce's case, as Gramsci remarks above, its content is (pure) thought, which forms a basis for posing ethical substance as pure assertion of self. For Gramsci, its content is (impure) spirit, i.e., historical error or specificity. This 'content' of the will, for Gramsci, is not meant to convey a pure assertion of self but exactly the

inverse: the 'specificity' of social being as historicized immanence. But for Croce's discussion of will in relation to (pure) selfhood, see *Aesthetic*, esp. ch. 7, pp. 89–99.

21 *Quaderni* II, 6: 86, 'Fase economica-corporativa dello Stato,' p. 762; *Prison Notebooks*, 'Economic-corporate Phase of the State,' p. 175

22 *Quaderni* III, 15: 50, p. 1810; *Prison Notebooks*, p. 170–1

23 *Quaderni* II, 10: 54, 'Introduzione allo studio della filosofia, Che cosa è l'uomo?,' p. 1344; *Prison Notebooks*, 'What Is Man?' p. 352, where Gramsci draws the argument specifically in reference to Marx's sixth thesis on Feuerbach

24 *Quaderni* III, 13: 1, p. 1559; *Prison Notebooks*, p. 130

25 *Quaderni* II, 7: 4, 'Scienza morale e materialismo storico,' p. 855; *Prison Notebooks*, 'Moral Science and Historical Materialism,' pp. 409–10. This remark made in reference to Marx's 'Preface' will be taken up in greater detail later in the chapter, but see K. Marx, 'A Preface to *The Contribution to a Critique of Political Economy.*'

26 *Quaderni* III, 13: 1, p. 1559; *Prison Notebooks*, p. 130

27 *Quaderni* II, 13: 16, p. 1577; *Prison Notebooks*, 'Prediction and Perspective,' p. 172 (parenthetical remarks by Gramsci; bracketed remarks, mine). In this passage, Gramsci is not merely identifying the will as 'political' or simply as a distinction between what is 'concrete' and what is 'abstract,' but rather as a marker between two concepts of what 'concretely' ought to be. As Gramsci puts it: 'The opposition between [a so-called practical politician] and Machiavelli is not an opposition between what is and what ought to be, but one between two concepts of what ought to be.'

28 *Quaderni* II, 6: 86, 'Fase economica-corporativa dello Stato,' pp. 760–1; *Prison Notebooks*, 'Economic-corporate Phase of the State,' pp. 174–5

29 Ibid

30 *Quaderni* III, 13: 1, p. 1559; *Prison Notebooks*, p. 130

31 *Quaderni* II, 11: 51, p. 1477; *Prison Notebooks*, 'Speculative Philosophy,' p. 371

32 Note here Nemeth's differing interpretation of the will in the *Quaderni*. He distinguishes Gramsci's use from that of Croce by insisting that Gramsci incorporates a distinct notion of the economic moment and the will as a function of philosophy, thereby suggesting that morality is not to be found in an historicization of 'truth' but, rather, in the degree to which 'will' remains 'free' of historical error. Cf. Nemeth, *Gramsci's Philosophy*, pp. 162–4.

33 *Quaderni* II, 10: 16–17, 28, 31, 41, pp. 1254–6, 1265–7, 1269–76, 1291–1301, respectively; and also the discussion in A. Lepre, *Gramsci secondo Gramsci*, pp. 95–9

34 With respect to this question of the diversity and its concomitant implications for a democratic society, it is worth nothing that, prior to the publication of the standard Italian edition, this insistence by Gramsci was often interpreted as a way to dismiss the radical pluralism inherent in that position, relying on a notion of the heterogeneity of the social as meaning, instead, 'alliance-building.' See, for example, the work of Massimo Salvadori, *Gramsci e il problema storico della democrazia*, esp. pp. 3–56.

35 *Quaderni* II, 10: 17, 28, 31, 40, pp. 1244–56, 1265–7, 1269–76, 1291–1301, respectively; and also the discussion in *Gramsci secondo Gramsci*, pp. 95–9

36 *Quaderni* II, 8: 191, 'Egemonia e democrazia,' p. 1056.

37 *Quaderni* II, 11: 67, pp. 1505–6; *Prison Notebooks*, 'Passage from Knowing to Understanding and Feeling and vice versa from Feeling to Understanding and Knowing,' pp. 418–19. Although this will be amplified shortly, it is worth recalling in this context that the 'leaders' and 'led,' indeed any social subject, is itself fractured, i.e., a function of historical truth, which is not an a priori, fully determined subject, but must be constituted as such.

38 *Quaderni* II, 10: 44, 'Introduzione allo studio della filosofia,' pp. 1330–2; *Prison Notebooks*, ' "Language," Languages and Common Sense,' pp. 348–51

39 Ibid, p. 1331; *Prison Notebooks*, p. 349 (emphasis mine)

40 *Quaderni* II, 11: 70, 'Antonio Labriola,' pp. 1507–9; *Prison Notebooks* "Antonio Labriola," pp. 386–88. Paggi clarifies the ethico-political moment as follows: 'Having abandoned the principle of linear causality ... the ethico-political dimension prevents historical forces from turning into fantastic shadows of a "hidden god". They become, instead, integral parts of a single social process. Thus, the establishment of the "cathartic moment", ie, the identification of the way in which the shift from economics to politics takes place becomes for Gramsci "the starting point of all the philosophy of praxis", and "the crux of all questions that have arisen around the philosophy of praxis"': L. Paggi, 'Gramsci's General Theory of Marxism,' in Chantal Mouffe, ed., *Gramsci and Marxist Theory*, pp. 139–40.

41 *Quaderni* II, 10: 12, pp. 1249–50; *Prison Notebooks*, pp. 365–6. In the original Italian, Gramsci uses the word 'gnoseological' rather than 'epistemological,' as translated here.

42 *Quaderni* II, 10: 7, 'Definizione del concetto di storia etico-politica,' pp. 1222–5

43 *Quaderni* II, 10: 7, 'Egemonia e democrazia,' p. 1056. See also *Quaderni* II, 11: 67, pp. 1505–6; *Prison Notebooks*, 'Passage from Knowing to Understanding and Feeling, and vice versa ... , pp. 418–9. It is worth

underscoring here that the 'process' and 'fact' of hegemony operate on a consensual basis with an underbelly of force; that is, force is not 'separate' from consent, nor consent from force: to use them as analytic tools in and of themselves would simply be involving conceptual instrumentalism. We will be returning to this point in chapter 5, but see, for example, *Quaderni* III, 19: 24, 'Il problema della direzione politica nella formazione e nello sviluppo della nazione e dello stato moderno in Italia,' pp. 2010–34; *Prison Notebooks*, 'The Problem of Political Leadership in the Formation and Development of the Nation and the Modern State in Italy,' pp. 55–83.

44 See, for example, G. Lichtheim, *Marxism: An Historical and Critical Study*, where he insists, in part, that Gramsci's emphasis on totality can lead to a reactionary politics.

45 See, for example, John Hoffman, *The Gramscian Challenge: Coercion and consent in Marxist Political Theory*, esp. pp. 21–3, 182–6, 193, where Gramsci's ethico-political will is seen by Hoffman as a 'general' will to be incorporated by and expressed in the totalizing state.

46 Gentile's 'actual idealism' is, according to Gramsci, just a more specific – but cruder – interpretation of Croce's 'history/anti-history dialectic,' a point Gramsci takes up at greater length in his sixth notebook, especially in *Quaderni* II, 6: 10, 'Passato e presente,' pp. 688–92; *Prison Notebooks*, 'Historical Belles-Lettres,' pp. 270–2 (partial translation).

47 G. Gentile, 'IX. The Totalitarian Nature of Fascist Doctrine' and 'XIII. The Fascist state as a democratic state,' in Adrian Lyttleton, ed., *Italian Fascisms: From Pareto to Gentile*, pp. 301–2, 310

48 *Quaderni* II, 6: 10, 'Passato e Presente,' p. 691; *Prison Notebooks*, 'Historical Belles-Lettres,' p. 271

49 It should be pointed out that Gramsci argues for a radicalization of a social totality, i.e., the posing of a 'non-sutured,' but nevertheless universalized whole. It is a decision that allows him to dismiss entirely the fascist logic discussed above. But, as we shall note shortly, the somewhat contradictory notion of an 'open-totality' does present him with a specific set of problems all its own.

50 *Quaderni* II, 10: 54, 'Che cosa è l'uomo?;' 7: 35, 'Materialismo e materialismo storico,' pp. 1343–6; and 883, respectively; *Prison Notebooks*, 'What Is Man?,' pp. 351–7 (combined translation)

51 *Quaderni* II, 7: 35, p. 883; *Prison Notebooks*, p. 354

52 These remarks could be seen, then, as an attack against the idealist acceptance of 'genius,' i.e., the resorting to locating 'external' factors outside the community in order to bring forward or account for creative possibilities/change. If one were not going to rely on an innate 'genius,' on the one side, or, on the other, a teleological unfolding of spirit towards an ethical idea (or both), then given the question of how

'real' events arise in history and create and institutionalize differences, for Gramsci, the answer could only be contextualized in terms of an ethico-political hegemony. See *Quaderni* II, 10: 7; and *Quaderni* III, 23: 3, 'Arte e lotta per una nuova civiltà'; and 23: 6, 'Arte e cultura,' pp. 1222–5, 2187–90, and 2192–3; *Cultural Writings*, pp. 104–7, 93–8, and 98, respectively.

53 *Quaderni* II, 11: 13, p. 1399, *Prison Notebooks*, 'Critical Notes on an Attempt at Popular Sociology,' p. 422; and *Quaderni* II, 7: 35, 'Materialismo e materialismo storico,' p. 884, *Prison Notebooks*, 'What Is Man?,' p. 355

54 *Quaderni* II, 10: 44, 'Introduzione allo studio della filosofia,' pp. 1331–2; *Prison Notebooks*, '"Language", Languages and Common Sense,' p. 350

55 *Quaderni* II, 10: 54, 'Che cosa l'uomo?,' p. 1346; *Prison Notebooks*, 'What Is Man?,' p. 353

56 Ibid, pp. 1345–46; *Prison Notebooks*, pp. 352–4

57 This is not to ignore or make light of the role that the economic system has in creating the subject 'man,' a point we shall endeavour to explore in chapter 5 when discussing the concept of economics in Gramsci's *Quaderni*. It is to insist on the point, however, that 'man' is not reducible to a single element, in this case 'labour,' but is rather the *ensemble* of historical circumstance.

58 *Quaderni* II, 8: 191, 'Egemonia e democrazia,' p. 1056

59 *Quaderni* II, 6: 88, pp. 763–4; *Prison Notebooks*, pp. 262–3 (parenthetical remarks by Gramsci; bracketed remarks, mine). The details of posing radical democracy as civil society (or ethico-political state/hegemony) will be drawn out shortly, and further in chapter 5.

60 *Quaderni* II, 11: 67, pp. 1505–6; *Prison Notebooks*, 'Passage From Knowing to Understanding and to Feeling and vice versa ... ,' pp. 418–19

61 As earlier mentioned, the concept of 'historic bloc' has been attributed to G. Sorel; we will return to Gramsci's particular elaboration of it in the following chapter when dealing specifically with the structure. But here it is meant to highlight Gramsci's usage of 'organic intellectual' (and, in that context, the role of the party) in forging that bloc. See further *Quaderni* III, 12: 1, pp. 1513–40; translated, in part, in *Prison Notebooks*, 'The Different Position of Urban and Rural-type Intellectuals,' pp. 14-33. See also *Quaderni* III, 13: 36, 'Sulla burocrazia,' pp. 1632–5; *Prison Notebooks*, 'On Bureaucracy,' pp. 185-90.

62 *Quaderni* II, 11: 67, pp. 1505–6; *Prison Notebooks*, 'Passage from Knowing to Understanding and Feeling and vice versa ... ,' p. 418 (my emphasis)

63 *Quaderni* III, 14: 72, 'Letteratura popolare. Contenuto e forma,' p. 1740; in A. Gramsci, *Selections from Cultural Writing*, 'Popular Literature. Content and Form,' p. 206

64 See also J. Hyppolite's summary remarks on Hegel's posing of absolute tyranny, in his 'Absolute Freedom and Terror: The Second Type of Spiritual Self,' in *Genesis and Structure of Hegel's* Phenomenology of Spirit, translated by S. Cherniak and J. Heckman (Evanston: Northwestern University Press 1974), pp. 453–4.

65 No. 68: 'Letter to Tani Schucht, 9 May 1932, Turi,' in Gramsci, *Letters from Prison*, pp. 237–8

66 As we shall later observe in the concluding chapter, it need not mean this at all. Though we will take this up in more detail later, see for example one of the more important theoretical contributions to choosing this path over the other by E. Laclau and C. Mouffe in *Hegemony and Socialist Strategy: Towards a Radical Democratic Politics*.

67 *Quaderni* II, 10: 48.II, 'Progresso e divenire,' p. 1338; *Prison Notebooks*, 'Progress and Becoming,' p. 360 (my emphasis)

Chapter Five

1 B. Croce, *Materialismo storico ed economia marxista* (1900 *Collected Works*, Vol. 2, ch. 4, p. 43), as referenced in *Prison Notebooks*, p. 460

2 *Quaderni*, 11 (II): 29, 'Lo "strumento tecnico",' p. 1440; *Prison Notebooks*, 'The "Technical Instrument,"' p. 460

3 Ibid. As we will note in this chapter, Gramsci, in rejecting the usefulness of 'the mode of production' as an explanatory category, does so by backing the claim that political and social content (and the state that may be said to exist) cannot be derived from the logic of its formal relations. For an excellent assessment of Gramsci's position and later writers such as Althusser, Poulantzas, as well as those involved with the neo-ricardian movement and Capital Logic school, see Bob Jessop, *The Capitalist State: Marxist Theories and Methods*, esp. 'Form and Functions of the State,' ch. 3, pp. 78–141.

4 *Prison Notebooks*, p. 336 n25, in reference to Marx's 'Preface to *The Contribution to the Critique*,' underscoring the point that social being determines consciousness rather than the reverse

5 The discussions regarding Gramsci's use of structure and superstructure are quite detailed in the non-English literature (particularly in the journals *Critica marxista*, *Dialectiques*, and *Rinascita*), often focusing on the question as to whether Gramsci should be considered a theorist who privileged ideological and cultural factors (the so-called superstructural movement) over economics, or vice versa. One of the points that will become clearer as we explore Gramsci's posing of the base is that, for Gramsci, structure cannot be separated as such; ideology and politics, indeed economics itself, are always constitutive concepts that

take on different meanings when cast in terms of a structure or superstructure or their synthetic unity. For an important critique of the position of Gramsci's presumed insistence on superstructure over that of the economic, see N. Badaloni, *Il marxismo di Gramsci*, and presenting an earlier and opposing view, E. Sereni, 'Blocco storico e iniziativa politica nell'elaborazione gramsciana e nella politica del P.C.I.' as referenced in C. Buci-Glucksmann, *Gramsci and the State*, pp. 276–7 n90. See also the debate between N. Bobbio, 'Gramsci and the Conception of Civil Society,' and J. Textier, 'Gramsci, Theoretician of the Superstructures,' in Chantal Mouffe, ed., *Gramsci and Marxist Theory*, pp. 21–47 and 48–79, respectively.

6 *Quaderni* II, 8: 182, 'Struttura e superstrutture,' and 11: 12.III, pp. 1051–2 and 1388–91, respectively; *Prison Notebooks*, 'Structure and Superstructure' (partly translated), and 'Note III,' pp. 366 and 325, respectively

7 *Quaderni* III, 12: 1 and 13: 10, pp. 1518–19 and 1568–70, respectively; *Prison Notebooks*, pp. 12, 136–8, respectively. Gramsci also insisted that the superstructure itself must be divided into two 'moments,' the one being civil society, the other the state. This distinction has contributed to a high degree of confusion around Gramsci's concept of a civil society as structural, a confusion well outlined in Perry Anderson's 'The Antimonies of Antonio Gramsci.' Lamentably it has led some scholars to miss completely the radical implications of re-posing the structure as constituted by the political moment, and thus has forced them to miss the radical implications of his concept of both the will and hegemony, not to mention the class-party, for the establishing of an 'open' and 'better' society. While we will refer to his work later, see, in particular, W. Adamson, 'The Autonomy of Politics,' in his *Hegemony and Revolution: Antonio Gramsci's Political and Cultural Theory*, esp. pp. 215–22.

8 *Quaderni* II, 11: 20, 'Oggettività e realtà del mondo esterno,' 11: 20, p. 1420; *Prison Notebooks*, 'The So-called "Reality of the External World,"' p. 448

9 *Quaderni* II, 8: 132, 'Machiavelli, La passione,' p. 1022

10 *Quaderni* III, 13: 18, 'Alcuni aspetti teorici e practici dell "economismo,"' pp. 1589–97; *Prison Notebooks*, 'Some Theoretical and Practical Aspects of "Economism," ' pp. 158–67

11 See, for example, Engels's letter to M. Bloch, 21 September 1890, where Engels, in rejecting an economic reductionist labelling, wrote: 'According to the materialist conception of history, the *ultimately* determining element in history is the production and reproduction of *real life*. More than this neither Marx nor I have ever asserted ... If someone twists

this into saying that the economic element is the *only* determining one, he transforms that proposition into a meaningless senseless phrase' (my emphasis), as referenced in *Prison Notebooks*, p. 427 n74. See also Marx's well-known attack against the (hegelian) posing of the state as the embodiment of the ethical idea in his early 'Critique of Hegel's *The Philosophy of Right*' and 'The 18th Brumaire of Louis Bonaparte'; and, of course, the classic by Engels, *The Condition of the Working Class in England*.

12 P. Worsely, 'The Model of Capitalism: British Political Economy,' in his *Marx and Marxism*, pp. 49ff. It should also be noted that while Marx's 'Preface' has been held out as an example of this kind of reductionism – a reading we shall next address – most offensive in this context seems to have been Marx's 'The General Law of Capitalist Accumulation,' in his *Capital: A Critical Analysis of Capitalist Production*, Vol. 1, pp. 574–665, and 'Manifesto of the Communist Party.'

13 K. Marx, 'Preface to *The Contributions to a Critique of Political Economy*, p. 503 (my emphasis)

14 See G.A. Cohen, *Karl Marx's Theory of History: A Defence*, ch. 3 and 8, pp. 63–87 and 216–48, respectively. Even Sorel, to whom Gramsci acknowledges a large debt, criticized those relying on the 1859 'Preface' to the exclusion of Marx's more economic studies: 'It seems to me the commentators on Marx were on the wrong path when they believed they had found the classic expression of their master's doctrine in the preface he wrote in 1859 ... This renowned text does not aim to furnish the rules for studying a particular period in history. It deals rather with the succession of civilizations; thus, the word "class" is not even mentioned. The phrases that describe the role of economics are extremely obscure, partially symbolic and, consequently, very difficult to interpret. Thus we need not be astonished that many liberties have been taken with this preface, which so many cite without ever having studied it seriously': Georges Sorel, 'Preface to the First Edition,' in his *The Illusions of Progress*, p. xli.

15 In keeping with Gramsci's own emphasis on this passage, we will refer mainly to the 'Preface,' though he also had access to Marx's *Economic and Philosophical Manuscripts of 1844* and *The Poverty of Philosophy: Answer to the 'Philosophy of Poverty' by M. Proudhon*. See as well Marx's *The German Ideology*, where he underscores the fluidity and constitutive nature of the 'structure': 'Civil society embraces the whole material intercourse of individuals within a definite stage of the development of productive forces. It embraces the whole commercial and industrial life of a given state and, in so far, transcends the State and the nation,

though, on the other hand again, it must assert itself in its foreign relations as nationality and inwardly must organise itself as State,' p. 78.

16 'Preface,' p. 503

17 The rejection of 'false consciousness' is a crucial contribution by Gramsci for its rejection underscores the point, for Gramsci, that people maintain a rational view of the world – whether or not in terms of simple 'common' sense or highly thought-out philosophical insight. To put it slightly differently, one's ideological commitment, however much bound by the negative features of one's culture or however much one might agree or disagree with it, it still 'real.' We will return to this point later in the chapter, but see *Quaderni* III, 13: 18, 'Alcuni aspetti teorici e practici dell "economismo",' p. 1595; *Prison Notebooks*, 'Some Theoretical and Practical Aspects of "Economism",' p. 164.

18 See A. Przeworksi, 'Proletariat into a Class: The Process of Class Formation from K. Kautsky's *The Class Struggle* to Recent Controversies,' in *Politics and Society* 7/4 (1977), pp. 343–401, expanded upon in his *Capitalism and Social Democracy*. Marx, of course, does incorporate into class (and class formation) 'fluidity' since they are precisely the embodiment of the 'law of motion' of capital and wage-labour. See, for example, Marx, *The Grundrisse*, pp. 120ff, and as well M. Weber's classic study, *The Theory of Economic and Social Organization*. Along similar lines see A. Giddens, *The Class Structure of Advanced Capitalist Societies*, and the critique of both Weber and Giddens by G. Therborn, *What Does the Ruling Class Do When It Rules?* In drawing out the implications on the fluidity of class formation, see the landmark work of E.P. Thompson, *The Making of the English Working Class*, which explores in graphic detail the constitutive experience of class and class struggle.

19 See for example E. Meiksins-Wood's *Retreat from Class*. Ironically this work, which explicitly sets out to condemn as 'a European left moving rightwards' (pp. 47ff) those analytic assessments that refuse ontological groundings, and pose power itself in terms of constitutive unities forged through political practice, ends by taking as a given what needs to be established; to wit: the historico-political aspect of power and the addendum aspects of political organization and class formation. Given her argument, we are thus forced to accept as revolutionary always already given 'truths' similar to the kind Gramsci sought to destroy. We will return to this and other similar discussions towards the conclusion of this chapter, but see also Norman Geras's summary discussion 'Post-Marxism?' and the reply by Ernesto Laclau and Chantal Mouffe, 'Post-Marxism without Apologies.'

20 *Quaderni* II, 7: 16, 'Guerra di posizione e guerra manovrata o frontale,' p. 866; *Prison Notebooks*, 'Political Struggle and Military War,' p. 238. We will be returning to this point in greater detail, but see also *Quaderni* II, 6: 138, 'Passagio dalla guerra manovrata (e dall' attacco frontale) alla guerra di posizione anche nel campo politico,' pp. 801–2; *Prison Notebooks*, 'The Transition from the War of Manoeuvre (Frontal Attack) to the War of Position – In the Political Field as well,' pp. 238–9.

21 *Quaderni* II, 11: 29, 'Lo "strumento tecnico," ' p. 1442; *Prison Notebooks*, 'The "Technical Instrument," ' p. 461

22 *Quaderni* III, 13: 18, p. 1595; *Prison Notebooks*, p. 164

23 This confusion happens particularly – though not exclusively – when Gramsci discusses, in certain fragments, the notion of civil society as being a moment of structure; in other fragments, as a moment of the superstructure; and, in other writings, as equated to the state. We will sort out the confusion in the last section of this chapter, but see, for example, *Quaderni* III, 13: 24, pp. 1613–17; 12: 1, esp. pp. 1518–20; 13: 18, p. 1590; *Prison Notebooks*, pp. 233–5, 12–13, and 160, respectively.

24 A parallel point based on the radical implications of Marx having posed surplus value (in terms of labour) as a 'process,' rather than in a flat and empirical sense of 'quantity,' has been best analysed in Dusan Pokorny, 'Marx's Philosophy of Surplus Value.' Here he raises the argument that since surplus value, understood in 'quantitative' terms, cannot fully articulate the exploitative relationship between worker and capitalist (since surplus value is, in part, the expression of the alienation of the worker – an alienation that clearly is qualitatively different from that of the capitalist), then some other way of accounting for that alienation must necessarily be considered.

25 *Quaderni* II, 7: 21, 'Validità della ideologie,' p. 869; *Prison Notebooks*, 'The Concept of "Ideology",' p. 377

26 *Quaderni* III, 13: 31, 'Il teorema delle proporzioni definite,' pp. 1626–8; *Prison Notebooks*, 'The Theorem of Fixed Proportions,' p. 190

27 *Quaderni* II, 11: 30, 'La "materia",' p. 1442; *Prison Notebooks*, '"Matter",' p. 466

28 As quoted in Jacques Textier, 'Gramsci: Theoretician of the Superstructures,' p. 59

29 *Quaderni* II, 11: 32, 'Quantità e qualità,' p. 1446; *Prison Notebooks*, 'Quantity and Quality,' p. 468

30 *Quaderni* II, 10: 52, p. 1342; *Prison Notebooks*, p. 347. But, see also *Quaderni* II, 10: 9, 'Immaneza speculativa e immanenza storicistica o realistica,' pp. 1246–8; *Prison Notebooks*, 'Speculative Immanence and Historicist or Realist Immanence,' pp. 399–401.

31 *Quaderni* II, 11: 32, 'Quantità e qualità,' p. 1446; *Prison Notebooks*,

'Quantity and Quality,' p. 469, especially where he writes: 'The most concrete theoretical-practical explanation, however, is that to be found in the first volume of *Capital*, where it is demonstrated that ... if every social aggregate is something more (and different) than the sum of its components, this must mean that the law or principle which explains the development of society cannot be a physical law, since in physics one does not get out of the quantitative sphere except metaphorically.'

32 *Quaderni* II, 10: 50, p. 1340; *Prison Notebooks*, p. 363

33 *Quaderni* II, 10: 41, pp. 1315–18. While these points will be discussed in greater detail shortly, it is worth noting here that Gramsci is following a similar path as had been described earlier, in chapter 2, in terms of truth and error (which together constitute Truth); or beauty and ugliness (which, taken together, constitute Beauty); or, finally, will and the intellect (which, taken together, constitute practical activity).

34 *Quaderni* II, 10: 12; 11: 29; *Quaderni* III, 13: 10, pp. 1249–50, 1439–41, and 1568–70, respectively; *Prison Notebooks*, pp. 365, 458–61, and 136–8, respectively. Here quantity is not directly oppositional to (or a negation of) quality; rather, these concepts are situated in a relation of contrariness. In this sense, their unity does not exhaust the entirety of field; but the quantity/quality nexus tries to address the whole of reality inasmuch as history is to be understood as an open and immanent totality. This posing of contrariness is discussed in reference to Kant by Lucio Colletti, *Marxism and Hegel*, p. 118, but one can draw this position, as did Hegel and Marx, directly from Spinoza. See also the discussion by L. Althusser in *Reading Capital*, esp. pp. 16–18, 92–105.

35 *Quaderni* II, 11: 32, 'Quantità e qualità,' p. 1447; *Prison Notebooks*, 'Quantity and Quality,' p. 469

36 *Quaderni* II, 10: 9, pp. 1246–8; *Prison Notebooks*, p. 401

37 *Quaderni* III, 13: 10, p. 1569, *Prison Notebooks*, pp. 137–8; and *Quaderni* II, 10: 10, p. 1248, *Prison Notebooks*, p. 401 (emphasis, mine).

38 *Quaderni* II, 11: 22, 'Questioni generali,' p. 1422; *Prison Notebooks*, 'The Constituent Parts of a Philosophy of Praxis,' pp. 431–2

39 *Quaderni* II, 13: 1, p. 1556; *Prison Notebooks*, p. 127. On Bergson's elaboration of *élan vital*, see his *Creative Evolution*, and as well H. Carr, *The Philosophy of Change: A Study of the Fundamental Principles of the Philosophy of Bergson*, esp. pp. 146–72.

40 *Quaderni* II, 10: 10, 'Introduzione alla studio della filosofia,' p. 1248; *Prison Notebooks*, 'Speculative Immanence and Historicist or Realist Immanence,' p. 401

41 *Quaderni* II, 11: 22, 'Questioni generali,' p. 1422; *Prison Notebooks*, 'The Constituent Parts of a Philosophy of Praxis,' p. 432 (translation slightly modified from the English edition)

42 *Quaderni* II, 8: 132, 'Machiavelli, La Passione,' p. 1022; *Prison Notebooks*, 'Politics as an Autonomous Science,' pp. 139–40
43 *Quaderni* II, 10: 57, 'Punti di meditazione sull'economia,' pp. 1350–1.
44 Ibid
45 *Quaderni* II, 13: 17, 'Analisi delle situazioni : rapporti di forza,' pp. 1578–85; *Prison Notebooks*, 'Analysis of Situations. Relations of force,' pp. 175–85
46 *Quaderni* III, 13: 2 and 13: 17, pp. 1561–63 and 1578–89; *Prison Notebooks*, pp. 175–77 and 177–85
47 *Quaderni* III, 13: 17, p. 1579; *Prison Notebooks*, p. 177. Indeed, this form of economism was precisely the trap he accused both the syndicalists and the liberals of having blindly accepted. 'Failure to consider the immediate moment of "relations of force" is linked to residues of the vulgar liberation conception – of which syndicalism is a manifestation – which thought itself more advanced when in reality it was taking a step backward. In fact the vulgar liberal conception ... was more advanced than syndicalism, [the latter of] which gave primordial importance to the fundamental socio-economic relation and only to that. [And yet, even though] the vulgar liberal conception took implicit account of this socio-economic relation ... [it] insisted more on the relation of the political forces [as if primordial and autonomous] rather than as an expression of the former and which, in reality, contained it. These residues of the vulgar liberal conception can be traced to a whole series of works purporting to be connected with the philosophy of praxis, [but in reality] have only given rise to infantile forms of optimism and folly'; *Quaderni* III, 13: 17, p. 1581; *Prison Notebooks*, p. 180.
48 *Quaderni* II, 13: 17, pp. 1578–9; *Prison Notebooks*, p. 177
49 *Quaderni* III, 13: 10, 13: 13, 13: 21, 14: 70, 15: 4, 17: 37, pp. 1568–70, 1572–6, 1601–2, 1732–5, 1752–5, 1939–40, respectively; *Prison Notebooks*, pp. 136–46 and 147–56 (combined fragment translations)
50 *Quaderni* III, 15: 4, 'Machiavelli. Elementi di politica,' p. 1752; *Prison Notebooks*, 'Elements of Politics,' p. 144 (parenthetical remarks, Gramsci's)
51 Though not directly referencing Gramsci, see, in particular, Sheldon Wolin, *Politics and Vision: Continuity and Innovation in Western Political Thought*. See also Steven Lukes, *Power: A Radical View*, crucial for its explication of 'power' as a relational and historical category. In this context, too, the path-breaking work of M. Foucault, *Discipline and Punish: The Birth of the Prison*, particularly in his discussion of the Benthamite panopticon. Stronger links between Gramsci and Foucault, as well as Derrida, will be discussed in the concluding chapter.

52 Machiavelli, *The Prince* (Harmondsworth: Penguin 1961), p. 99, as referenced in *Prison Notebooks*, p. 170 n71

53 *Quaderni* III, 13: 17, p. 1581; *Prison Notebooks*, p. 179. In his last notebook, Gramsci references linguistics to sustain this point, *Quaderni* III, 29: 1–9, pp. 2341–51.

54 This point is amplified in C. Buci-Glucksmann's 'Hegemony and Consent,' in Anne Showstack-Sassoon, ed., *Approaches to Gramsci*, pp. 116–26

55 *Quaderni* III, 15: 14, 'Machiavelli. Elementi di politica,' pp. 1752–53; *Prison Notebooks*, 'Elements of Politics,' pp. 144–5

56 *Quaderni* II, 10: 41, pp. 1315–17

57 *Quaderni* III, 13: 17, 'Analisi delle situazioni : rapporti di forza,' pp. 1578–89, esp. pp. 1583ff; *Prison Notebooks*, 'Analysis of Situations, Relations of force,' pp. 177–85

58 This is not to suggest, as mentioned earlier, that the structure should now be privileged over the superstructure, nor for that matter, that the superstructure would have no connection to concepts of hegemony or political organization and struggle. It is rather to criticize, as did Gramsci, the kind of reductionism that placed everything political or even 'cultural' as being 'outside' the economic and hence exiled into the upper nether regions of a superstructural moment.

59 But, see in particular, Chantal Mouffe, 'Hegemony and Ideology in Gramsci,' in her *Gramsci and Marxist Theory*, pp. 168–204, where the concept of hegemony is no longer developed along the usual descriptions of it as a tactical device and is instead set in relation to the political and ideological moment. For an important survey of the historico-political and social evolution of the concept itself, see her later 'Hegemony: The Genealogy of a Concept,' co-authored with E. Laclau, in their *Hegemony and Socialist Strategy: Towards a Radical Democratic Politics*, pp. 7–46.

60 For an assessment of the difficulties involved in translating the concept, see, in particular, translation note 5 by Hoare and Smith in *Prison Notebooks*, pp. 55ff.

61 V.I. Lenin, *Two Tactics of Social Democracy in the Democratic Revolution*. An elaboration of this point can be found in Joseph Femia, *Gramsci's Political Thought: Hegemony, Consciousness, and the Revolutionary Process*.

62 Although Gramsci wrote several earlier drafts of this position (including some before his imprisonment), see, in particular, *Quaderni* III, 19: 24, 'Il problema della direzione politica nella formazione e nello sviluppo della nazione e dello Stato moderno in Italia,' pp. 2010–35; *Prison Notebooks*, 'The Problem of Political Leadership in the Formation and Development of the Nation and the Modern State in Italy,' pp. 55–85.

63 *Prison Notebooks*, p. 57 n5

64 See, for example, Perry Anderson, 'The Antinomies of Antonio Gramsci,' p. 15ff.

65 Gramsci's 'Notes on Italian History,' scattered throughout the *Quaderni*, are particularly relevant: *Quaderni* II, 10: 1, 9, 41.XI, 61; *Quaderni* III, 15: 11, 17, 59, 62, 19: 24, 25, 27, 28, 25: 2, 5. (In the *Prison Notebooks*, these various fragments are often interspersed with each other and in no particular order, but see pp. 52–120.) These notes establish, among other important insights, the concept of 'passive revolution,' a concept that underscored the ability for the state to transform during the Risorgimento without any specific leadership. 'What was involved,' explains Gramsci, 'was not a social group which "led" other groups, but a State which, even though it had limitations as a power, "led" the group which should have been "leading" ': *Quaderni* III, 15: 59, 'Risorgimento Italiano,' p. 1822; *Prison Notebooks*, 'The Function of Piedmont,' p. 105. Gramsci's discussion of alliances and coalitions and the general weaknesses emerging from those alliances for the Italian nation-state spawned heated debates in the late 1950s and early 1960s, particularly around the question as to whether or not agrarian reform (or the lack thereof) was likely to create a stronger, more homogeneous industrial class. The question of a passive revolution also underlay many of the debates on dependency, particularly with regard to the increasing occurrence of the military *coup d'état*. See, for example, the detailed analysis of J. Nun, 'Latin America: Hegemonic Crisis and the Military Coup.'

66 This acceptance of a notion of hegemony based on an already formed internality of political groups (which, taken together, would form a coalition or power bloc) has had serious ramifications for a variety of leftist strategies. Often tending to organize against the dominant groups in power by forging so-called alliances with a variety of 'communities,' i.e., seemingly unproblematic 'whole' categories of people, in this case, 'women,' 'working class,' 'gays,' 'people of colour,' 'students,' etc., the introduction of coalition politics has, at times, not only perpetuated the myth of exclusivity towards each other's 'community,' establishing, in so doing, a kind of 'hierarchy of oppressions,' but has tended to perpetuate a stereotypic notion of subjectivity within those groups. One finds, for example, that the 'women's community' has consequently tended to mean white, middle class, heterosexual, anti-porn, and anti-masculinist; the 'gay community' has tended to mean white, middle class, male, sexually active, and so forth. Not only does this stereotyping effectively disenfranchise those within the respective groups who do not seem 'to fit' these identities, it masks the

actual power relations that commence in order to produce a unified 'expression' of those diverse interests. Gramsci recognized explicitly the severe implications of taking as a given the 'already formed internality' of social groups, as his profound rethinking of hegemony bears out.

67 *Quaderni* II, 10 (II): 12, 'Introduzione allo studio della filosofia,' p. 1249; *Prison Notebooks*, 'Structure and Superstructure,' p. 365

68 *Quaderni* III, 13: 17, 'Analisi delle situazion : rapporti di forza,' pp. 1578–89; *Prison Notebooks*, 'Analysis of Situations. Relations of Force,' pp. 177–85. See also Stuart Hall, 'Politics and Ideology: Gramsci.'

69 *Quaderni* II, 10: 12, 'Introduzione allo studio della filosofia,' pp. 1249–50; *Prison Notebooks*, 'Structure and Superstructure,' p. 365–6

70 *Quaderni* II, 8: 21, 'Validità delle ideologie,' p. 869; *Prison Notebooks*, 'The Concept of "Ideology",' p. 377

71 *Quaderni* II, 11: 12.IV, pp. 1377–95; *Prison Notebooks*, pp. 325–43. See also David Cheal, 'Hegemony, Ideology and Contradictory Consciousness.'

72 *Quaderni* III, 13: 23, 'Osservazioni su alcuni aspetti della struttura dei partiti politici nei periodi di crisi organica,' pp. 1602–13; *Prison Notebooks*, 'Observations on Certain Aspects of the Structure of Political Parties in Periods of Organic Crisis,' pp. 210–18

73 *Quaderni* II, 7: 19, 'Ideologie,' p. 868; *Prison Notebooks*, 'The Concept of "Ideology",' p. 376

74 *Quaderni* II, 11: 17, 'La cosí detta "realtà del mondo esterno",' p. 1413; *Prison Notebooks*, 'The So-called "Reality of the External World",' p. 442. For a similar point rejecting the argument that each fluctuation of politics and ideology is, ipso facto, an immediate 'expression' of the economic 'base,' see also 7: 24, pp. 871-73.

75 *Quaderni* II, 7: 19, 'Ideologie,' p. 868; *Prison Notebooks*, 'The Concept of "Ideology",' p. 376 (parenthetical remarks, Gramsci's; bracketed remarks, mine)

76 *Quaderni* II, 7: 19, pp. 868–9; *Prison Notebooks*, pp. 376–77

77 Ibid, p. 869; *Prison Notebooks*, p. 377, (parenthetical remarks, Gramsci's)

78 The terms 'common sense' and 'good sense' are often cited in Gramsci's work, albeit his usage of these terms is vague and contradictory. Often their value seems to lie more in their polemic and even strategic sense than in theoretical usages, strictly speaking. But see *Quaderni* II, 11: 12, p. 1378–81; *Prison Notebooks*, p. 326–29, where he clarifies what the meaning of 'good sense' as being the practico-political and reasoned 'overcoming bestial and elemental passions through a conception of necessity which gives a conscious direction to one's activity. This is the healthy nucleus that exists in "common sense", the part of it which can be called "good sense" and which deserves to be made more

unified and coherent ... [It is thus a] problem of preserving the ideological unity of the entire social bloc which that ideology serves to cement and unify' (p. 1380/328). See also *Quaderni* II, 11: 13 and *Quaderni* III, 15: 20, pp. 1396–1401 and 1598–1601, respectively; only portions are translated in *Prison Notebooks*, but see pp. 419–24, 133–6, respectively. The discussion of 'common sense' in Gramsci's notebooks and its importance to revolutionary politics have been examined at length, with some exploring, in the main, the reactionary nature; see, for example, Geoffrey Nowell-Smith, 'Common Sense.' Others have developed from the posing of common and good sense a framework for an analysis of the role of intellectuals in creating a progressive society; see, for example, Alvin Gouldner's *The Future of Intellectuals and the Rise of the New Class: A Frame of Reference.*

79 *Quaderni* II, 11: 13, pp. 1396, 1397; *Prison Notebooks*, p. 419
80 *Quaderni* III, 13: 16, p. 1577–8; *Prison Notebooks*, 'Prediction and Perspective,' p. 172
81 *Quaderni* II, 6: 88, 'Stato gendarme – guardino notturno, ecc,' pp. 763–4; *Prison Notebooks*, pp. 262–3; see also *Quaderni* III, 17: 51, pp. 1947–8; *Prison Notebooks*, pp. 266–7.
82 *Quaderni* II, 10: 15, 'Noterelle di economia,' pp. 1253–4; *Prison Notebooks*, p. 208 83 *Quaderni* II, 6: 88, 'Stato gendarme – guardino notturno, ecc,' p. 263 (parenthetical remarks, Gramsci's; bracketed remarks, mine)
84 *Quaderni* I, 3: 34, p. 312, *Prison Notebooks*, p. 276 (emphasis, Gramsci)
85 *Quaderni* III, 12: 1, p. 1523; *Prison Notebooks*, p. 16; and, as well, *Quaderni* III, 13: 21, pp. 1601–2; *Prison Notebooks*, pp. 147–8. As we noted earlier, this task would lead to a new ethico-political outcome: 'Where these conditions exist, "the solution of the tasks becomes 'duty', will becomes 'free'." Morality would then become a search for the conditions necessary for the freedom of the will in a certain sense, aimed at a certain end, and the demonstration that these conditions exist.' *Quaderni* II, 7: 4, p. 855; *Prison Notebooks*, p. 410.
86 *Quaderni* III, 17: 37, 'Machiavelli,' p. 1939; *Prison Notebooks*, pp. 148–9
87 *Quaderni* III, 12: 1, esp. pp. 1520–2; *Prison Notebooks*, pp. 14–16
88 Ibid, p. 1522; *Prison Notebooks*, p. 15
89 Ibid, pp. 1513–30; *Prison Notebooks*, 'The Intellectuals,' pp. 5–25; *Quaderni* III, 19: 24 and 19: 25, pp. 2010–34, 2034–5; *Prison Notebooks*, pp. 55–84. Gramsci's development of the concept of the organic intellectual is being examined only in terms of the party (understood in its broader sense as social subject). Here it should be stated that there is no intention of replacing a vanguardist notion of class (or of party) with that of the category of intellectuals – a replacement suggested by certain academics often mesmerized with the importance of their own

lectures. For an assessment of the concept that differs markedly from either Lukacs's posing of the intellectual-as-vanguard or Jean-Paul Sartre's of the intellectual-philosopher (as the repository of the negative), see Christine Buci-Glucksmann, 'From the Question of the Intellectuals to the Question of the State,' in her *Gramsci and the State*, pp. 19–46. For an assessment of the role of intellectuals as the particular (class) bearers of the social totality, whose role has direct implications for creating a democratic society/state, see, for example, Alvin Gouldner's 'Prologue to a Theory of Revolutionary Intellectuals,' and as well his more recent *Against Fragmentation: The Origins of Marxism and the Sociology of Intellectuals*. For a brief assessment of Gramsci's pre-prison discussion on the distinction between an organic intellectual land a cult figure/personality, see Palmiro Togliatti, *On Gramsci and Other Writings*, as well as Alastair Davidson, *The Theory and Practice of Italian Communism*, Vol. 1.

90 Specific notes on the 'modern prince' were most often classed in notebooks 13 and 14; under the broader heading 'Note Sul Machiavelli, Sulla Politica E Sullo Stato Moderno' (which included the well-known discussions on Americanism and Fordism); notebooks 2, 6, 8, 17, and 22 remain particularly relevant.

91 *Quaderni* III, 13: 20, pp. 1600–1; *Prison Notebooks*, pp. 135–6 (bracketed remarks, mine)

92 See, for example, where he writes: 'Machiavelli merges with the people, becomes the people; not, however, some "generic" people, but the people whom he, Machiavelli has convinced by the preceding argument – the people whose consciousness and whose expression he becomes and feels himself to be, with whom he feels identified. The entire "logical" argument now appears as nothing other than auto-reflection on the part of the people ... whose conclusion is a cry of passionate urgency ... and makes it a kind of "political" manifesto': *Quaderni* III, 13: 1, p. 1556; *Prison Notebooks*, pp. 236–7.

93 Ibid, pp. 1553–61; *Prison Notebooks*, pp. 125–33. See also Leonardo Paggi, 'Machiavelli e Gramsci [1969],' reprinted in his *Le strategie del potere in Gramsci*, pp. 287–426.

94 Gramsci thus surmised, 'If one had to translate into modern political language the notion of "Prince", as used in Machiavelli's work, one would have to make a series of distinctions: the "Prince" could be a Head of State, or the leader of a government, but it could also be a political leader whose aim is to conquer a State, or to found a new type of State; in this sense, "Prince" could be translated in modern terms as "political party" ': *Quaderni* I, 5: 127, 'Machiavelli,' pp. 661–2; *Prison Notebooks*, pp. 252–3.

95 With this, we return once again to Marx's third thesis on Feuerbach,

but this time with a more layered answer to the question 'Who educates the educator?': it is the political party/organ intellectual of a people-nation, itself subjective to and expressing a politics-history, immanent in its expression.

96　Georges Sorel's, *Reflections on Violence*, as quoted in *Prison Notebooks*, p. 126 n4

97　*Quaderni* III, 13: 21, pp. 1601–2; *Prison Notebooks*, pp. 147–8

98　*Quaderni* II, 10: 7, 13, pp. 1222–4 and 1235–7, respectively.

99　*Quaderni* III, 13: 1, p. 1556; *Prison Notebooks*, p. 126

100　*Quaderni* III, 13: 17, pp. 1578–89, esp. pp. 1583–84; *Prison Notebooks*, pp. 177–85

101　Ibid, pp. 1583–4; *Prison Notebooks*, p. 181, where Gramsci writes: 'The first and most elementary of [the relation of political forces] is the economic-corporate level: a tradesman feels *obliged* to stand by another tradesman, a manufacturer by another manufacturer, etc; but the tradesman does not yet feel solidarity with the manufacturer; in other words, the members of the professional group of its unity and homogeneity, and of the need to organise it, but in the case of the wider social group this is not yet so.'

102　*Quaderni* III, 13: 1, p. 1556; *Prison Notebooks*, p. 127 (parenthetical remarks, Gramsci's; emphasis and bracketed remarks, mine)

103　*Quaderni* II, 11: 52, 'Regolarità e necessità,' pp. 147–81, esp. pp. 1480–1; *Prison Notebooks*, 'Regularity and Necessity,' pp. 411–14, esp. pp. 413–3

104　*Quaderni* III, 13: 17, pp. 1578–89; *Prison Notebooks*, pp. 177–85

105　Ibid, p. 1584; *Prison Notebooks*, pp. 181–2

106　There is significant discussion in the Italian and French literature, less so in the English, on the concept of the historic bloc, particularly in terms of whether the meaning of historic bloc were to extend to the formation of the social totality itself or remain a function of consolidating class interest per se. On presenting the historic bloc as the expressive form of social totality – but doing so by privileging this unity over the specific relations of force from which it was constituted – see, for example, the discussion by H. Portelli, *Gramsci et le bloc historique*. A useful summary of a number of those debates can be found in Buci-Glucksmann's *Gramsci and the State*, pp. 273–90. It would seem from Gramsci's argument that historic bloc would mean neither a homogenization of a particular set of interest per se nor a synonym for a social totality, if, by that totality, the element of full closure were in any way implied.

107　*Quaderni* II, 8: 182, 'Struttura e superstrutture,' pp. 1051–2; *Prison Notebooks*, 'Structure and Superstructure,' p. 366

108　This is not to say that a trade union itself (or, for that matter, as stated earlier, a newspaper, a theatre group, etc.) could not become 'party.' It is merely to emphasize that any group whose goals were determined issue by issue, i.e., as a kind of 'trade unionism,' could never become 'organic' in the fullest sense of the word.

109 *Quaderni* III, 13: 1, pp. 1556–61; *Prison Notebooks*, pp. 128–33. See also Chantal Mouffe, 'Hegemony and the Integral State in Gramsci: Toward a New Concept of Politics.'

110 *Quaderni* III, 17: 51, 'Machiavelli,' pp. 1947–8; *Prison Notebooks*, 'Religion, State, Party,' p. 267 (parenthetical remarks, Gramsci's)

111 This is a complex point, perhaps better understood by way of an example. If we take the oppression of women and, with it, feminism as an organized (however much diverse) political movement intent on destroying that oppression, we must rethink the very meaning of 'woman' herself. Would this not mean, as Gramsci's argument here clearly suggests, that the ethico-political universalizing of this entity called 'woman' would mean precisely not only the disappearance of the category and concept of woman in its particularized and antagonistically (misleading) opposition to 'man,' but, indeed, that of the movement itself through which that liberation was founded? And does this not mean, finally, that the concrete universal of a 'humanity' in which it is resolved is one that is never 'closed' or fully sutured, but maintains its cohesive subjectivity – that, by necessity, always involves a specificity and negation, in this case along open and immanent lines – of that very identity? A gramscian logic would lead one to say, yes.

112 *Quaderni* III, 14: 70, 'Machiavelli. Quando si può dire che un partito sia formato e non possa essere distrutto con mezzi normali,' pp. 1732–3; *Prison Notebooks*, 'Political Parties,' p. 152

113 *Quaderni* III, 13: 21, p. 1601; *Prison Notebooks*, p. 147 (parenthetical remarks, Gramsci's)

114 *Quaderni* III, 13: 18, 'Alcuni aspetti teorici e practici dell' "economismo",' p. 1590; *Prison Notebooks*, 'Some Theoretical and Practical Aspects of "Economism",' p. 160. See also *Quaderni* III, 26: 6, 'Lo Stato "veilleur de nuit",' pp. 2302–3; *Prison Notebooks*, p. 261. But in *Quaderni* III, 12–1, pp. 1518–19, *Prison Notebooks*, p. 12, Gramsci also writes that the state does not equal civil society, and indeed that they make up two distinct moments in the *superstructure*. Elsewhere he suggests that the 'State = political society + civil society, in other words, hegemony protected by the armour of coercion.' Are these contradictory statements and/or major vacillations on the problem? The short answer is no. In the first case he is attempting to articulate in practical-theoretic terms how a new state (as party) could be born – and indeed, must be born – on the fractured, discontinuous terrain of history, so that it can become the bearer of a new world-view, rooted in the 'necessary-rational-real'

terrain of history, as noted earlier, in chapter 3. We can see that, in this case, the state would, consequently, be distinct from, but not equal to, civil society; taken together they would form the unity of a superstructural moment. In the second case, Gramsci was attempting to underscore how the 'party-as-integral-state' must be pitted against the reality of the actual power relations and processes entrenched in the old society itself. Those power relations exist precisely because they are hegemonic, that is, precisely because they are based both on the legitimate consent of 'the led,' and as such elicit that consent with the underbelly of violence. Thus, in this case, Gramsci insists on posing the state as political + civil society; that is, as the constitutive unity that emerges from the relations of forces and crises inherent in its first moment (the structure), and which, in being so constituted, implies a notion of power, and, in particular, state power, which is never homogeneously contained.

115 *Quaderni* II, 6: 88, 'Stato gendarme–guardiano notturno, ecc,' pp. 763–4; *Prison Notebooks*, 'The State,' pp. 262–3

116 Thus the state disappears (or withers away): we are left with the *law* of civil society as opposed to the *rule* of authoritarian logic. Thus he concludes that with this 'hegemonic state' (i.e., civil society), 'it is only possible to create a system of principles asserting that the State's goals is its own end, its own disappearance, in other words the re-absorption of political society into civil society': *Quaderni* I, 5: 127, 'Machiavelli,' p. 662; *Prison Notebooks*, 'Politics and Constitutional Law,' p. 253.

117 *Quaderni* II, 8: 191, 'Egemonia e democrazia,' p. 1056 (parenthetical remarks, Gramsci's; underlining, mine). See also 10: 44, pp. 1330–2, where Gramsci suggests that the philosophy of praxis is, accordingly, best understood as a 'democratic' philosophy.

118 *Quaderni* III, 22: 15, 'Civiltà americana ed europea,' p. 2179; *Prison Notebooks*, 'American and European Civilization,' p. 317

119 *Quaderni* II, 10: 40, p. 1291; *Prison Notebooks*, p. 368. But, see also *Quaderni* II, 11: 35, 'La teleologia,' p. 1450; *Prison Notebooks*, 'Teleology,' p. 470-1.

120 *Quaderni* I, 5: 127, p. 657; *Prison Notebooks*, p. 249 (my emphasis)

121 *Quaderni* II, 11: 23, 'La teleologia,' p. 1426

122 *Quaderni* II, 10: 48.II, 'Progresso e divenire,' p. 1338; *Prison Notebooks*, 'Progress and Becoming,' p. 360 (my emphasis)

123 *Quaderni* II, 11: 15, 'Il concetto di "scienza",' pp. 1405–6; *Prison Notebooks*, 'The Concept of Science",' p. 440

124 *Quaderni* II, 9: 68, 'Machiavelli. Centralismo organico e centralismo democratico,' pp. 1138–40; *Quaderni* III, 13: 36, 'Sulla burocrazia,' pp. 1632–5.

Chapter Six

1 Scholars such as Walter Adamson typify this kind of (misleading) interpretation. He writes, in part: 'As in the German Idealist traditions, Gramsci tended philosophically toward a unitarist rather than a pluralist position; he seemed to believe in a kind of anthropological impetus immanent in history which supports political movements and forms of political organization tending toward uniformity and against diversity ... In comparison, Gramsci's was a far simply world [sic] – one which led to a "pessimism of the intelligence" but which still promoted an "optimism of the will"': *Hegemony and Revolution*, pp. 240, 246.

2 *Quaderni* III, 14: 72, 'Contenuto e forma,' p. 1740; *Cultural Writings*, 'Content and Form,' p. 206

3 The claim that Gramsci is so clearly the precursor to discourse theory might imply that the latter exists as a fairly cohesive theoretical approach. Nothing could be farther from the truth; indeed, it could be said that the trajectories of what has come to be diagnosed as 'postmodernism' are almost as voluminous as are the myriad texts written for and against it. We will narrow our discussion to the work by Foucault, Derrida, Laclau, and Mouffe, and set the reasons for that choice below. But, for a general introduction of the depth and breadth of the field, see in particular Linda Hutcheon, *The Politics of Postmodernism*, and the more recent, extremely important reader by Peggy Kamuf, ed., *A Derrida Reader: Between the Blinds*.

4 Ernesto Laclau and Chantal Mouffe, 'Hegemony and Radical Democracy,' in their *Hegemony and Socialist Strategy*, pp. 176–78, 192–3

5 Or as Antonin Artaud put it in *Cahiers de Rodez*, 'we must rid ourselves of all static, ontological 'truths': We must make reason shit.' On this general point, see Rosalind Krauss, *The Originality of the Avant-Garde and Other Modernist Myths*, and Jacques Derrida, *The Truth in Painting*.

6 Michel Foucault, *This Is Not a Pipe*, p. 16 (parenthetical remarks, Foucault's; bracketed remarks, mine)

7 Jacques Derrida, 'The Hinge,' in his *Of Grammatology*, pp. 65–73.

8 M. Foucault, *Maurice Blanchot: The Thought from Outside*, pp. 9–11

9 Ibid, pp. 13, 21–2. On this point, see also Gilles Deleuze, *Foucault*, pp. 86–102; and J.W. Bernauer, *Michel Foucault's Force of Flight: Towards an Ethics for Thought*, pp. 46–61.

10 For a detailed critique of the philosophy of (self) reflection and extremely clear exposition on the way in which Derrida sought to go 'beyond' (or, perhaps, 'beside') it, see Rodolphe Gasché, *The Tain of the Mirror: Derrida and the Philosophy of Reflection*.

11 Foucault, *Thought from the Outside*, pp. 23–4
12 Ibid, p. 24
13 Ibid, pp. 21–2
14 M. Foucault, 'Introduction to a Non-Fascist Life,' pp. xiii–xiv (parenthetical remarks, Foucault's)
15 Jacques Derrida, 'The Double Session,' in his *Dissemination*, p. 216.
16 Ibid, p. 215
17 On this point, see for example, Ernesto Laclau, 'New Reflections on the Revolution of Our Time' and 'Letter to Aletta' in his *New Reflections on the Revolution of Our Time*, pp. 29–31 and 160–1, respectively.
18 *Quaderni* I, 3: 34, p. 311; *Prison Notebooks*, p. 276

Bibliography

Books

Adams, Henry Packwood. *The Life and Writings of Giambattista Vico*. London: George Allen and Unwin Ltd. 1935

Adamson, Walter. *Hegemony and Revolution: A Study of Antonio Gramsci's Political and Cultural Theory*. Berkeley: University of California Press 1980

Albee, E. *A History of English Utilitarianism*. London: Swan Sonnenschein and Co. 1902

Alcara, R. *La formazione e i primi anni del Partito comunista italiano nella storiografia marxista*. Milan: Jaca 1970

Althusser, L., and E. Baliber. *Reading Capital*. Translated by Ben Brewster. London: New Left Books 1970

Anderson, Perry. *Arguments within English Marxism*. London: Verso 1980

– *Considerations on Western Marxism: A Critical Reader*. London: New Left Books 1977

Ascoli, Max, and Fritz Lehmann (eds.). *Political and Economic Democracy*. New York: W.W. Norton and Company Inc. 1937

Auciello, Nicola. *Socialismo ed egemonia in Gramsci e Togliatti*. Bari: De Donato 1974

Avineri, Shlomo. *Hegel's Theory of the Modern State*. London: Cambridge University Press 1972

Badaloni, N. *Il problema dell'immanenza nella filosofia politica di Gramsci*. Venezia: Arsenale 1988

– *Il marxismo di Gramsci*. Torino: Einaudi editore 1975

Badaloni, N., L. Gruppi, C. Buci-Glucksmann, G. Nardone, E. Agazzi,

190   Bibliography

A. Natta, and S. Antonielli. *Attualita di Gramsci: L'egemonia, lo stato, la cultura, il metodo, il partito.* Milano: Il Saggiatore 1977

Baldan, Attilio. *Gramsci come storico: Studio sulle fonti dei 'Quaderni del carcere.'* Bari: Dedalo Libri 1978

Barber, Benjamin. *Strong Democracy: Participatory Politics for a New Age.* Berkeley: University of California Press 1984

Bauman, Z. *Culture as Praxis.* London: Routledge and Kegan Paul 1973

Beck, L.W. (ed.). *Kant's Theory of Knowledge: Selected Papers from the Third International Kant Congress.* Dordrecht, Holland: D. Reidel Publishing Co. 1974

Beer, Max. *A History of British Socialism* (in two volumes). London: G. Bell and Sons 1929

Bellingeri, Edo. *Dall'intellettuale al politico: Le 'Cronache Teatrali' di Gramsci.* Bari: Dedalo Libri 1975

Bergami, Giancarlo. *Il giovane Gramsci e il marxismo 1911–1918.* Milano: Feltrinelli Economica 1977

Bergson, Henri. *Creative Evolution.* Translated by A. Mitchell. New York: Henry Holt and Co. 1911

– *The Creative Mind.* Translated by M.L. Andison. New York: The Philosophical Library 1946

– *Matter and Memory.* Translated by Nancy Margaret Paul and W. Scott Palmer. London: George Allen and Unwin/Humanities Press 1911, 1970

Berlin, Isaiah. *Four Essays on Liberty.* Oxford: Oxford University Press 1969

– *Vico and Herder: Two Studies in the History of Ideas.* London: Hogarth Press 1976

Bernauer, J.W. *Michel Foucault's Force of Flight: Towards an Ethics for Thought.* London: Humanities Press 1990

Bernstein, E. *Evolutionary Socialism: A Criticism and Affirmation.* New York: Schocken Books 1961

Bloomfield, Jon (ed.). *Class, Hegemony, and Party.* London: Lawrence and Wishart 1977

Bobbio, Norberto. *The Future of Democracy.* Translated by Roger Griffin and edited by Richard Bellamy. Cambridge: Polity Press 1987

Boggs, Carl. *Gramsci's Marxism.* London: Pluto Press 1976

– *The Two Revolutions: Gramsci and the Dilemma of Western Marxism.* Boston: South End Press 1984

Bowles, Samuel, and Herb Gintis. *Democracy and Capitalism: Property, Community, and the Contradictions of Modern Social Thought.* New York: Basic Books 1986

Brown, Merle E. *Neo-Idealist Aesthetics: Croce-Gentile-Collingwood.* Detroit: Wayne State University Press 1966

Buci-Glucksmann, Christine. *Gramsci and the State*. Translated by David Fernbach. London: Lawrence and Wishart 1980

Bukharin, N. *Historical Materialism: A System of Sociology*. Moscow: Progress Publishers 1925

Burke, Edmund. *Reflections on the Revolution in France (1790)*. Edited and translated by F.G. Selby. London: Macmillan 1930

Burnheim, John. *Is Democracy Possible? The Alternative to Electoral Politics*. Cambridge: Polity Press 1985

Calabro, G. P. *Antonio Gramsci: La 'transizione' politica*. Napoli: Edizioni scientifiche italiane 1982

Cammett, John M. *Antonio Gramsci and the Origins of Italian Communism*. Stanford: Stanford University Press 1967

Carr, H. Wilden. *The Philosophy of Benedetto Croce: The Problem of Art and History*. New York: Macmillan 1917

– *The Philosophy of Change: A Study of the Fundamental Principle of the Philosophy of Bergson*. London: Macmillan 1914

Cavalcanti, Pedro, and Paul Piccone. *History, Philosophy, and Culture in the Young Gramsci*. Translated by P. Molajoni, M.A. Aiello-Peabody, P. Piccone, and J. Thiem. St Louis: Telos Press 1975

Clark, Martin. *Antonio Gramsci and the Revolution That Failed*. New Haven: Yale University Press 1977

Cohen, G.A. *Karl Marx's Theory of History: A Defence*. Princeton: Princeton University Press 1978

Colletti, Lucio. *From Rousseau to Lenin: Studies in Ideology and Society*. Translated by John Merrington and Judith White. London: New Left Books 1972

– *Marxism and Hegel*. Translated by Lawrence Garner. London: Verso/New Left Books 1973

Connerton, Paul. *The Tragedy of the Enlightenment: An Essay on the Frankfurt School*. Cambridge: Cambridge University Press 1980

Coward, R., and J. Ellis. *Language and Materialism: Developments in Semiology and the Theory of the Subject*. London: Routledge and Kegan Paul 1977

Cozens, Phil. *Twenty Years of Antonio Gramsci: A Bibliography of Gramsci and Gramsci Studies Published in English 1957–1977*. London: Lawrence and Wishart 1977

Croce, Benedetto. *Aesthetic as Science of Expression and General Linguistic* (Volume 1 of *The Philosophy of Spirit*). Translated by Douglas Ainslie. London: Macmillan 1900, 1904, 1909

– *The Conduct of Life*. Translated by Arthur Livingston. New York: Harcourt Brace and Co. 1924

– *Historical Materialism and the Economics of Karl Marx*. Translated by C.M. Meredith. London: Howard Latimer Ltd 1919

- *History as the Story of Liberty.* London: George Allen and Unwin 1941
- *Logic as a Science of Pure Concept* (Volume 2 of *The Philosophy of Spirit*). Translated by Douglas Ainslie. London: Macmillan 1917
- *My Philosophy: Essays on the Moral and Political Problems of Our Time.* Translated by E.P. Carritt. New York: Collier Books 1962
- *The Philosophy of Giambattista Vico.* Translated by R.G. Collingwood. London: Howard Latimer 1913
- *The Philosophy of the Practical (Economic and Ethic)* (Volume 3 of *The Philosophy of Spirit*). Translated by Douglas Ainslie. London: Macmillan 1913
- *Philosophy, Poetry, History: An Anthropology of Essays.* Translated by Cecil Sprigge. London: Oxford University Press 1966
- *Politics and Morals.* Translated by Salvatore J. Castiglione. New York: Philosophical Library 1945
- *What Is Living and What Is Dead in the Philosophy of Hegel.* Translated by Douglas Ainslie. London: Macmillan 1915
Croly, Herbert. *Progressive Democracy.* New York: Macmillan 1914
Cunningham, Frank. *Democratic Theory and Socialism.* Cambridge: Cambridge University Press 1987
Cutler, A., B. Hindess, P. Hirst, and A. Hussain (eds.). *Marx's 'Capital' and Capitalism Today.* London: Routledge and Kegan Paul 1977
Dahl, Robert. *Dilemmas of Pluralist Democracy: Autonomy vs. Control.* New Haven and London: Yale University Press 1982
- *A Preface to Democratic Theory.* Chicago: University of Chicago Press 1956
Davico-Bonino, Guido. *Gramsci e il teatro.* Torino: Einaudi editore 1972
Davidson, Alastair. *Antonio Gramsci: Towards An Intellectual Biography.* London: Merlin Press 1977
- *The Theory and Practice of Italian Communism,* Vol. 1. London: Merlin Press 1982
Davis, John A. (ed.). *Gramsci and Italy's Passive Revolution.* London: Croom Helm 1979
Deleuze, Gilles. *Foucault.* Translated by Sean Hand. London: Athlone Press 1988
Derrida, Jacques. *Dissemination.* Translated with an introduction by Barbara Johnson. Chicago: University of Chicago Press 1981
- *Of Grammatology.* Translated and with an introduction by Gayatri Chakravorty Spivak. Baltimore: Johns Hopkins University Press 1976
- *Margins of Philosophy.* Translated by Alan Bass. Chicago: University of Chicago Press 1982
- *Speech and Phenomena and Other Essays on Husserl's Theory of Signs.* Edited and translated by David B. Allison. Evanston, Ill.: Northwestern University Press 1973

– *The Truth in Painting.* Translated by Geoff Gennington and Ian McLeod. Chicago: University of Chicago Press 1987

Dewey, John. *The Quest for Certainty.* New York: Capricorn 1960

Dilthey, W. *Pattern and Meaning in History: Thoughts on History and Society.* Edited by H.P. Rickman. New York: Harper Torchbooks 1962

Duncan, G. (ed.). *Democracy: Theory and Practice.* Cambridge: Cambridge University Press 1983

Dunn, John. *The Political Thought of John Locke: An Historical Account of the Argument in 'Two Treatises of Government.'* Cambridge: Cambridge University Press 1969

Engels, F. *The Condition of the Working Class in England.* Translated by W.O. Henderson and W.H. Chaloner. Oxford: Blackwell 1958

– *Dialectics of Nature.* Translated by Clemens Dutt. Moscow: Progress Publishers 1976

Felice, Franco de. *Fascismo, democrazia, fronte populare.* Bari: De Donato 1973

Femia, Joseph. *Gramsci's Political Thought: Hegemony, Consciousness and the Revolutionary Process.* Oxford: Clarendon Press 1981

Ferrata, G., and N. Gallo (eds.). *2000 pagine di Gramsci* (two volumes). Milano: Il Saggiatore 1971

Fichte, Johann Gottlieb. *The Science of Knowledge.* Translated by A.E. Kroeger. London: Trubner & Co., 1889

Fiori, Giuseppe. *Antonio Gramsci: Life of a Revolutionary.* New York: E.P. Dutton & Co. 1971

Foucault, Michel. *The Care of the Self* (Volume 3 of *The History of Sexuality*). Translated by Robert Hurley. New York: Vintage Books 1986

– *Discipline and Punish: The Birth of the Prison.* Translated by A. Sheridan. New York: Vintage/Random House 1979

– *Foucault Live: Interviews, 1966–84.* Translated by J. Johnston. New York: Semiotext(e) 1989

– *Maurice Blanchot: The Thought from Outside.* Translated by B. Massumi. New York: Zone Books 1987

– *The Order of Things: An Archaeology of the Human Sciences.* New York: Random House 1973

– *This Is Not a Pipe.* Translated and edited by James Harkness, with illustrations and letters by René Magritte. Berkeley: University of California Press 1982

Freeman, Michael, and D. Robertson (eds.). *The Frontiers of Political Theory.* New York: St Martin's Press 1980

Friedman, Milton. *Capitalism and Freedom.* Chicago: University of Chicago Press 1962

Gallino, L., A. Pizzorno, N. Bobbio, A. Gramsci, and R. Debray. *Gramsci y la sciencias sociales / cuadernos Pasado y Presente.* Mexico: PYP 1978

Gasché, Rodolphe. *The Tain of the Mirror: Derrida and the Philosophy of Reflection.* Cambridge, Mass.: Harvard University Press 1986

Gentile, Giovanni. *Genesis and Structure of Society.* Translated by H.S. Harris. Urbana: University of Illinois Press 1960

– *Origini e dottrina del fascismo.* Quaderni dell'istituto nazionale fascista di cultura (serie seconda). Roma: Liberia del Littorio 1929

– *The Philosophy of Art.* Translated by G. Gullace. Ithaca: Cornell University Press 1972

– *The Theory of Mind as Pure Act.* Translated by H. Wilden Carr. London: Macmillan 1922

Giddens, Anthony. *The Class Structure of Advanced Capitalist Societies.* London: Hutchison 1981

Giorgi, Pietro Leandro di. *Fondazione 'marxista' dell'analisi socio-economica nei 'Quaderni del carcere.'* Firenze: Antonio Lalli 1981

Gouldner, Alvin. *Against Fragmentation: The Origins of Marxism and the Sociology of Intellectuals.* New York: Oxford University Press 1985

– *The Coming Crisis of Western Sociology.* London: Heinemann 1970

– *The Future of Intellectuals and the Rise of the New Class: A Frame of Reference.* New York: Continuum 1980

– *The Two Marxisms: Contradictions and Anomalies in the Development of Theory.* New York: Seabury Press 1980

Graham, Keith (ed.). *Contemporary Political Philosophy: Radical Studies.* London: Cambridge University Press 1982

Gramsci, Antonio. *A Gramsci Reader: Selected Writings 1916–1935.* Edited by David Forgacs. London: Lawrence and Wishart 1988

– Arte e folclore, *a curi di Guiseppe Presipino.* Roma: Newton Compton editori 1976

– *La costruzione del partito comunista 1923–1926.* Torino: Einaudi 1971

– *Lettere dal carcere.* A cura di Sergio Caprioglio e Elsa Fubini. Torino: Einaudi 1965

– *Letters from Prison.* Selected and translated by Lynne Lawner. London: Jonathan Cape 1975

– *Lettere antifascisti dal carcere e dal contino.* Roma: Editori Riuniti 1975

– *The Modern Prince and Other Writings.* Translated by Louis Marks. New York: International Publishers 1957

– *New Edinburgh Review: Gramsci's Letters from Prison* (in three volumes). Translated by Hamish Henderson. Edinburgh: University of Edinburgh Press 1947

– *Quaderni del carcere* (edizione critica dell'Istituto Gramsci, 4 vols.). A cura di V. Gerratana. Torino: Einaudi 1975

– *Scritti Politici.* A cura di Paolo Spriano. Roma: Riuniti 1967

– *Selections from Cultural Writings.* Edited by D. Forgacs and G. Nowell-

Smith, translated by W. Boelhower. Cambridge, Mass.: Harvard University Press 1985

- *Selections from Political Writings 1910–1920.* Selected and edited by Q. Hoare; translated by J. Matthews. New York: International Publishers 1977

- *Selections from Political Writings 1921–1926.* Edited and translated by Q. Hoare. New York: International Publishers 1978

- *Selections from the Prison Notebooks.* Edited by Quintin Hoare and Geoffrey Nowell-Smith. New York: International Publishers 1971

Green, Thomas H. *Lectures on the Principles of Political Obligation (and Other Writings).* Edited by Paul Harris and John Marrow. Cambridge: Cambridge University Press 1986

Grimaldi, Alfonsina. *The Universal Humanity of Giambattista Vico.* New York: S.F. Vanni 1958

Gruppi, L. *Socialismo e democrazia: La teoria marxista dello Stato.* Milano: Edizioni del Calendario 1969

Halevy, E. *The Growth of Philosophic Radicalism.* Translated by Mary Morris. London: Faber and Faber 1952

Hegel, G.W.F. *Phenomenology of Spirit.* Translated by A.V. Miller. Oxford: Clarendon Press 1977

- *Philosophy of Mind* (Being Part 3 of the *Encyclopaedia of the Philosophical Sciences, 1830*). Translated by W. Wallace; foreword by A.V. Miller and J.N. Findlay. Oxford: Clarendon Press 1977

- *Philosophy of Right.* Translated by T.M. Knox. Oxford: Clarendon Press 1942

Held, David. *Models of Democracy.* Stanford: Stanford University Press 1987

Hibbin, Sally (ed.). *Politics, Ideology and the State.* London: Lawrence and Wishart 1978

Hindess, Barry. *Philosophy and Methodology in the Social Sciences.* London: Harvester Press 1977

Hindess, Barry, and P. Hirst. *Mode of Production and Social Formation.* London: Macmillan 1977

Hobbes, Thomas. *Leviathan.* Edited by C.B. Macpherson. New York and London: Penguin Books 1968

Hobsbawn, Eric. *The Italian Road to Socialism: An Interview with Giorgio Napolitano of the Italian Communist Party.* Translated by John Cammett and Victoria De Grazia. New Haven, Conn.: Lawrence & Hill Co. 1977

Hoffman, John. *The Gramscian Challenge: Coercion and Consent in Marxist Political Theory.* Oxford: Basil Blackwell 1984

Holloway, J., and S. Picciotto (eds.). *State and Capital: A Marxist Debate.* London: Edward Arnold 1978

Horowitz, Asher. *Rousseau, Nature, and History.* Toronto: University of
Toronto Press 1987

Horowitz, G., and A. Horowitz. *Everywhere They Are in Chains: Political
Theory from Rousseau to Marx.* Toronto: Nelson 1988

Horowitz, Irving Louis. *Radicalism and the Revolt against Reason: The Social
Theories of Georges Sorel.* London: Routledge and Kegan Paul 1961

Howard, Dick. *From Marx to Kant.* New York: State University of New York,
Albany 1985

Howard, Dick, and Karl E. Klare (eds.). *The Unknown Dimension: European
Marxism since Lenin.* New York: Basic Books 1972

Hughes, H. Stuart. *Consciousness and Society: The Reorientation of European
Social Thought 1890–1930.* New York: Knopf 1958

Hunt, Alan (ed.). *Marxism and Democracy.* London: Lawrence and Wishart
1980

– *Class and Structure.* London: Lawrence and Wishart 1977

Hutcheon, Linda. *The Politics of Postmodernism.* London: Routledge and
Kegan Paul 1989

Hyppolite, J. *Genesis and Structure of Hegel's* Phenomenology of Spirit.
Translated by Samuel Cherniak and John Heckman. Evanston: Northwestern University Press 1974

Jay, Martin. *Marxism and Totality: The Adventures of a Concept from Lukacs to
Habermas.* Berkeley: University of California Press 1984

Jessop, Bob. *The Capitalist State: Marxist Theories and Methods.* Oxford: Basil
Blackwell 1982, 1984

Jocteau, G.C. *Leggere Gramsci: Una guida alle interpretazioni.* Milano: Feltrinelli 1975

Joll, James. *Gramsci.* Glasgow: W. Collins 1977

Kamuf, Peggy (ed.). *A Derrida Reader: Between the Blinds.* London: Harvest-
er/Wheatsheaf 1991

Kant, Immanuel. *The Critique of Judgement.* Translated by James Creed
Meredith. Oxford: Oxford University Press 1928

– *Critique of Pure Reason.* Translated by Norman Kemp Smith. London:
Macmillan 1934

Kilminster, R. *Praxis and Method: A Sociological Dialogue with Lukacs, Gramsci,
and the Early Frankfurt School.* London: Routledge and Kegan Paul 1979

Kolakowski, Lezek. *Main Currents of Marxism* (three volumes). New York:
Oxford University Press 1982

Korsch, Karl. *Marxism and Philosophy.* London: New Left Books and Monthly Review Press 1970

Kosik, Karel. *Dialetics of the Concrete: A Study on Problems of Man and World.*
Translated by Karel Kovanda with James Schmidt. Boston: D. Reidel
Publishing Co. 1976

Krauss, Rosalind. *The Originality of the Avant-Garde and Other Modernist Myths*. Cambridge, Mass.: MIT Press 1985

Kuhn, Thomas. *The Structure of Scientific Revolutions*. Chicago: University of Chicago Press 1962

Labriola, Antonio. *Socialism and Philosophy*. Introduced by Paul Piccone. St Louis: Telos Press 1980

Lacasta, J. Ignacio. *Revolucion socialista e idealismo en Gramsci*. Madrid: Editorial revolucion 1981

Laclau, Ernesto. *Politics and Ideology in Marxist Theory: Capitalism–Fascism–Populism*. London: New Left Books 1977

– *New Reflections on the Revolution of Our Time*. London: Verso 1990

Laclau, Ernesto, and Chantal Mouffe. *Hegemony and Socialist Strategy: Towards a Radical Democratic Politics*. London: Verso 1985

Laski, Harold. *Democracy in Crisis*. London: G. Allen 1933

Lefebvre, Henri. *The Sociology of Marx*. Translated by Norbert Guterman. New York: Pantheon Books 1968

Lenin, V.I. – *Collected Works* (Vols. 4 and 38). Moscow: Progress Publishers 1961

– *The Selected Works of V.I. Lenin*. Moscow: Progress Publishers 1968

– *Two Tactics of Social Democracy in the Democratic Revolution*. New York: International Publishers 1935

Lepre, Aurelio. *Gramsci secondo Gramsci*. Napoli: Liguori 1978

Lichtheim, Georg. *Marxism: An Historical and Critical Study*. London: Routledge and Kegan Paul 1961

Lipsett, Seymour Martin. *Political Man: The Social Bases of Politics*. New York: Anchor Books 1963

Lively, J. *Democracy*. London: Basil Blackwell 1975

Lively, J., and J. Rees (eds.). *Utilitarian Logic and Politics: James Mill's 'Essay on Government', Macaulay's Critique, and the Ensuing Debate*. Oxford: Clarendon Press 1978

Locke, John. *An Essay Concerning Human Understanding*. Edited by A.S. Pringle-Pattison. Oxford: Clarendon Press 1924

– *Two Treatises of Government*. Edited by Peter Laslett. Cambridge: Cambridge University Press 1967

Lo Piparo, Franco. *Lingua, intellettuali, ed egemonia in Gramsci*. Bari: editori Laterza e Figli 1979

Loria, Achille. *Karl Marx*. Authorized translation from the Italian with foreword by Eden and Cedar Paul. London: George Allen and Unwin 1920

Lukacs, Gyorgy. *History and Class Consciousness: Studies in Marxist Dialectics*. Translated by Rodney Livingstone. Cambridge, Mass.: MIT Press 1971

Lukes, Steven. *Marxism and Morality*. Oxford: Clarendon Press 1985

– *Power: A Radical View*. London: Macmillan 1974

Lyttleton, Adrian (ed.). *Italian Fascisms: From Pareto to Gentile*. New York: Harper and Row Publishers 1975

Macciocchi, Maria-Antonietta. *Pour Gramsci*. Paris: Editions du Seuil 1975

Machiavelli, Niccolo. *The Prince and the Discourses*. Edited by Bernard Crick and translated by Leslie Walker. Harmondsworth: Penguin Books 1970

Macpherson, C.B. *Democratic Theory: Essays in Retrieval*. London: Oxford University Press 1973

– *Edmund Burke*. Oxford: Oxford University Press 1980

– *The Life and Times of Liberal Democracy*. London: Oxford University Press 1977

– *The Political Theory of Possessive Individualism: Hobbes to Locke*. Oxford: Oxford University Press 1962

– *Property*. Oxford: Basil Blackwell 1978

– *The Real World of Democracy*. Toronto: Canadian Broadcasting Corporation 1965

– *The Rise and Fall of Economic Justice and Other Papers*. Oxford: Oxford University Press 1985

McPherson, T. *Political Obligation*. London: Routledge and Kegan Paul 1967

Maiello, R. *Vita di Antonio Gramsci*. Torino: ERI 1980

Maier, Bruno. *Antonio Gramsci: Introduzione e guida allo studio dell'opera gramsciana*. Firenze: Le Monnier 1978

Mariani, Umberto (ed.). *Italian Quaterly: Special Issue on Gramsci*. Rutgers University, No. 97–8 (Summer/Fall 1984)

Martinez-Lorca, Andres. *El Problema de los intelectuales y el concepto de cultura en Gramsci*. Malaga: Universidad de Malaga 1981

Marx, Karl. *Capital: A Critical Analysis of Capitalist Production*. 3 Vols. Translated by S. Moore and E. Aveling, edited by F. Engels. Moscow: Progress Publishers n.d.

– *Critique of Hegel's Philosophy of Right*. London: Cambridge University Press 1970

– *Economic and Philosophic Maniscripts of 1844*. Translated by D. Struik. New York: International Publishers 1964

– *The German Ideology*. Moscow: Progress Publishers, 1964

– *The Grundrisse: Foundations of the Critique of Political Economy*. Translated by M. Nicolaus. New York: Vintage Books 1973

– *The Poverty of Philosophy: Answer to the 'Philosophy of Poverty' by M. Proudhon*. Moscow: Progress Publishers 1975

Marx, Karl, and F. Engels. *Selected Works in Three Volumes*. Moscow: Progress Publishers 1970

Marzani, Carlo. *The Open Marxism of Antonio Gramsci*. New York: Cameron Associates 1957

Matteucci, Nicola. *Antonio Gramsci e la filosofia della prassi*. Milano: Giuffre 1977

Mautino, Aldo. *La formazione della filosofia politica di Benedetto Croce*. Bari: Latzera 1953

Michels, Robert. *Political Parties* (1911 edition). Translated by Eden and Cedar Paul. Glencoe: The Free Press 1958

Miliband, Ralph. *Class Power and State Power: Political Essays*. London: Verso 1983

– *Marxism and Politics*. Oxford: Oxford University Press 1977

– *The State in Capitalist Society: An Analysis of the Western System of Power*. London: Quartet Books 1976

Mill, James. *Elements of Political Economy*. London: Baldwin 1826

– *An Essay on Government*. Cambridge: Cambridge University Press 1937

– *Essays in Government, Jurisprudence, Liberty of the Press and Law of Nations*. New York: Doubleday-Doran and Co. 1935

Mill, J.S. *Essays on Economics and Society*. Edited by John Robson. Toronto: University of Toronto Press 1967

– *Principles of Political Economy with Some of Their Application to Social Philosophy*. London: Longmans, Green 1909

– *A System of Logic: Rationcinative and Intuitive, Being a Connected View of the Principle of Evidence and the Methods of Scientific Investigation* (in 2 vols.). London: J. W. Parker 1843

– *Three Essays: On Liberty (1851), Representative Government (1861) and The Subjection of Women (1869)*. Oxford: Oxford University Press 1975/85

Moore, Barrington. *The Social Origins of Dictatorship and Democracy: Lord and Peasant in the Making of the Modern World*. Boston: Beacon Press 1967

Mosca, Gaetano. *The Ruling Class: Elementi di scienza politica*, 3rd ed. Translated by Hannah D. Kahn. New York: McGraw-Hill 1939, 1965

Mouffe, Chantal (ed.). *Gramsci and Marxist Theory*. London: Routledge and Kegan Paul 1979

Mussolini, B. *My Autobiography*. Translated by Richard Washburn-Child. New York: Charles Scribner's Sons 1927

Nagel, H. *The Structure of Science*. New York: Harcourt Brace and World 1961

Nemeth, Thomas. *Gramsci's Philosophy: A Critical Study*. Sussex: Harvester Press 1980

Orfei, Ruggero. *Antonio Gramsci: Coscienza critica del marxism*. Varese: Relazioni sociali 1965

Paggi, Leonardo. *Antonio Gramsci e il moderno principe: Nella crisi del socialismo italiano*. Roma: Editori Riuniti 1970

– *Le strategie del potere in Gramsci: Tra fascismo e socialismo in un solo paese 1923–1924*. Roma: Editori Riuniti 1984

200   Bibliography

Paine, Thomas. *Rights of Man*. London: J.M. Dent and Sons 1930
Palmer, L.M., and H. S. Harris (eds.). *Thought, Action and Intuition as a Symposium on the Philosophy of Benedetto Croce*. Hildesheim: Georg Olms Verlag 1975
Pareto, Vilfred. *The Mind and Society*. Tanslated by Arthur Livingstone. New York: Harcourt Brace 1935
Parsons, Talcott. *The Structure of Social Action*. Glencoe, Ill.: The Free Press 1949
Pateman, Carol. *Participation and Democratic Theory*. Cambridge: Cambridge University Press 1970
– *The Problem of Political Obligation: A Critical Analysis of Liberal Theory*. New York: John Wiley and Sons 1979, 1985
Paul, E.F., F. Miller, J. Paul, and J. Ahrens (eds.). *Marxism and Liberalism*. Oxford: Basil Blackwell 1986
Pelczynski, Z.A. (ed.). *The State and Civil Society: Studies in Hegel's Political Philosophy*. Cambridge: Cambridge University Press 1984
Pellicani, Luciano. *Gramsci: An Alternative to Communism?* Stanford: Hoover Institution Press 1976
Piccone, Paul. *Italian Marxism*. London, Berkeley: University of California Press 1983
Piotte, Jean-Marc. *La pensée politique de Gramsci*. Ottawa: Les Editions Parti Pris 1970
Portelli, H. *Gramsci e le bloc historique*. Paris: Presses universitaires de France 1974
Poulantzas, Nicos. *Political Power and Social Classes*. Translated by T. O'Hagan. London: New Left Books 1968, 1975
– *State, Power, Socialism*. Translated by P. Camiller. London: New Left Review Books 1978
Pozzolini, A. *Antonio Gramsci: An Introduction to His Thought*. Translated by Anne Showstack. London: Pluto Press 1970
Prior, Mike (ed.). *The Popular and the Political*. London: Routledge and Kegan Paul 1981
Przeworski, A. *Capitalism and Social Democracy*. Cambridge: Cambridge University Press 1985
Raptis, Michael. *Socialism, Democracy and Self-Management*. London: Allison and Busby 1980
Rawls, John. *A Theory of Justice*. Oxford: Oxford University Press 1972
Ritter, Joachim. *Hegel and the French Revolution: Essays on the Philosophy of Right*. Translated by Richard Dien Winfield. Cambridge, Mass., London: MIT Press 1982
Romano, Federico. *Gramsci e il liberalismo – antiliberale*. Roma: Edizioni cremonese 1973

Rorty, Richard. *Philosophy and the Mirror of Nature*. Princeton: Princeton University Press 1979

Rossi, Pietro (ed.). *Gramsci e la cultura contemporanea: Atti del Convegno internazionale di studi gramsciani tenuto a Cagliari il 23–27 aprile 1967* (Vols. 1 and 2). Roma: Editori Riuniti – Istituto Gramsci 1969, 1975

Roth, Jack J. *The Cult of Violence: Sorel and the Sorelians*. Berkeley: University of California Press 1979

Rousseau, Jean Jacques. *The Social Contract and Discourses*. Translation and introduction by G.D.H. Cole. London: J.M. Dent and Sons 1973

Salamini, Leonardo. *The Sociology of Political Praxis: An Introduction to Gramscian Theory*. London: Routledge and Kegan Paul 1981

Salvadori, Massimo L. *Gramsci e il problema storico della democrazia*. Torino: Einaudi 1970

Sanguineti, Federico. *Gramsci e Machiavelli*. Roma: Laterza 1982

Sassoon, Anne Showstack. *Approaches to Gramsci*. London: Writers and Readers Cooperative 1982

– *Gramsci's Politics*. London: Croom Helm 1980

Saussure, Ferdinand de. *Course in General Linguistics [1916]*. Translated by W. Baskin. London: Fontana 1974

Schmidt, Alfred. *History and Structure: An Essay on Hegelian-Marxist and Structuralist Theories of History*. Translated by Jeffrey Herf. Cambridge: MIT Press 1981

Schumpeter, Joseph. *Capitalism, Socialism and Democracy*. New York: Harper and Row 1942, 1962

Shklar, Judith N. *Freedom and Independence: A Study of the Political Ideas of Hegel's Phenomenology of Mind*. Cambridge: Cambridge University Press 1976

Simon, Roger. *Gramsci's Political Thought*. London: Lawrence and Wishart 1982

Sorel, Georges. *Degenerazione capitalista e degenerazione socialista*. Edizione per cura e con prefazione di Vittorio Racca. Milano: Remo Sandron 1907

– *From Georges Sorel: Essays in Socialism and Philosophy*. Edited and with introduction by John Stanley, and translated by John Stanley and Charlotte Stanley. New York: Oxford University Press 1976

– *The Illusions of Progress*. Translated by John Stanley and Charlotte Stanley. Berkeley: University of California Press 1969

– *Reflections on Violence*. Translated by T.E. Hulme and J. Roth, with an introduction by E.A. Shils. Glencoe, Ill.: The Free Press 1950

– *Scritti politici e filosofici*. A cura di Giovanni Cavallari. Torino: Einaudi 1975

Spriano, Paolo. *Gramsci and the Party: The Prison Years*. Translated by John Fraser. London: Lawrence and Wishart 1979

Steiner, George. *On Difficulty and Other Essays*. New York: Oxford University Press 1978

Tagliacozzo, G., M. Mooney, and D. P. Verne (eds.). *Vico and Contemporary Thought*. New York and London: Macmillan 1980

Taylor, Charles. *Hegel*. Cambridge: Cambridge University Press 1975

Therborn, G. *What Does the Ruling Class Do When It Rules? State Apparatuses and State Power under Feudalism, Capitalism, and Socialism*. London: New Left Books 1978

Thomason, Burke. *Making Sense of Reification: Alfred Schutz and Constructionist Theory*. Translated by Tom Bottomore. London: Macmillan 1982

Thompson, E.P. *The Making of the English Working Class*. Harmondsworth: Penguin 1963

– *The Poverty of Theory and Other Essays*. New York: Monthly Review Press 1978

Timpanaro, Sebastiano. *On Materialism*. Translated by Lawrence Garner. London: New Left Books 1975

Tocqueville, Alexis de. *Democracy in America* (in two volumes). Edited by J.P. Mayer; translated by G. Lawrence. New York: Doubleday and Co. 1975

Togliatti, Palmiro. *Gramsci*. Roma: Editori Riuniti 1967

– *Lectures on Fascism*. New York: International Publishers 1976

– *On Gramsci and Other Writings*. Edited and with an introduction by Donald Sassoon. London: Lawrence and Wishart 1979

Unger, Roberto M. *Knowledge and Politics*. New York and London: The Free Press 1975

Vacca, Giuseppe. *Saggio su Togliatti e la tradizione comunista*. Bari: De Donato 1974

Vico, Giambattista. *The New Science of Giambattista Vico: Translated from the Third Edition (1744)*. Translated by Thomas G. Bergin and Max H. Fisch. New York: Cornell University Press 1948

– *The Selected Writings of Giambattista Vico*. Edited and translated by Leon Pampa. Cambridge: Cambridge University Press 1982

Volpe, Galvano della. *Logic as a Positive Science*. Translated by J. Rothschild. London: New Left Books 1980

– *Rousseau and Marx: And Other Writings*. Translated by J. Fraser. London: Lawrence and Wishart 1978

Watson, Gary (ed.). *Free Will*. Oxford: Oxford University Press 1982

Weber, Max. *The Protestant Ethic and the Spirit of Capitalism*. London: George Allen and Unwin 1930

– *The Theory of Economic and Social Organization*. Edited by T. Parsons; translated by A.M. Henderson. New York: Oxford University Press 1947

Williams, Gwyn. *Proletarian Order: Antonio Gramsci, Factory Councils and the Origins of Italian Communism*. London: Pluto Press 1975

Williams, Raymond. *Marxism and Literature*. Oxford: Oxford University Press 1977

– *Problems in Materialism and Culture*. London: Verso 1980

Wolfe, A. *The Limits to Legitimacy: Political Contradictions of Contemporary Capitalism*. New York: Free Press 1977

Wolin, Sheldon. *Politics and Vision: Continuity and Innovation in Western Political Thought*. Boston: Little, Brown 1960

Wood, Ellen Meiksins. *Retreat from Class: A New 'True' Socialism*. London: Verso 1986

Worsley, Peter. *Marx and Marxism*. London: Tavistock Publishers 1982

Articles

Abercrombie, N., and B. Turner. 'The Dominant Ideology Thesis,' *British Journal of Sociology* 29/2 (June 1978), 149–69

Anderson, Perry. 'The Antinomies of Antonio Gramsci,' *New Left Review* 100 (November–January 1976–7), 5–78

Andrew, E. 'Marx's Theory of Classes: Science and Ideology,' *Canadian Journal of Political Science* 8/3 (September 1975), 454–66

Badaloni, N. 'Il fondamento teorico dello storicismo gramsciano.' In *Gramsci e la cultura contemporanea*, Vol. 2, a cura di P. Rossi, pp. 73–80. Roma: Editori Riuniti-Istituto Gramsci 1970

Bates, Thomas. 'Gramsci and the Theory of Hegemony,' *Journal of the History of Ideas* 36/2 (April–June 1975), 351–66

Bay, C. 'Foundations of the Liberal Make-Believe: Some Implications of Contract Theory versus Freedom Theory,' *Inquiry* 14/3 (1971), 213–37

Bobbio, Noberto. 'Gramsci and the Conception of Civil Society.' *Gramsci and Marxist Theory*, edited by Chantal Mouffe, pp. 21–47. London: Routledge and Kegan Paul 1979

– 'Is There a Marxist Theory of the State?' *Telos* 35 (Spring 1978), 5–16

Bowles, S., and H. Gintis. 'The Invisible Fist: Have Capitalism and Democracy Reached a Parting of the Ways?' *American Economic Review* 68/2 (1978), 358–63

Buci-Glucksmann, Christine. 'Del consentimiento como hegemonía: la estrategia gramsciana,' *Revista Mexicana de Sociología* Abril–Junio 1979, 379–89

Calzolari, Andrea. 'Structure and Superstructure in Gramsci,' *Telos* Spring 1969, 33–42

Cerroni, Umberto. 'Democracy and Socialism,' *Economy and Society* 7/3 (1978), 241–83

Cheal, David. 'Hegemony, Ideology and Contradictory Consciousness,' *The Sociological Quarterly* 20/1 (Winter 1979), 109-17

Colletti, Lucio. 'Antonio Gramsci and the Italian Revolution,' *New Left Review* 65 (January–February 1971), 87–94

– 'Marxism and The Dialectic,' *New Left Review* 93 (September–October 1975), 3–29

Converse, Peter E. 'The Nature of Belief Systems in Mass Publics.' In *Ideology and Discontent*, edited by D. E. Apter, pp. 206–61. London: Collier-Macmillan 1964

Dahrendorf, R. 'On the Origins of Social Inequality.' In *Philosophy, Politics, and Society*, edited by Peter Laslett and W.G. Runciman, pp. 88–110. Oxford: Basil Blackwell 1962

Davidson, Alastair. 'Gramsci and Lenin 1917–1921.' In *Socialist Register, 1974*, edited by Ralph Miliband and John Saville, pp. 125–50. London: The Merlin Press 1974

– 'Gramsci and Reading Machiavelli,' *Science and Society* 27/1 (Spring 1973), 56–80

– 'The Varying Seasons of Gramscian Studies,' *Political Studies* 2/4 (December 1972), 448–61

Debray, Regis. 'Schema for a Study of Gramsci,' *New Left Review* 59 (January–February 1970), 48-52

Donzelli, Carmine. 'Introduzione a Gramsci.' In A. Gramsci, *Quaderno 13, 'Notrelle sulla politica del maciavelli'*, pp. ix–cii. Torino: Einaudi 1981

Duncan, G., and S. Lukes. 'The New Democracy,' *Political Studies* 11/2 (1963), 156–77

Engels, F. 'Ludwig Feuerbach and the End of Classical German Philosophy (1886).' In Karl Marx and Frederich Engels, *Selected Works in Three Volumes*, Vol. 3, pp. 335–76. Moscow: Progress Publishers 1970

– 'The Peasant Question in France and Germany.' In Karl Marx and Frederich Engels, *Selected Works in Three Volumes*, Vol. 3, pp. 457–76. Moscow: Progress Publishers 1970

– 'Socialism: Utopian and Scientific.' In Karl Marx and Frederich Engels, *Selected Works in Three Volumes*, Vol. 3, pp. 95–151. Moscow: Progress Publishers 1970

Femia, Joseph. 'Elites, Participation, and the Democratic Creed,' *Political Studies* 27/1 (March 1979), 1–20

– 'Hegemony and Consciousness in the Thought of Antonio Gramsci,' *Political Studies* 23/1 (March 1975), 29–48

Finochiaro, Maurice. 'Gramsci's Crocean Marxism,' *Telos* 41 (Fall 1979)

– 'Science and Praxis in Gramsci's Critique of Bukharin,' *Philosophy and Social Criticism* 6/1, 25–56

Foucault, M. 'Introduction to a Non-Fascist Life.' In G. Deleuze and F. Guattari, *The Anti-Oedipus: Capitalism and Schizophrenia*, pp. xi–xiv. Minneapolis: University of Minnesota Press 1983

Gallie, William B. 'Essentially Contested Concepts,' *Proceedings of the Aristotelian Society* 56, 157–91

Genovese, E. 'Review of John Cammett's *Antonio Gramsci and the Origins of the Italian Communist Party*,' *Studies on the Left* (March–April 1967), 83–107

Geras, Norman. 'Post-Marxism?' *New Left Review* 163 (May–June 1987) 40–82

Giachetti, Romano. 'Antonio Gramsci: The Subjective Revolution.' In *The Unknown Dimension: European Marxism since Lenin*, edited by Dick Howard and Karl E. Klare, 147–68. New York: Basic Books 1972

Glasso, Giuseppe. 'Gramsci e il problema della storia italiana.' In *Gramsci e la cultura contemporanea*, edited by P. Rossi, pp. 305–54. Roma: Editori Riuniti/Istituto Gramsci 1969

Golding, S. 'The *Concept* of the Philosophy of Praxis in Gramsci's *Quaderni del carcere*.' In *Marxism and the Interpretation of Culture*, edited by C. Nelson and L. Grossberg, pp. 543–63. Champagne-Urbana: University of Illinois Press 1988

Gouldner, A. 'Prologue to a Theory of Revolutionary Intellectuals,' *Telos* 26 (Winter 1975–6), 3–36

Graham, W. 'Re-discovering Gramsci's Optism of the Will.' *Italian Quarterly* Special Issue on Gramsci, edited by H. Mariani, 97/98 (Summer/Fall 1984), 183–8

Gramsci, Antonio. 'In Search of the Education Principle,' translated and introduced by Q. Hoare, *New Left Review* 32 (July–August 1965), 55–62
– 'Science and "Scientific" Ideologies,' translated by M.A. Finocchiaro, *Telos* 39 (Spring 1979), 151–5

Hall, Stuart. 'Debate: Psychology, Ideology, and the Human Subject,' *Ideology and Consciousness* 3 (Spring 1978), 113–27
– 'The Hinterland of Science.' In *On Ideology*, edited by S. Hall, B. Lumley and G. McLennan, pp. 7–32. London: Hutchison 1978

Hall, Stuart; Bob Lumley, and Gregor McLennan. 'Politics and Ideology: Gramsci.' In *On Ideology*, pp. 45–77
– 'Rethinking the "Base-Superstructure" Metaphor.' In *Class, Hegemony, and Party*, edited by Jon Bloomfield, pp. 43–72. London: Lawrence and Wishart 1977

Hartley, William. 'Approaching Gramsci's Cultural Politics,' *Italian Quarterly* 97–8 (Summer/Fall 1984), 171–81

Hawley, James P. 'Antonio Gramsci's Marxism: Class, State and Work,' *Social Problems* 27/5 (June 1980), 584–600

Held, D. 'Introduction: Central Perspectives on the Modern State.' In *States and Societies*, edited by D. Held, pp. 1–55. Oxford: Martin Robertson 1983

Hindess, Barry. 'The Concept of Class in Marxist Theory and Marxist Politics.' In *Class, Hegemony, and Party*, edited by Jon Bloomfield, pp. 95–108. London: Lawrence and Wishart 1977

Hoare, Quintin. 'What Is Fascism?' *New Left Review* 20 (Summer 1963), 99–111

Hobsbawn, Eric. 'Gramsci and Marxist Political Theory.' In *Approaches to Gramsci*, edited by A. Showstack-Sassoon, pp. 20–36. London: Writers and Readers Publishing Cooperative Society 1982

– 'The Great Gramsci,' *New York Review of Books*, 21 April 1974

Holloway, J., and S. Picciotto. 'Introduction: Towards a Marxist Theory of the State.' In *State and Capital: A Marxist Debate*, edited by J. Holloway and S. Picciotto, pp. 1–31. London: Eward Arnold 1978

Hoy, David C. 'Taking History Seriously: Foucault, Gadamer, Habermas,' *Union Seminary Quarterly Review* 34/2 (Winter 1979), 85–95

Hunt, Geoffrey. 'Gramsci, Civil Society and Bureaucracy,' *Praxis International*, 6/2 (July 1986), 206–19

Inwood, M.J. 'Hegel, Plato and Greek "*Sittlichkeit*."' In Z. A. Pelczynski, *The State and Civil Society: Studies in Hegel's Political Philosophy*, pp. 55–76. Cambridge: Cambridge University Press 1984

Jessop, Bob. 'The Gramsci Debate: Assimilating Gramsci Is a Key Aspect in the Revival of the Left,' *Marxism Today*, February 1980, 23–5

– 'The Political Indeterminacy of Democracy.' In *Marxism and Democracy*, edited by Alan Hunt, pp. 55–80. London: Lawrence and Wishart 1980

Jones, Phil. 'The People, Democracy and Ideology in Marxist Theory,' *Marxism Today*, February 1978, 57–62

Karabel, Jerome. 'Revolutionary Contradictions: Antonio Gramsci and the Problem of Intellectuals,' *Politics and Society* 6/2 (1976), 123–72

Kolakowski, Leszek. 'Karl Marx and the Classical Definition of Truth,' In *Marxism and Beyond*. London: Paladin 1971

Laclau, Ernesto. 'Democratic Antagonisms and the Capitalist State.' In *Frontiers of Political Theory*, edited by M. Freeman and D. Robertson, pp. 101–39. New York: St. Martin's Press 1980

– 'The Impossibility of Society,' *Canadian Journal of Political and Social Theory* 7/1–2 (1983), 21–4

– 'Metaphor and Social Antagonisms.' In *Marxism and the Interpretation of Culture*, edited by Cary Nelson and Lawrence Grossberg, pp. 249–57. Champagne-Urbana: University of Illinois Press 1988

– 'New Social Movements and the Plurality of the Social.' In *The New Social Movements in Latin America*, edited by D. Slater, pp. 27–42. Amsterdam: Centre for L.A. Research and Documentation 1985

– 'Popular Rupture and Discourse,' *Screen Education* 34 (Spring 1980), 87–93

Laclau, Ernesto, and Chantal Mouffe. 'Post-Marxism without Apologies,' *New Left Review* 166 (December 1987), 79–106

Lenin, V.I. 'On the Question of Dialectics.' In *Collected Works*, Vol. 38, pp. 355–64. Moscow: Progress Publishers 1961

– 'Once More on the Theory of Realisation.' In *Collected Works*, Vol. 4, pp. 74–93. Moscow: Foreign Languages Publishing House 1969

– 'State and Revolution: The Marxist Theory of the State and The Tasks of the Proletariat in Revolution.' In *Selected Works*, Vol. 7, pp. 3–112. Moscow: Progress Publishers 1968

Lukes, Steven. 'The Real and Ideal Worlds of Democracy.' In *Powers, Possessions, and Freedom: Essays in Honour of C.B. Macpherson*, edited by A. Kontos, pp. 139–52. Toronto: University of Toronto Press 1979

Macaulay, Thomas Babington. 'Mill's *Essay on Government*: Utilitarian Logic and Politics,' *Edinburgh Review* 97; reprinted in J. Lively and J. Rees, eds., *Utilitarian Logic and Politics: James Mill's 'Essay on Government', Macaulay's Critique and the Ensuing Debate*, pp. 97–129. Oxford: Clarendon Press 1978

Macpherson, C.B. 'Elegant Tombstones: A Note on Friedman's Freedom.' In *Democratic Theory: Essays in Retrieval*, pp. 143–56. London: Oxford University Press 1973

– 'Locke: The Political Theory of Appropriation.' In *The Political Theory of Possessive Individualism: Hobbes to Locke*, pp. 194–262. Oxford: Oxford University Press 1962

– 'Post-Liberal Democracy?' In *Democratic Theory: Essays in Retrieval*, pp. 170–84

– 'Needs and Wants: An Ontological or Historical Problem?' In *Human Needs and Politics,* edited by R. Fitzgerald, pp. 26–35. Australia: Pergamon Press 1977

Mann, Michael. 'The Sociological Cohesion of Liberal Democracy,' *American Sociological Review* 35/3 (1970), 423–39

Martinelli, A. 'In Defense of the Dialectic: Antonio Gramsci's Theory of Revolution,' *Berkeley Journal of Sociology* 13 (1968)

Marx, Karl. 'Critique of the Gotha Programme.' In *Selected Works (in Three Volumes)*, Vol. 3, pp. 9–10. Moscow: Progress Publishers 1970

– 'The 18th Brumaire of Louis Bonaparte.' In *Selected Works (in Three Volumes)*, Vol. 1, pp. 394–487. Moscow: Progress Publishers 1969

– 'The General Law of Capitalist Accumulation.' In *Capital: A Critical Analysis of Capitalist Production* (in three volumes), Vol. 1, pp. 574–665. Moscow: Progress Publishers n.d.

– 'Manifesto of the Communist Party.' In *Selected Works (in Three Volumes)*, Vol. 1, pp. 98–137. Moscow: Progress Publishers 1969

– 'Preface to *The Contribution to a Critique of Political Economy.*' In *Selected Works (in Three Volumes)*, Vol. 1, pp. 502–6. Moscow: Progress Publishers 1969

– 'Theses on Feuerbach.' In Karl Marx and Friedrich Engels, *Selected Works (in Three Volumes)*, Vol. 1, pp. 13–15. Moscow: Progress Publishers 1969

Maya, Carlos. 'El concepto del Estado en los cuadernos de la carcel,' *Cuadernos Politicos* 33 (Mexico: July–September 1982), 7–19

Meiksins, P., and E. Meiksins-Wood. 'Beyond Class? A Reply to Chantal Mouffe,' *Studies in Political Economy*, Summer 1985, 141–65

Merrington, John. 'Theory and Practice in Gramsci's Marxism.' In *Socialist Register 1968*, edited by Ralph Miliband and John Saville, pp. 145–76. New York: Monthly Review Press 1968.

Mill, John Stuart. 'The Claims of Labour' (1845), in *Collected Works [of J.S. Mill]*, Vol. 4, edited by J.M. Robson, pp. 363–89. Toronto and London: University of Toronto Press 1967

– 'Principles of Political Economy.' In John Stuart Mill, *Collected Works*, Vol. 3, edited by J.M. Robson, pp. 705–9, 752–66, 880–971. Toronto and London: University of Toronto Press 1965

Morrow, Raymond. 'Gramsci in Germany,' *Telos* 22 (Winter 1974–5), 174–81

Mouffe, Chantal. 'Democracy and the New Right.' In *Politics and Power: Law, Politics and Justice*, pp. 221–36. London: Routledge and Kegan Paul 1981

– 'Hegemony and New Political Subjects: Toward a New Concept of Democracy.' In *Marxism and the Interpretation of Culture*, edited by Cary Nelson and Lawrence Grossberg, pp. 89–104. Champagne-Urbana: University of Illinois Press 1988

– 'Hegemony and the Integral State in Gramsci: Towards a New Concept of Politics.' In *Silver Linings*, edited by G. Bridges and R. Brunt, pp. 167–87. London: Lawrence and Wishart 1981

– 'Working Class Hegemony and the Struggle for Socialism,' *Studies in Political Economy* 312 (Fall 1983), 7–26

Mouffe, Chantal, and A. Showstack-Sassoon. 'Gramsci in France and Italy: A Review of the Literature,' *Economy and Society* 6/1 (1977), 31–69

Müller, W. and C. Neusüss. 'The Illusion of State Socialism and the Contradiction between Wage Labour and Capital (1970),' *Telos*, 25 (1975), 13–90

Mure, G.R.G. 'The Economic and Moral in the Philosophy of Benedetto Croce,' delivered before the Centre for Advanced Study of Italian Society in the University of Reading 8 November 1966, and reprinted in *Occasional Papers* [1]. Reading: University of Reading 1967

Nemeth, Thomas. 'Gramsci's Concept of Constitution,' *Philosophy and Social Criticism* 5/3–4 (1978), 295–318

Nowell-Smith, Geoffrey. 'Common Sense,' *Radical Philosophy* 7 (Spring 1974)

Nun, Jose. 'Elements for a Theory of Democracy: Gramsci and Common Sense,' revised edition of a paper presented at the International Seminar on Gramsci and Latin America, organized by the Gramsci Institute, Ferrara, 11–13 September 1985

– 'Latin America: Hegemonic Crisis and the Military Coup' (monograph). Berkeley: Institute of International Studies: University of California 1969

Offe, C. 'Political Authority and Class Structure – An Analysis of Late Capitalist Societes,' *International Journal of Sociology* 2 (1972), 73–108

O'Neill, J. 'On the History of the Human Senses in Vico and Marx.' In *Vico and Contemporary Thought*, edited by G. Tagliacozzo, M. Mooney, and D.P. Verne, pp. 179–86. New York and London: Macmillan 1980

Pereyra, Carlos. 'Gramsci: Estado y sociedad civil,' *Cuadernos Politicos* 21 (Mexico: July–September 1979), 66–74

Piccone, Paul. 'From Spaventa to Gramsci,' *Telos* 31 (Spring 1977), 35–67

– 'Gramsci's Hegelian-Marxism,' *Political Theory* 2/1 (February 1974), 32–45

– 'Gramsci's Marxism: Beyond Lenin and Togliatti,' *Theory and Society* 3/4 (1976), 485–512

Pitkin, Hannah. 'Obligation and Consent.' In *Philosophy, Politics, and Society*, 4th series, edited by P. Laslett, W.G. Runciman, and Q. Skinner, pp. 43–85. Oxford: Basil Blackwell 1972

Plant, Raymond. 'Community: Concept, Conception, and Ideology,' *Politics and Society* 8/1 (1978), 79–107

Pokorny, Dusan. 'Marx's Philosophy of Surplus Value,' *The Philosophical Forum* 16/4 (Summer 1985), 274–92

Przeworski, Adam. 'Proletariat into a Class: The Process of Class Formation from K. Kautsky's *The Class Struggle* to Recent Controversies,' *Politics and Society* 7/4 (1977), 343–401

Richardson, T. 'Science, Ideology and Common Sense: On Antonio Gramsci and Louis Althusser.' In *Politics, Ideology and the State*, edited by Sally Hibbin, pp. 99–122. London: Lawrence and Wishart 1978

Rose, Nikolas. 'Fetishism and Ideology: A Review of Theoretical Problems,' *Ideology and Consciousness* 2 (London: Autumn 1977), 27–56

Rosengarten, Frank. 'Three Essays on Antonio Gramsci's *Letters from Prison*,' *Italian Quarterly* 97–8 (Summer/Fall 1984), 7–40

Rosiello, Luigi. 'Problemi linguistici negli scritti di Gramsci.' In *Gramsci e la cultura contemporanea [II]*, edited by Pietro Rossi, pp. 347–67. Roma: Editori Riuniti 1970

Salamini, Leonardo. 'Gramsci and the Marxist Sociology of Knowledge: An Analysis of Hegemony, Ideology and Knowledge,' *Sociological Quarterly* 15/3 (Summer 1974), 359–80

– 'Language and Hegemony,' unpublished mimeograph, 1982

- 'The Specificity of Marxist Sociology in Gramsci's Theory,' *The Sociological Quarterly* 16/1 (Winter 1975), 65–86
Sassoon, Anne Showstack. 'The "Gramsci Boom": A Reflection on the Present Crisis? ' In *Power and Politics* [no. 1], pp. 203–11. London: Routledge and Kegan Paul 1980
- 'Gramsci: A New Concept of Politics and the Expansion of Democracy.' In *Marxism and Democracy*, edited by A. Hunt, pp. 81–100. London: Lawrence and Wishart 1980
Skinner, Q. 'The Empirical Theorists of Democracy and Their Critics: A Plague on Both Their Homes,' *Political Theory* 1/3 (1973), 287–306
Suvin, Darko. 'On Two Notions of "Science" in Marxism.' In *Brave New Universe*, edited by T. Henighan, pp. 27–43. Ottawa: Tecumseh Press 1980
Textier, Jacques. 'Gramsci: Theoretician of the Superstructures.' In *Gramsci and Marxist Theory*, edited by Chantal Mouffe, pp. 48–79. London: Routledge and Kegan Paul 1979
Todd, N. 'Ideological Superstructure in Gramsci and Mao Tse-Tung,' *Journal of the History of Ideas*, 205/1 (January–March 1974)
Wallerstein, Immanuel. 'The State and Social Tranformation: Will and Possibility,' *Politics and Society* May 1971, 359–64
Williams, Raymond. 'Base/Superstructure in Marxist Cultural Theory,' *New Left Review* 82 (November–December 1973); reprinted in R. Williams, *Problems in Materialism and Culture*, pp. 31–49. London: Verso Press 1980
Wood, Neal. 'Some Reflections on Sorel and Machiavelli,' *Political Science Quarterly* 83 (March 1968), 76–91
Wright, Eric Olin. 'Class Boundaries in Advanced Capitalist Societies,' *New Left Review* 98 (July–August 1976), 3–41

Index

absolute historicism, 4, 44, 45, 67, 70, 88, 126; as central feature of the philosophy of praxis, 61, 129, 162n85; dilemma with, 129–31, 154n9

actual idealism, 79; *see also* Gentile, G.

aesthetic: individual, judgment, 30; as science of expression 26–7, 35–6

Archimedean point: as external authority, 5, 10, 126; obligation as, 6–7

Artaud, Antonin, 186n5

Austro-marxists, 50–2, 158n41

base: as dialectical, open structure, xvi–xvii; as one-dimensional economic system, xvi; and quantity/quality, 95; and superstructure relation, 90–4, 126, 151n67; *see also* structure

becoming: Croce's interpretation of, 28–9, 36; and democracy, 85, 128–9; as a hegemonic process, 128; as historical realism, 63–4; as

historicized immanence, xv, 62, 74; as individual (subjective) and social ought, 62–4, 83, 85; and the rational and real, 62; and will, 77; *see also* hegemony; immanence

Bergson, Henri, 20, 69, 98, 147–8n24

Boggs, C., 145n4

Bukharin, N.: Gramsci's critique of, 56–7, 88, 159n56; and naïve metaphysics, 41, 53; *see also* economism

bureaucracy, 68

Burke, Edmund, 7, 139n2, 142n16

Cartesianism, and self-referentiality, 134

cathartic moment, 66, 78, 168n40; *see also* hegemony; historic bloc; structure

change: by accident, vanguard, or genius, xvii, 81, 169–70n52; and error and necessity, 44–5, 65; expression of the political moment, 44–6, 81–2; permanent, 92, 98; and possibility, 64; real or

moment of certainty, 23–5, 135; as 'thought from outside' (fiction), 134–5

tyranny of majority, 4, 11

utilitarianism, xiii, 11–13, 142n16

Utopian socialists, 51–2

Verum ipsum factum, 23–4, 25, 27, 30

Vico, G., xiv, 18, 20, 23–6, 27, 34, 37, 46, 54, 146–7n12, 147nn13, 23, 147–8n24

war of position, 93

will: as the art of politics, 76, 125; as base of philosophy, 33–4, 71–3, 75; concrete, 160–1n66; as condition for ethico-political society, 39–40, 42, 68, 88, 100–1, 125–6; debates on, 69–71, 165n3; as discursive, 124–5; as 'disturbing element,' 100, 124; and duty/ freedom, 74, 148n25; as (economic) practical activity, 32–5, 167n32; as *élan vital*, 98; and fascism, 79–82; the general, 12; as ground and horizon of 'is/ ought,' xii, 18, 70–1, 74–6, 121, 124; as ground and vehicle for

social cohesion, 15–18, 75–6, 77–9, 83; as impure, 166–7n20; and necessity, 56–7, 130; as 'operative awareness,' 70; 'pessimism of the intellect, optimism of the,' 69, 156n5, 186n1; as politics/knowledge terrain, 70, 77–8, 81, 100; practico-political, xvi, 47, 72–4, 83; and radical autonomy of the moral subject, 11–13, 144n30; the rational, 13, 33; and 'real' democracy, 68, 79, 84–5; and 'real' dialectic, 70, 73, 76, 78, 85; rational, 33–4, 56–8; and *Sittlichkeit*, 14–17, 70, 78, 120–2, 130; subjective, 81; and transcendence, 69; triumph of the, 69, 166n10; as will-power, 70, 76, 80, 85, 125; *see also* collective will; democracy; political party

Wood, E. Meiksins, 174n19

working class, xvii–xviii; and essentialism, 87; as ethical ground, 85–6, 101, 103, 120–2; historic mission of the, 121, 130; and struggle, 89; as 'those not in the know,' 112, 113; *see also* class; class struggle